Alfred von Tirpitz

My Memoirs

Volume 1

Alfred von Tirpitz

My Memoirs

Volume 1

ISBN/EAN: 9783954272501
Erscheinungsjahr: 2012
Erscheinungsort: Bremen, Deutschland

MY MEMOIRS

BY

GRAND ADMIRAL
VON TIRPITZ

VOLUME I

NEW YORK
DODD, MEAD AND COMPANY
1919

PREFACE

THE despair that seized upon all patriotically minded Germans when the Empire which we had thought invincible collapsed has also wrecked many people's faith in our nation and in the continuity of its historical development. It seemed to me my duty therefore to write down my reminiscences, because I can show proofs that the old structure of our state was not antiquated and rotten, but was capable of any development, and moreover that the political legend of a ruthless autocracy and a bellicose military caste having let loose this war is an insult to truth. The Kaiser in particular did not want the war, but did his utmost to prevent it when he realized the danger.

If history is just and cannot be perverted by the fabrication of legends, it should show that by far the greater measure of the responsibility for this war rests with our enemies. The rule of the road at sea puts the blame in collisions on the person who causes the danger of the situation, and not on the one who makes a mistake through incorrect judgment at the last moment in his endeavour to escape from it. Our misfortune, however, did not proceed from the acquisition of power, but from the weakness which did not know how to use that power either for the purpose of preserving or concluding peace, and in addition, from our illusions about our enemies, the nature of their war aims, their conduct of the war, and the nature of the economic war.

In order to make myself understood, I must speak the truth to the best of my knowledge. I am compelled, therefore, to present the actions of persons who are alive according to my own views, which will probably differ from theirs, and consequently give rise to some pain. Nothing is farther from my mind than to impute to them ignoble ends, or any blame in the general sense of the word.

It is only Germany's desperate position which forces me against my own inclination to publish these facts during my lifetime.

Now that the writing of my reminiscences is finished, I feel that I must heartily thank all those who have helped me in my task. Besides my friends and my comrades, both young and old, who have examined the correctness of my statements in the light of their own information, these thanks are due especially to the Professor of History in the University of Frankfort, Dr. Fritz Kern, who has stood at my side from the very beginning in the most sympathetic and untiring way. Lastly, I should like to thank the publisher, Dr. Koehler, for the friendly interest that he has shown in the book.

A. VON TIRPITZ.

JAGDHAUS ZABELSBERG,
   April, 1919.

CONTENTS OF VOLUME I

CHAPTER I

IN THE PRUSSIAN NAVY

CHAPTER II

THE STOSCH ERA

CHAPTER III

THE CAPRIVI ERA

CHAPTER IV

TECHNICAL MATTERS

CONTENTS

CHAPTER V

THE NEW COURSE

CHAPTER VI

TACTICAL WORK

CHAPTER VII

NAVY SCHEMES

CHAPTER VIII

TSINGTAO

CHAPTER IX

AT THE ADMIRALTY

CONTENTS

CHAPTER X

WITH BISMARCK

CHAPTER XI

THE NAVY BILLS

CHAPTER XII

BUILDING THE FLEET

CHAPTER XIII

UNDER THE KAISER

.CHAPTER XIV

ADMIRALTY AND FOREIGN POLICY

CONTENTS

CHAPTER XV

ENGLAND AND THE GERMAN FLEET

CHAPTER XVI

THE OUTBREAK OF THE WAR

MY MEMOIRS

MY MEMOIRS

CHAPTER I

IN THE PRUSSIAN NAVY

1. Entering the Service. Prussian Navy and Prussian politics, 1866-1870. Warfare then and now.—2. Foreign political currents. Relations with England. More at home in Plymouth than in Kiel. The superiority of the English. "But you are not a sea-going nation."

I

WHEN I was a boy there was scarcely any trace left of the enthusiasm for the navy which the Revolution of '48 aroused in Germany, although it flickered up once more in the year 1864 after the Battle of Jasmund. My going into the navy was not the result of a passionate fondness for it, but was the unintentional product of my father's educational ideal, which was ahead of his time. As my father felt in himself the lack of a knowledge of the exact sciences, he sent my brother and me to the *Realschule* of our native town Frankfort-on-the-Oder, instead of to the *Gymnasium,* intending to let us change schools when we reached the top form. But in view of the slight undeveloped state of the *realschule* at that time, this school proved

inadequate; I have felt the effects of this all my life.
Our teachers were so old-fashioned that they spoke
a language which we really did not understand. As
a scholar I was very mediocre, and at Christmas, 1864,
my certificate was " Moderate." My school friend
Maltzahn had expressed his intention of entering the
navy, and so it óccurred to me that it might mean a
certain relief for my parents if I too were to take
up the idea. At first my proposal was received in complete silence at home, but after some weeks my father
called me to him and told me that my depressed state
of mind had been noticed. My mind seemed to be
set on the navy, he said, and if I wanted to go, no
obstacle would be placed in my way. Nobody could
have been more suprised than I; but what was I to
do? I kept to my word, and in the spring of 1865
I presented myself at the age of sixteen for the entrance examination at the Naval Cadets' Institute of
those days in Berlin, passed, to everybody's surprise,
fifth on the list, and became a sailor.

The attractions of the navy were, as I have said,
slight at that time. In 1861 the corvette *Amazone* had
gone down with almost all the cadets on board who
constituted the supply of officers for many years to
come. This event reduced the applications for naval
cadetships to three the following year, and compelled
the conditional acceptance even in my year of several
candidates who had failed, in addition to the ten as-
pirants who were successful. The grasp of naval affairs possessed by the Prussian *intelligentsia* of those

days, as well as the hereditary German tendency to regard everything from the standpoint of domestic party politics, is indicated by an article which appeared at the time in the *Gartenlaube*. It described in novelistic form how the Prussian Junker party attempted to destroy the liberal institution of the navy by bribing a Danish captain to ram the *Amazone*. The author of this malicious piece of foolery seemed to overlook the fact that the majority of the cadets who were drowned were themselves "Junkers"; Prince Adalbert was very careful in his choice of prospective officers.

Moreover, I occasionally found in my earlier presentations of the Navy Estimates to Parliament that certain Conservative circles distrusted the idea of a fleet. It was not considered to be in keeping with the Prussian tradition, it competed in some degree with the army, it seemed too closely related with industry and commerce in view of the agricultural distress of that time and the great economic conflicts of the parties. Individual members of the extreme Right even voted against the Second Navy Bill of 1900, against the "horrible Fleet," as a Conservative leader called it,—whilst overwhelmingly sympathetic support was to be found from the outset among the Liberal *bourgeoisie,* side by side with some of the bitterest opposition to the Bill.

The immediate result of the sinking of the *Amazone* was to increase still further the confusion of personalities in our Naval Officers Corps in 1864. Portions

of this corps had been previously transferred from
the army, whence cavalrymen in particular brought
with them the youthful independence necessary for
naval service; others came from the German or
Danish navies: others again had been trained in
England, America, or Holland. In addition the so-
called Dantzig *stuerkes* were enlisted from the merchant sailing ships in order to fill the gaps which the
war with Denmark had revealed in the Officers' Corps.
Indeed Dantzig was still our real port. These seamen usually only sailed on the short voyage between
Dantzig and England, whilst the better sorts went up
into the North Sea. The influx of these uneducated
sea-dogs from the merchant service of those days
brought many a joke into our mess; we called them
Hilfsbarone, and they included some remarkable characters who were removed after 1870, several of them
after proceedings had been taken by a court of honour.
Their authority was often not recognized by the crews,
whilst the officer from the Cadet Institute always remained the master, although he was in a certain sense
more of a comrade to the ordinary sailor. Washing-
ton's principle of only taking gentlemen for his officers
proved its wisdom to us also. It is only bravery in
face of the enemy that can make up for lack of education. In general, the naval cadets of those days
were short of teachers who could be considered edu-
cators. According to the good Prussian tradition,
there was no lack of drudgery: we were dragged from
one course to another until we obtained officers' rank

after four and a half years. But the teachers had little
idea of handling this human material. Many of the
old Prussian naval officers therefore went their own
way or became cranks; at the best they were self-
taught. My year, however, was favoured: we had
excellent superiors, to whom I look back with gratitude. Admiral Batsch was our commander at that
time. It is said with some justice that it depends
upon the way cadets are handled in the first year
whether the crew turns out well or not.

Duty centred in the main in learning how to handle
rigging. The art of navigation as evolved through
the centuries required long training for officers and
ratings. As was usual in the days of sailing ships, we
had adventures on many occasions during our training voyages, which made us understand the days of
Marryat and Nelson as though we had seen them ourselves.

It was seldom that the paths of the Prussian Navy
crossed those of Prussian politics. When it did happen, it was generally in the way related to us by those
who took part in the voyage of the *Gazelle* to Japan
in 1864. A German ship had gone ashore in the neighbourhood of Yokohama, and had been looted. The
commander of the *Gazelle,* Captain von Bothmer,
went thither with a landing party to protect it. On
the way he met a *daimio* who demanded kowtow.
Our commander refused. The *daimio* was surrounded
by 3,000 Japanese knights in steel armour, with lowered heads, and arms crossed over their swords. Fi-

nally the captain got out of the difficulty by offering
the salute which is given to a royal prince in Prussia.
An agreement was made on the formula: a march past
at the double with rifles at the slope.

The ships were also used for reprisals against ex-
otic states. As a rule, however, in those days we went
on instructional voyages with no other end in view
than that of training the Fleet.

There was an atmosphere of the Middle Ages about
our actions in war-time too. The *Niobe* had to reckon
with meeting the Austrian steam corvette *Erzherzog
Friedrich* in the Channel in 1866, and, being a sailing-
ship, had to avoid a fight. I was then No. 3 at the
muzzle-loading gun, and it was my duty to put in the
cannon balls; by my side lay my pike, ready to hand
in case the enemy should grapple and press through
the port-hole. Other people stood ready with pole-
axes which they were to strike into the hull of the
enemy vessel, and use as steps. Off the Scilly Islands
we sighted a ship lying-to, resembling the Austrian in
build. It got under way and was evidently bearing
down upon us; it then hoisted up its funnel and pursued us under steam. Fog separated us during the
night. When it lifted near Plymouth, and we stood
by, cleared for action, the frigate hoisted the Nor-
wegian flag, and we youngsters were disappointed in
our joyful anticipation of a fight. Later we lay at
Kiel with loaded guns off the streets of the old town,
which lead down to the water-side, when the Prussians
under Manteuffel were advancing across the canal at

Holtenau, and it seemed questionable whether the Austrians under Gablentz would put up a resistance or not. Gablentz, however, entrained and went off, our band playing meanwhile. The Austrian officers had been very much liked in Kiel; their many promises were now broken, but they had won all hearts, whilst the Prussians, who looked as though they had swallowed their ram-rods, came to disturb the desired formation of an independent little state of Slesvig-Holstein. In spite of the existing state of war we rejoiced at Tegetthoff's sea victory at Lissa almost as though he were one of ourselves. In 1864, the Austrian fleet had fought very valiantly at our side in the heavy engagement near Heligoland, and Austria was still looked upon by us as a German brother-country; in those days Austria's Czechs and Poles were completely overlooked.

Our reputation abroad increased considerably in 1866. Once before we had felt humiliated at the way we had been looked down upon in Cadiz when the Spanish officer kept us waiting for the quay-side inspection. But in Marseilles in 1867 the people came rushing on board to see the Prussians. In Nice needle-guns were exhibited in the fair-booths. To be sure the French officers gave us a foretaste of 1870 partly by their arrogance and partly by ill-concealed vexation.

In the spring of 1870 our first armoured squadron was formed of four different ships, and I was a sub-lieutenant on board the flagship *König Wilhelm*.

Prince Adalbert, who had begged to be allowed to command the squadron, was no longer in the zenith of his power, but after some hesitation the King granted his request—to celebrate his resignation, so to speak —and we went to the Azores. Instruction on these armoured ships was still influenced by the customs of the sailing-ships: we even tried to sail on this voyage, but the hulks refused to move. The position of the Prussian Navy at that time is characterized by the fact that we had no dockyards for big ships in German harbours. When the ships were commissioned sufficient weight was not given to the fact that an iron ship must be docked every year to be cleaned. When the war with France began to smoulder, our squadron had not been docked for several years; we calculated later that the *König Wilhelm* had over sixty tons of mussels on its sides which had reduced its speed from fourteen to ten knots. An engine defect compelled us to run into Plymouth for a lengthy period of repair and the English admiral offered us his dock. It is still not clear to me why we did not accept it; it was stated in the officers' mess at the time that the Prince was the difficulty, because he could not stay all the time in the dockyard. However that may be, we steamed back through the Channel in the middle of July, without having been into dock, and in daily expectation of being attacked by the French, against whom our only defence would have been practice shot (filled with peas) and a fuse which misfired at every opportunity.

On July 16th we arrived in Wilhelmshaven, where the mobilization was in full swing, but we could not enter the harbour because the locks were not yet completed; so we remained in the roads. The dangers of being without a dockyard crippled the squadron; any damage to the ship's bottom was irreparable and meant incapacity for battle. We now went through a hard time in the outer roads. We were to be thrown into the fight if Hamburg or any other place on the North Sea was attacked. We also put out to sea twice; once as far as the Dogger Bank to watch the two new French armoured vessels which had been sent to reinforce the French Eastern Squadron; and the second time when we expected to find the French fleet scattered after a storm, to the leeward of Heligoland. On neither occasion did we come to blows. The army reproached us for not attacking the whole French fleet when it suddenly appeared off Wilhelmshaven on its way home. We youngsters were also indignant at not being let loose on the enemy, but this caution was correct. We were three armoured ships to their eight, and we could only do 10 knots; and even if Captain Werner had advertised the *König Wilhelm* in the *Gartenlaube* as the strongest ship in the world, this was not sufficient to counterbalance a threefold superiority. In view of the lack of any possibility of refitment we should have had to expect the loss of our whole fleet, without reaping any advantage thereby. It was also difficult for the lay mind to understand why we did not at least attempt a raid. An engage-

ment begun at sea, however, cannot be broken off if
the enemy has the greater speed. In any case the
navy was blamed for its inactivity, and we were not
even allowed to count these years as war service.

In 1870 we had some excellent Lloyd steamers
which we could have armed for privateering warfare.
We kept, however, to the declaration which we had
made at the beginning of the war, that we would not
privateer. When the French seized our merchant-
men, we ultimately changed our standpoint, but it
was then too late for the necessary preparations.

The maritime law of these days, based on the Paris
Convention of 1856, prevented the French from bom-
barding open towns; though if they had done so we
could have taken reprisals. Any disarming of our
warships lying in foreign waters was also against the
law. Our ships coaled in Vigo whilst the French
ships lay outside the harbour, and a French sloop
was actually within the harbour watching us. In the
open roads of Fayal in the Azores the French armoured
vessel *Montcalm* circled round our sloop *Arcona* which
was lying at anchor there, without doing it any harm.
In short, it was a naval war without the English. In
the later world-war the lawyers of the Foreign Office
and the Reichstag still placed the greatest hopes in the
niceties of maritime law, whilst the English passed
them over with sovereign power, and will strive after
the war for a new maritime law which will stabilize
their police control of the seas.

The campaign which had been so glorious for the

army lay heavy on the navy.   In addition, our in-
active war service in the outer roads had been a heavy
strain.   We were prepared for an attack at any time
under unfavourable conditions.   Our mine barrier
troubled us more than the enemy; the bad mines
broke loose in a heavy sea and drifted about in the
roads.   For months I went on the watch for four
hours every night on the projecting ram of the *König
Wilhelm,* to look out for our own mines, although
this would have been just as useless for catching loose
mines in the misty autumn weather as the floating
wooden barricade attached to the bowsprit of the
ship.

The greatest achievement of our squadron, however,
was its entry into the locks of Wilhelmshaven when
the winter compelled us to leave the outer roads.   The
harbour was unfinished; sheep were still grazing on
the bottom of the basins on July 16th.   The fairway
into the harbour had not yet been dredged sufficiently;
therefore in order to enter we had to abandon muni-
tions and coal to lighten the vessel.   During a lull in
the weather on December 22nd, a heavy ice-drift set
in and the floes rose as high as the batteries and cut
the anchor chains.   It was impossible for coal-barges
to come into the roads.   The entry had to be attempted,
for apart from the fact that the exit from the
roads at Wangeroog was dangerous, we had no more
fuel on board to take us to Norway.

The entry was effected with great difficulty: on
December 23rd everything that we possessed lay in

the harbour basin, and therewith the war ended as far
as we were concerned.

But it was not in keeping with the Prussian character to allow us to enjoy our irresponsible existence
in idleness.   Partly in order to maintain discipline,
and partly because it was thought that the navy ought
to be tackled in a more military manner and brought
up to a more soldierly standard, a tremendous amount
of infantry drill was carried out in the winter months.
The Stosch era was casting its shadow before.

II

My feelings towards England were determined by
my family and my profession.   The *milieu* in which
I grew up was steeped in memories of the Wars of
Liberation; my great-uncle had been orderly officer to
York von Wartenburg; and even in my childhood's
days patriotic sentiment pointed out anybody whose
behaviour in '13 had not been above suspicion.   There
was still a strong preference for our old ally, England.
That had not been permanently dimmed even by
Palmerston's much-resented rejection of Germany's
naval aspirations, nor by the reconnoitring services
which the British performed round Heligoland for the
Danes, against Tegetthoff in 1864.   At all events my
father, who inclined to liberal views in home politics,
shared the resentment which was growing up in the
Gneisenau circle against selfish Great Britain, and
cherished his own youthful memories of the other
allies of Prussia's regeneration, the Russians.   The

difference of opinion among the great ones at home naturally reacted upon us children, and I can remember acting in a little play at a party at home in which my sister played the Englishman, my brother (who inherited the disposition of our two refugee grandmothers) played the Frenchman, and I as the Russian received the blows which represented the Crimean War.

As a sea-cadet I soon found from my own experience that the Prussians were still esteemed in England. Between 1864 and 1870 our real supply base was Plymouth, where Nelson's three-deckers and the great wooden ships of the line of the Crimean War lay in long rows up the river. Here we felt ourselves almost more at home than in the peaceful and idyllic Kiel, which only grumbled at Prussia and whose harbour was crossed at that time by one little steamer only, which brought flour from the water-mill at Swentin.

In the Navy Hotel at Plymouth we were treated like British midshipmen, even in regard to prices. As we poor brothers in arms of Waterloo had not yet offended England by our economic power we were suffered with friendly condescension. Our tiny naval officers' corps looked up to the British navy with admiration, and our seamen sailed in those days quite as much on English ships as on German. The majority of our ratings served for twelve years on the English model and only a small section were recruits, but these latter had sailed in every merchant service,

part of them indeed in the American navy, and all
spoke English. We officers were on the best of terms
with the English, and kept up this comradeship right
into the last few years before the world-war, when
the younger British officers began to pay less attention to manners (the result of the lowering of the
social standard among the recruits), and to alter their
behaviour towards us in consequence of the agitation
against us.

The seeds of Britain's displeasure were sown on
September 2nd, 1870. When our squadron anchored
off Dover in July, 1870, in view of the threat of war,
we were welcomed by innumerable steamers, closely
packed with people, who shouted in a friendly way:
" It is all settled between France and Prussia," because they believed that peace was assured after the
Hohenzollern's candidature for the throne had been
withdrawn.

The general attitude then was still: Poor Prussia!
if only it is not swallowed up by Napoleon! We were
looked upon as the attacked party. It was after the
battle of Sedan that English feeling changed round,
though it did not affect the navy, which still continued
to treat us as professional brethren. It struck me,
however, that the upper classes of English society
abandoned our side immediately the war was over, a
change which was helped by the much closer tie between their civilization and Paris, and by their coolness
towards what was felt to be German lack of form.

The Prussian navy had little tradition of its own.

The expedition to Eastern Asia still stood out as a kind of famous deed, and then there was the war against Denmark (in which, however, the lack of a proper fleet was keenly felt when the support desired by Prince Friedrich Karl for the transportation of troops to Alsen broke down owing to the bad weather, the weak engines of our gunboats, and the superiority of the Danish fleet). We grew up on the British navy like a creeping plant. We preferred to get our supplies from England. If an engine ran smoothly and without a hitch, if a rope or a chain did not break, then it was certain not to be a home-made article, but a product of English workshops—a rope with the famous red strand of the British navy. In those ships which we had built ourselves things broke with uncomfortable readiness. When I came to Berlin in the winter of 1869 for the Artillery Test Commission, the great national question of Krupp *v.* Armstrong, which had just been decided in Krupp's favour, was still throbbing in people's minds. The navy had been for Armstrong. In those days we could not imagine that German guns could be equal to English.

When an Englishwoman saw our crews on board the *Friedrich Karl* at Gibraltar in 1873, she said in astonishment, "Don't they look just like sailors?" For our men were superior to the British at that time, just as I believe they were at the beginning of the world-war. When I asked her how else they should look, she replied in a most decided tone, "But you are not a sea-going nation."

On the whole Bismarck's words to Geelach in a letter of 1857 hold good for the relationship between us. . . . " A's for foreign countries I have had all through my life a sympathy for England and its inhabitants, and it comes over me even now from time to time. But these people do not want to let themselves be liked by us."

CHAPTER II

1. In Hamburg, 1871. German fishermen under foreign flag. Foreign service. Carthagena.—2. "Those are soldiers." The militarization of the Navy. The Naval Academy. The Naval Staff. Stosch's plan for the foundation of a navy.—3. We explore. Manysidedness of maritime interests.

I

FROM 1871 to 1888 the navy worked under landsmen. Lieut.-General von Stosch relieved Prince Adalbert of the supreme command in 1871, and at the same time took over the Naval Department of the War Ministry. General von Caprivi succeeded him as Chief of the Admiralty from 1883 up to the beginning of the William II era.

When the fine flag with the eagle was hauled down on our ships in 1867, and the flag of the North German Federation, more on the English pattern, was hoisted in its place, we ensigns were pained, it is true, at the disappearance of the Prussian colours, but we foreboded a great historical change, and emptied our glasses with mixed feelings. The year 1871 pushed the memory of Prussia farther back; we became Imperial officers and the navy received the black-white-and-red cockade.

We of the navy were in touch with the Hanseats at a time when they were anti-Prussian and refused military service. In 1871 I was a lieutenant on the *Blitz* in the Elbe, where Prussia had put a guardship in 1866 to watch the annexationist tendencies of Hamburg. This outpost was left on the frontier, forgotten; we had light river-duties and harbour-police duties; in general, however, we were purely demonstrative—and enjoyed Hamburg's friendship until Stosch found out that we were idling there, and cancelled the command. The harbour of Hamburg, full of poetry —the maze of sailing ships lay along the quay-side, for the docks had not yet been built—still had all the character of an import harbour. The shipping was chiefly in English hands, and one could perceive how much Germany's chief port had formerly been an English agency. It was not until the year 1895 that the German flag predominated for the first time over the English in the Hamburg harbour. When the *Blitz* lay in the Elbe, the Hamburgers, feeling themselves to be merely a passive commercial centre, still inclined towards England, upon whom indeed they were absolutely dependent, whilst Germany had to take their coffee and tobacco at any cost, so that even long afterwards the Hamburgers struggled against their incorporation in the Customs Union (1888).

Stosch started from the idea of developing Germany's maritime interests, of strengthening and protecting " Germandom " and German labour in the world. This policy was first brought home to me when I was first officer of the gunboat *Blitz,* by an order to protect the fisheries.

Along with greater things the German herring fisheries had gone to ruin during the centuries of our weakness and our poverty. Stosch was the first man to support the first herring fishing association which was re-formed in Emden. The enterprise laboured under a disadvantage, because we had a longer way to go to the herring grounds than the foreign fishermen, and the tax of one thaler upon every ton of herrings—dating from Frederick the Great's administration in Eastern Friesland—did not allow so young a business to thrive with unskilled labour.

Before the world-war, we unfortunately imported foreign fish, mostly herrings, to the value of far more that Mk. 100,000,000. A higher tariff which was aimed at was wrecked by the catchword "the poor man's herring," although the tax would have been scarcely noticeable on each herring at the retail dealers. For it is the middleman between Emden and Berlin who doubles the price of herrings.

The five Emden trawlers who first ventured out herring fishing asked for military protection, because neither their lives nor their nets were safe among the Scottish and Dutch fishermen who fished in hundreds on their customary grounds. Our old wooden gunboat had at the same time to study the best way of making catches and the best stations for the herring shoals. Owing to the breaking of a mast we arrived late at the grounds—it was June, and as light as day

at midnight at more than 60° longitude; the sea was
calm and covered with fishing boats, Dutchmen, Scots,
and a few French—but when we looked round for
our boats we could not find our charges for days. At
last we saw a few trawlers which agreed with our
description, and we actually recognised through the
telescope the thin black-white-and-red strip which had
been given us as a mark of recognition. When we
approached them, however, the nearest trawler set
sail and made off. We sent a shot after it, whereupon
it lowered its sail. When we asked the men why they
denied their German nationality, they said that it
would have been too unsafe for them, that they would
have run the risk of the strangers sailing through their
nets and tearing them in two. Our good Emdeners
as a matter of fact sailed under the Dutch flag, and
were afraid of acknowledging the German colours.
In Lerwick we did meet one who hoisted the German
flag at our approach, dutifully brought us a ton of
herrings, but then immediately put to sea and vanished.
The officer of a Dutch warship lying there then told
us that this trawler which had acted like a German
that day had come in only the night before disguised as
a Dutchman, and had gone to the Dutch vessel for
a doctor and medicine. The Herring Association had
itself recommended this peculiar proceeding to its
members.

Thus we saw in the most illuminating way how in-
timidated a great nation can become without sea-power
and how cut off we were from the riches which the

sea offered us. It was not very long since Palmerston had threatened to treat any ship flying the German flag as a pirate. When we were at Amrum in the same year (1872), several trawlers from Finkenwerder hid themselves behind the island because the English North Sea fishing fleet with eighty or ninety boats was covering the sea in front of Amrum. We advised the people of Finkenwerder to put out because we should have liked nothing better than to be able to seize one of those foreign fishermen for any transgression of the three-mile limit. The men replied, however, that they would not dare to do this because we were not always there to protect them. This was the state of our national pride and prestige along our own coasts. How we had fallen since the days of the Hanseatic League!

Stosch's increasing endeavour to further Germany's maritime interests in all directions was pursued under great difficulties from the beginning of his period of office. Foreign service at this time almost overstrained the resources of the navy. Every commander, however, could reckon upon Stosch's consistent support in his activities abroad, even in the often independent and difficult decisions which foreign service required as a result of the scarcity of cable connections. But this was not done without some friction with the Imperial Chancellor. In 1873, when I was officer of the watch on the *Friedrich Karl,* we received orders to protect Germans in the ports of Southern Spain where there was civil war. While doing so we seized a sloop that had been captured by the insurgents and was flying a red flag; but this did not meet with Bismarck's approval. Then again our commander, Werner, in conjunction with the British armoured vessel *Swiftsure,* was asked by the Germans and also by the Spanish municipal authorities of Malaga to seize the insurgent ships *Almansa* and *Victoria;* he did so, and put their *personnel,* together with their leader, General Contreras, on shore at Carthagena. But an order came from Berlin for the dismissal of Werner, and for the recall of our squadron from the roads of Carthagena. We heard afterwards that in Berlin, both Stosch and Moltke had supported Werner, whilst Bismarck insisted upon his dismissal and actually wanted to bring him before a court martial.

In Carthagena we had been co-operating with British ships, which to our shame we had now to leave in the lurch. At Gibraltar, Werner was relieved of his command. When he left the ship he read us a few letters from Stosch, and ended with the words, "That's what the man writes to me." He rebelled, so to speak. Hitherto we had been held in high esteem; it had been enough for our flag to show itself; when it was said "Frederico Carlos està qui," the whole coast, filled as it was with insurgents, became quiet. But our position declined so much with the sacrifice of Werner, that we afterwards experienced great difficulties, and not only with the insurgents. Whilst many Germans had previously remembered their nationality, and whilst their numbers on the

consular lists was constantly increasing (in Malaga
it had actually been trebled in a week), the Germans
were henceforward badly treated everywhere, and ultimately their houses were looted in Carthagena. Hereupon we receivd orders to proceed against the fortress
of Carthagena. Now this was difficult from a military
point of view with the *Friedrich Karl* and one gunboat. Our new commander telegraphed to Stosch
that it was doubtful whether he could carry out the
order with the forces at his disposal. Stosch's reply
was phrased with the classic pungency which was characteristic of him. He said that other ships would be
commissioned for our support, but that for the rest
he would suggest that it was not ships but men that
did the fighting. We proceeded, therefore, and the
order was promptly executed. But our reputation
along the coast had sunk for once; this was not without its consequences, nor without its economic disadvantages also.

The English are not accustomed to abandon an officer, either politically or militarily, no matter whether
his action exceeds the prescribed limits or not.
Whether it is the annihilation of the Turkish fleet
at Navarino or the struggle for the Taku forts,
whether it is the flight of the daughter of the Sultan
of Zanzibar, whether it is a planned murder like that
of Sir Roger Casement, the " King Stephen" incident, or even the " Baralong " affair, which they have
probably condemned in private, the English protect
their people on principle, in order to strengthen the

regard for Britons in the world, and their inclination
to act on their own initiative. In the English foreign
service attention is paid to liberty of action, and as
a precaution risky enterprises are carried out as far
as possible by subordinatees and not by chiefs of mis-
sions. With us the hierarchical order is inviolably
preserved.

In this case Bismarck's motives were not known to
us younger sailors, and the exposure of Werner was
incomprehensible in so far as in our view it could
only be welcomed by the legitimate Spanish Government, if the protection of the quite considerable German interests on the south coast at the time weakened
the insurgents. Our reverence for Bismarck did not
suffer from the incident any more than from his
other disagreements with Stosch. His peculiar greatness carried with it perhaps the disadvantage that our
knowledge of politics, like that of the majority of
Germans, was not very highly developed, since everything connected with politics seemed to be provided
for, so to speak, for all time by the figure of the old
master who had given us the Empire.

II

In addition we had no time for politics. Apart from
the development of Germany's maritime interests,
Stosch's second fundamental idea by which he left
his mark on the navy was that he taught it to *work*. I
do not mean work without mistakes; that was impossible with a nation that was estranged from the sea

and its nature; but work in its real sense. The more
mature the navy became, and the more our nation
came to understand the great prospects in the sea, the
more fruit did this capacity for work bear. I remembered the astonished remarks of English officers when
we lay in our old tubs alongside the modern English
vessels at Malta in 1890, and drilled and drudged the
whole day long. If they demanded so much of their
people, they said, there would be mutiny. They could
not understand this stringent regimen, particularly
as, in consequence of the short period of service of
the German crew, it did not altogether lead to efficiency. The year before, we had paraded a landing
division before the Queen in the park at Osborne;
the British naval officers exclaimed in astonishment,
" These are soldiers." The impression was not quite
correct, but it was significant.

Under Prince Adalbert strict care had been taken that
the customs copied from the English navy should be
naval and not military. For example, when the Prince
made a tour of inspection the sailor had to wear his
gigantic shining hat on the back of his head and stand
with his legs apart; people stepping on to the quarter-
deck had to salute the flag; on board, the seaman
saluted his officer by taking off his cap, the petty officer by lifting his cap, and so on with many other
bits of etiquette; but there was no standing stiffly to
attention, nor could one keep one's hands to one's
trouser seams in the old sailing days. The crews
had strenuous and dangerous but individual duties,

and the petty officers often acted on their own initiative up aloft. When the ship rolled, everybody had to look to himself. The army training did not exist in the service in the days of training ships.

When we lay in the Wilhelmshaven basin in the winter of 1870, and the rigging was all down, we were, as I said, drilled to exhaustion. The military tendency increased too abruptly under General Stosch. Many of the older officers grumbled: there used to be one spot left in Prussia where one could live, they said, and that was the navy; this state of things could not be borne any longer. There were others, however, who carried the infantry training and the drill farther than Stosch had probably intended, in order to further their own reputations. The slight attraction of the navy under Stosch also led him to accept less suitable officer recruits. This fact, and the impossibility of getting any tactical schooling for the navy of those days, are together responsible for the scarcity of personality among the admirals of the beginning of the twentieth century. Stosch's personality was as sharp as jagged iron. He frequently amused us during inspection by strong reprimands which often cut to the root of the matter. I can remember one criticism at the end of an inspection, which began with the cutting words: "Sheer slop—from the commander to the lowest ship's boy!" It is true that the commander had had the honour and the misfortune to entertain Prince Friedrich Karl on board for four weeks during the summer: a kind of visit which Stosch regarded as distracting to the service. His forceful intervention in the whole development of the navy was helped by the fact that he practically united in himself both the supreme executive command and the administration, so that internal obstacles could be easily brushed aside by him.

In the twelve-year ratings—long-service men—the old Prussian navy possessed a *personnel* which we have never since obtained. Stosch introduced the three years', or more correctly the two and a half years' service, more ruthlessly than was adapted to the requirements of voyages.

In spite of all the zeal, the frequent retirement of experts and the short-dated periods of service rendered the achievements demanded by the Admiralty quite impossible. We were brought into a well-nigh dangerous situation by the abolition of the petty officers' categories. Thus the whole of the quartermaster's *personnel* was done away with and replaced by men from the crew, so that the duties of the quartermaster had to be put upon the officers.

Just as this abolition of necessary specialists and the introduction of the two and a half years' service period (which was too short for a training in navigation) did not suit the material and personal characteristics of the navy, so, inversely, the land training was screwed up to an importance which it did not possess.

The summer squadrons were not put into commission until May; they were expected to do the utmost at once, and they dispersed again in the autumn before they could do anything at all. Then in the autumn the crews came ashore, mostly to the depots, but they were not arranged in categories as was done later— but treated just like regiments. There was no time left during the short summer manœuvres for any battle, or even squadron, training, and indeed scarcely any time for the roughest training in ordinary ship routine. In the words of one admiral, the squadron training in battle tactics resembled "an attempt to mould something solid out of loose sand."

Strict watch duties, in the military sense, were introduced on board the ships and devoured time and energy without having any real use. We had to wear the uniform with the hussar's sash introduced by Stosch, even on watch in the tropics, until one officer fainted on the bridge; then white drill appeared once more. Further, mobilization on army lines was introduced. Formerly the commissioning of ships had lasted several weeks, but later on we gave it up, so to speak, and kept the ships permanently in commission. Stosch, on the other hand, demanded that since a regiment was mobilized in three days, the same should be done with the ships. The fact that the complicated microcosm of technical matters which a ship represents, interspersed with the most varied requirements and considerations, does not form an organism if all the material is thrust on board within three days, was passed over at this period with a big sponge. Stosch was never a sailor, and in addition, his advisers who were not always well chosen, neglected to translate his military ideas into our terms, and if necessary even to oppose him. There were too many commands, and too few questions, and consequently the sinking of the *Grosser Kurfürst* in 1878, which was partly due to this militarization of the navy, brought the storm of criticism to the surface. From that time onwards more attention was paid to the requirements of a voyage, and to the ship as an organism. Later, Caprivi and I raised the standard of training in the fleet; in particular, by re-introducing a greater continuity in the *personnel*—in so far as the shortened period of service permitted. In the naval academy which Stosch founded at Kiel he inspired the right idea of teaching fewer special subjects, and promoting general education and independent study. A great deal of mathematics was taught, besides philosophy, natural and nautical science (regarding which we sent many observations to the museums during our voyages), and astronomy, which in any case can be reckoned among the special sciences. The history of naval warfare was insufficiently taught in those days and little was to be gained from maritime law; political economy was only added under my administration. In the course of years the academy has assumed a more specializing character, although I have always urged against its being made a purely preparatory school for the Naval Staff, and against being allowed to rear scholars who were not capable of turning out spick and span. I also tried to confine the technical side of the teaching at the schools

—including the academy—more to special courses, in which they had more facilities for keeping up with the new developments in technical matters than they had at the academy, with its restricted time and limited supply of models. More fruitful than the technical instructions in the naval schools were the scientific shipbuilding and engineering sections. It is not that the officer has to make these things, but he must be able to criticize their construction. The technical side is so subdivided to-day that the constructor himself is ignorant of the details. In addition the mind of the pure technician is not absolutely adapted to other tasks. There are indeed from time to time engineers with a universal grasp at the head of great undertakings, but the organising vein is more often found in lawyers or merchants. In addition to the military questions, however, particularly those of increasingly complicated tactics, the naval officer has other matters, such as organizing, legal and political, to attend to. The higher naval officer must have spent some part of his life in the great world. The higher mathematics, so valuable as mental gymnastics, are, to a certain degree, dangerous for the naval officer. The subject is too absorbing in its inexhaustibility, and its exactness can, like any other theory, lead a man to underestimate the *imponderabilia,* and to forget that the art of generalship is not a logical science, but is born of intuition, and formed primarily of personality. Therefore those categories which rise to the highest positions ought not to be trained as specialists.

It is good for them to have specialized in some work and to know what it means and the sum total of mental and physical labour that it contains; but their own line should diverge from the technical.[1] Specialization became more and more dangerous to the navy. So much the more do I consider Stosch's educational system, which aimed at an all-round training, to be correct.

Among Stosch's efforts to establish a similarity with the army, he instituted a Naval Staff Course, and extended the Naval Staff which he had created, actually giving it a badge of its own on the lines of the "qualification stripe" of the General Staff. In the navy, however, one must not remain long ashore or else one forgets one's seamanship. Moreover the navy's active service is much more varied than that of the army. The General Staff permeates the whole army like a vitalizing nerve-cord, as a second safeguard side by side with the hierarchy of the commanders, as an assistant reporter for the commanders, and depending with them upon the personal connection between the Corps Staff and the great General Staff. Such a second nerve-system is inconceivable in the navy. The holding together of great masses,

---

[1] Apropos, I mention here the principle introduced by Lord Fisher in England of standardizing the officers' corps so that the gentleman who had been trained to engineering could serve just as well on the bridge. The British naval attaché in 1913 gave as the reason for this so-called Selborne system the desire to weaken the advancing democratic influence of the trade unions in the engine-room by giving it a military point. This system does not imply any military progress.

questions connected with advances, and similar problems disappear here; there are only a few individuals,
namely, the ships, to lead. Even in the epoch of wireless telegraphy, the fact still remains in naval warfare
that the commander must be sole ruler on board his
ship; and in just the same degree the chiefs of the
squadron staffs cannot have gentlemen under them
who have outside connections. Stosch's Naval Staff
course was therefore put on one side again; those
officers who are now appointed to the Naval Staff are
preferably taken from the fleet. This very proper
abolition of the Naval Staff course rendered it more
difficult to promote gifted young leaders to responsible
posts at an early age, but this difficulty could be overcome by other means in case of necessity.

How far Stosch proceeded from the standpoint of
a land-general is indicated by the scheme for the establishment of a fleet that he drew up on taking over
office. His ship-building programme aimed at a small
concentrated raiding or " sally " fleet as the kernel of
the navy—the " sally " was a land term to begin with
—whilst the remaining ships were to be distributed
along the coast as a kind of garrison facing the sea.
The nature of the Baltic harbours then made it necessary to construct these ships with flat bottoms, thus
producing a cross between a sea-going ship and a
coastal-defence vessel without any outstanding character. The idea of distributing a portion of the forces
along the coast was not a good one, for when the
moment came to strike they all had to be concentrated

again. The army model of distribution of effectives
is not adaptable to the fleet; for a ship is in itself an
instrument of attack. Stosch passed over such things
in his dominating manner.

III

If the beginnings of the Imperial navy were hampered by the dominating prestige of the army, yet
Stosch, as I said, was ahead of his time in the energy
with which he pushed forward our sea power that had
been neglected for centuries.

He attached great value to the posting of cruisers
to foreign stations, and rightly too in his time. For
the political conditions in the South American States,
for example, or in China and Japan, were not yet so
far developed as to allow diplomatic or consular procedure to suffice in every case; the actual power on
the spot decided the day.

As far back as the seventies Stosch was convinced
that we must acquire colonies, and that we could not
continue in existence without some means of expansion. He considered that the prosperity of the young
Empire would only be ephemeral if we did not counterbalance the decided disadvantage of our position and
history overseas before it was too late.

At that time we could have obtained better colonies
more easily than was the case later. Apart too from
colonial ambitions, the navy was permeated by a striving after knowledge of world economics, all the more
since the news service was only feebly devoloped by

professional consuls. When we were abroad with the
Friedrich Karl in 1872 we had orders to " explore,"
to report on all places both as to what they were
suited for and what economic importance they might
have for us. I still remember how I reconnoitred the
island of Porto Grande in the Cape Verd Islands; it
was almost barren, high rocks with a few scattered
palms, but it was the natural coaling-station between
Cape Town, Europe, and South America.

During our visit to Curaçoa we got the impression
that the purchase of the island was being considered,
and it is possible that our next year's commission, a
voyage to Hawaii, was connected with something similar. But in the seventies Germany did not understand
such symptoms. Moreover, the shameful fact that
we had to let the bulk of our increasing population
emigrate abroad, as we were not yet in a position to
export goods instead of human beings, stood in peculiar contrast to our political reputation. Stosch
busied himself with all imperial questions that were
connected with the sea, particularly the development
of our stunted mercantile marine. He met with a
good deal of opposition, but succeeded in setting the
standard for shipping affairs in the Federal Council;
he made use of the Hydrographic Office, the Naval
Observatory, and of our relations with the Hanseatic
Ambassadors in order to strengthen his position.
Sailors' schools, in which the navy was directly interested on account of its supply of recruits, pilots, ton-
nage questions, lighthouses, surveys, the fisheries of

which I spoke above, all consular affairs—in short, all the petty matters of the sea were this indefatigable man's field of activity. He broke down in ruthless fashion the old tradition of giving preference to the machinery of foreign countries, and of England in particular. Even if this youthful period of German industry brought to the fore abundant cases of the so-called " children's ailments " of machinery, the succeeding period has been grateful to our old chief for his policy.

Stosch took up again the broken thread of the Hansa; he was the first to feel his way towards a future for Germany overseas. He did a great deal also to breathe a belligerent spirit into the navy. Mistakes were made, but in those days it was not a trifling matter; a grave earnestness characterized our work.

CHAPTER III

1. Caprivi's fundamental idea. Preparations for the approaching war on two fronts. Coastal defence. The twelve tactical questions. The Naval Staff. Our first plan of operation. The lack of a shipbuilding programme.—2. Caprivi, Imperial Chancellor.

I

In spite of the strenuous drill, the chances of war were really very slight during the Stosch era, in view of the international situation during the seventies. In those days the young Imperial eagle made its first flight across the sea in peace. While we had to keep two things in mind at the beginning of the twentieth century, the enormous and yet so vulnerable importance of Germany's peaceful labour throughout the world, and the dangers of war which threatened the mother country on all sides, Stosch had not to reckon with any immediate enemies. The first real manœuvres held by Stosch, which were on the smallest scale, took place in 1882 shortly before his resignation. As a matter of fact it was scarcely possible to carry out manœuvres in a tactical sense since we had not yet been trained to such a pitch; it was really only an exercise in the simple multiplication table, so to speak. Much time was expended on artillery exercises and simple shooting practice, but the most important feature then was the firing of concentrated broadsides at a range of only 200 and 500 yards, a fact which speaks for itself.

In Caprivi we had a new chief at the head of the Admiralty in 1883, who adapted all his work to the idea of war, under the influence of international conditions, although he also followed his own bent. Caprivi was the typical General Staff officer. This man, who was understood by very few people, lived and weaved his plans in the state of mind which he often expressed to me as follows: " Next year we shall have a war on two fronts." Every year he expected it the next spring. He was far less a politician than Stosch. When he was afterwards summoned by the Emperor William II, some time after Bismarck's departure, to take over the Chancellorship according to command, he said bitterly to Field-Marshal Loë on the way to the Castle, " I am now going to bury my military fame." In the words of Prince Friedrich Karl, he was " a good man spoiled " for the navy, and ought really to have been Chief of the General Staff.

Under his influence the navy acquired a politico-military character. Whether this was right or not may be left out of the question, but it was at least an idea. Under Stosch the navy had not known for what strategic end it was working. The bulk of it was absorbed in the formalities which may be called going through " evolutions "; it was practising what is known

as wheeling to the right and the left in company drill.
The mobilization existed only on paper. Caprivi held
an inspection in the spring of 1883, and was overcome
by the enormous working activity which was going on
without any proper guiding idea.

As it was impossible to do anything on a very big
scale with any speed, and as the weakness of the navy
under Stosch had always lain in the fact that it was
expected to attempt more than it could perform, Caprivi restricted himself until the next war to the
preparation of strong coastal defences against Russia
and France. If this "two-front" idea is not taken
into consideration, it is easy to make unjust criticisms
of his imperfect realization of the navy's tasks. He
said to himself: First of all the war which is coming
the day after to-morrow must be settled and then we
can go on developing the navy. He proceeded to get
into close personal touch with the work, and even conducted the manœuvres, which were now held every
autumn, with various general and special projects as
in the army. They were generally directed against the
coast, the one party attacking it and the other defend-
ing it.

At that time I had already won a certain position
in the navy, as the creator of the torpedo section, and
could permit myself some criticism of the backwardness of our tactics. Besides, I was related to Caprivi,
which fact, however, was rather dangerous with one
of his nature, so that I really never got away from
the tie. But I could speak frankly, and I said to

him: what we especially lack is some grasp of tactics; we do not know how we should fight. Caprivi did everything in his power to take up this suggestion. He put the so-called " twelve tactical questions " to a series of officers whose judgment he respected. It was always premised that the French were against us, and the questions were then asked: How will the advance be regulated? What order of battle should we adopt? How would one behave in the *mêlée* which (in Caprivi's opinion) would ensue under any circumstances? [1]

Caprivi instituted Naval Staff tours, during which problems were set on the following lines: Russia and France declare war upon us; the Russian fleet wants to join the French, and we are to prevent it. It was from such situations, which served as the guiding line of the discussion, that a gradual advance was made from mere coastal defence to the demand for a High Sea Fleet. Caprivi's activities culminated in his working out personally our first plan of operation after he had instructed himself in the matter; then he brought me in for consultation. The plan consisted roughly as follows: I was to run a torpedo division into Cherbourg the moment war was declared, and then the battle fleet which we possessed was to proceed to Cherbourg and bombard the place. Caprivi is also the real originator of our mobilization.

[1] For my part I still considered it probable that a kind of cavalry engagement must develop if a battle were fought to a finish.

In spite of his grasp of tactics, Caprivi had no definite shipbuilding programme. It is true he saw that
the Navy could not live from hand to mouth. On the
one hand, however, he had been too far removed from
naval matters all his life, and on the other, the views
that prevailed in the naval officers' corps itself were
far too vague to allow a definite shipbuilding policy
to crystallize. Caprivi was amazed at the chaos of
shipbuilding schemes. I explained to him, in reply
to his frequent questions, that a decision on the composition of the fleet could only proceed from clarity in
tactical ideas, which had not yet been obtained. Finally
the political ideas of the chiefs crippled shipbuilding.
On the occasion of the introduction of the two years'
service period in the Army Bill of 1893, Caprivi, who
was the Imperial Chancellor, said to me: " We must
not think of the creation of a strong German navy
until the international and psychological necessity of
a war with Russia, whom France will join, has been
concluded." Our continental orientation, which had
been one-sided for centuries, made us overlook far
too easily before 1896—what Bethmann overlooked
in July, 1914—that England's European policy of the
Balance of Power would have intervened if we had
beaten the Dual Alliance.

His activity as Chancellor must likewise be interpreted pre-eminently by his idea of the " two-front "
war, for politics as politics were not in his line. His
friendliness towards the Poles had its root in his endeavour to establish an element there which would

not be too hostile to us in the event of war. When I was spending some weeks with King Humbert of Italy in 1893, Caprivi commissioned me to say to him, "The decision will take place on the Rhine." At the dissolution of the reinsurance treaty, Caprivi, as I happen to know from him personally, was actuated by the feeling that the treaty was not quite honourable in view of the unavoidable war: in addition it was depriving us of Austria's confidence. Caprivi had once gone with Prince Friedrich Karl on an official visit to Russia after 1870. While there he felt everywhere the hatred and the jealousy of the St. Petersburg officers towards the widely famed Prussian army, which I myself can confirm from my own experiences. We had won too many victories. Caprivi used to tell how Czar Alexander II disregarded the German officers quite noticeably, until he suddenly rushed up to them in one of the rooms and said to Caprivi, "You have no idea how I like you, but I daren't show it here." Knowing Caprivi as I do, I consider it inconceivable that he was subject to any English or court influences on the occasion of the dissolution of the reinsurance treaty. In order to bind Austria more firmly to us in the event of war, he concluded the commercial treaty of 1891 with her on terms that were unfavourable for our agriculture.

Caprivi found no time to cultivate our maritime interests as Stosch had done, neither did his own personality urge him to do so. He belonged to the class of the sons of officers and government officials whose thoughts are far removed from economics, and who are not attracted by the subject. The lonely man, with no requirements of his own, brought with him little sympathy for the development of industry. He was therefore an opponent of colonial expansion at first, although when ' ordered he performed the military share of the acquisition of colonies with skill and energy.

II

When I attempted during my period of office to do justice to the money-making classes, and in the spirit of Stosch to revive once more the cutlivation of maritime interests that had been broken off in 1883, I ran up against many of the irregularities which have arisen during the course of German history. Misplaced economy and petty bureaucratic narrowness have made our way into the world difficult. The navy had more ample occasion to feel and realize this than the army. Its duties on the whole gave it a certain world-perspective. Until the great war, the army took the study of the world, and particularly of England, much less to heart. In all essentials it marched into the world-war with the old ideas of a "two-front" war, and with a natural superiority which it possessed over the navy in consequence of the prevailing land tradition in Germany; it still looked upon the fleet indeed as a kind of pioneer detachment of the army, unmindful of the fact that the real main front was the sea front,

now that a grave but not hopeless fate had made us
the target of a world-coalition. In short, this insistence on Caprivi's standpoint under completely altered
conditions was one of the historical reasons for the
war taking the course it did. But more of this later.

In contrast to the land officer, the naval officer was
referred to the study of overseas forces. Intercourse
with foreigners moreover rounded off the rough Prussian edges in him, without killing his appreciation
of the indispensable traditions of the State. For it
must never be forgotten that Prussia has fashioned in
her officers one of the few fixed German types, and
moreover the type which has enabled us to appear
as free men in the world again, since our complete
lapse into foreign slavery after Frederick the Great.

> "La vie au roi,
> L'honneur pour soi,
> Sacrifiant son bien,
> Chicane pour un rien,
> Voilà l'officier prussien."

Between 1870 and 1914 the German State was
too young to fashion a German type of its own.
This fact did us harm in the world.

The relations of the English naval officers' corps
with their German comrades were still free from jealousy in Caprivi's time. The prevailing tendency in
official policy at that time to regard the British fleet
as the complement of the Triple Alliance almost
brought our relations to that pitch of friendliness
which such an alliance implies, but this was con-

stantly avoided by England when practical issues were broached. The prestige we gained in 1870 helped us over our naval inferiority in our relations with the French. We admired in the French the pride of a beaten people which never forgets its honour for a moment, and we smiled many a time at the *romance verve* of their desire for revenge.[1]

Feeling against the Germans became intensified after the nineties owing to various reasons. We older men remember with peculiar feelings those days under William I, when we were still distinguished people in the world, and were well received. But this gloom which settled around us could hardly have been relieved by the "victory on both fronts" of Caprivi's imagination, and even of the General Staff's plans in 1914. For it arose especially from the un-exampled growth of our overseas trade, and from

---

[1] One little scene is characteristic of this. When we fell in with a French squadron off Salonika in 1876, both of us seeking satisfaction for the murder of consuls, the French were not allowed to mix in our society; they were not allowed to accept a glass of wine even when they were on active duty with us for several hours. Once when a French commander came on board I paraded the crew, and since he was impressed by it he could not but invite me to see the same on his ship. I went, and all the formal courtesies were gone through. When we went into the battery, however, gun-drill was taking place there, and the officer in charge gave the order: "Direction: Babord contre la frégate turque, tribord contre la frégate Kronprinz!" Whereupon the gun crews turned round and grinned at me with pleasure. The commander, however, dealt with the officer in private. No painful scenes occurred then as they did later during the public celebration of the opening of the North-East Canal in 1895 (a demonstration which was distasteful to me), when the French and the Russians behaved so unpleasantly.

the irritation created by Germany's conquest of the world's market. The annoyance of the English at our upward movement was scarcely to be felt during the Caprivi era, but it had come to light in all its strength ten years afterwards, about the middle of the nineties, long before the beginning of our real naval construction.

The accession of the Emperor William II closed the epoch of the naval generals. Stosch and Caprivi belonged to the flower of the Prussian army in Germany's greatest epoch; they had taken leading parts in the wars of union. I was honoured by co-operation with these great-minded masters, and when I took over the Imperial Admiralty in 1897 I tried to collect into one volume the varied lines of thought which they had both displayed, under more spacious conditions. For various reasons, however, the naval administration by no means prospered in the interim, but sank into chaos for nearly a decade.

CHAPTER IV

I

Since I was twenty-nine I have had the good fortune
to be employed uninterruptedly in positions of independence, among which in fact there was not one
of those " soft jobs " that now and again fall to the
lot of members of the General Staff. My rise is
bound up with the development of the torpedo arm.
Whitehead in Fiume had invented the automatic torpedo which brought within firing range those vital
parts of a ship below the water line, which could only
be attacked hitherto with the ram of a vessel; it thus
promised a revolution in naval tactics and shipbuilding. Stosch had introduced the fish torpedo over-
hastily, and had bought large numbers of them before they were really serviceable for war. The use
of it still constituted " a greater danger to the man
who launched it than to his enemy." People were
too optimistic about it, and, as is often the case with
new weapons, had anticipated the change before the
new idea was really practicable.

When Stosch realized this he asked for special reports in the autumn of 1877 from the chief of the torpedo section and certain of his subordinate officers, and these he read himself. My report drew his attention to me. In the winter of 1877-78 I was sent to Fiume to deal with Whitehead about the torpedos, which we did not consider of any use. I succeeded in getting rid of half our order, which Whitehead sold elsewhere.[1]

From May onwards I led the torpedo section as commander of the *Zieten*. I began, so to speak, with nothing at all, and often worked partly like a mechanic with my own hands, making myself an apparatus. When the Crown Prince and the Emperor inspected the navy in 1879 and 1880 I was allowed to demonstrate in torpedo-firing, and the unexpected and certain success of this helped to strengthen Stosch's position again, which had been shaken by the *Grosser Kurfürst* catastrophe.

I proceeded with the torpedo section, just as I did later with all new inventions, whether airship, submarine, or anything else. I refrained from the premature

[1] On this occasion the threatening war between Britain and Russia in 1878 (in which I was ordered to support the Russians as far as I could) produced a peculiar impression of Hungary's relations with Austria. Whitehead, who was a thorough Englishman, refused to supply the Russians; the Hungarian Government under Tisza prohibited the export of torpedoes, so that we were compelled to try to take the torpedoes, which we had already bought, across the Austrian frontier, which was only an hour distant, on the recommendation of Austrian gentlemen, although they were German property. The Hungarians then set up honved outposts, so that the matter had to be settled diplomatically.

adoption of new devices, but acted energetically as
soon as I saw that the matter contained some real
possibility of development. I have always found this
method to be the only right one. It was very often
a difficult part of my duties to prevent myself, as Secretary of State, from getting agitated by the impatient
throng of inventions which came rushing in from all
sides during this epoch; but it was also a very important one, if we were to set up a first-class navy with
our limited means in the short time instead of a mu-
seum of experiments. We were overwhelmed with
unripe inventions which had first to be sifted by instinct, so as not to fritter away and overburden the
energies of the authorities. Once I was unable to
put on the brake, and the success of the construction
of the fleet was endangered by haste, which was our
greatest enemy in the whole undertaking.[1]

In my work in the torpedo section I first set myself
to perfect the technical accuracy which is necessary
in everything connected with shipping, and which in

[1] An example of this. When wireless telegraphy came in it
promised to fulfill a long-felt need in the navy for the trans-
mission of orders from ship to ship at long distances. Everybody pressed therefore for its introduction on a grand scale—the
navy, the firm directly interested in it, and of course the Emperor.
And yet it was not ripe for use at sea, nor was the introduction of business competition at all desired. During my absence
in America, however, its installation was carried through in
spite of the opposition of my deputy. The consequence was
that the necessary development came to a standstill for the time
being; moreover, we had to spend a great deal of money quite
unnecessarily on the installation, and had endless trouble with
these technical difficulties. Naturally I got the blame and I
was now attacked because of its ineffectiveness.

all my labours I continuously kept in view. The Whitehead torpedo was all right as far as the idea went; but it still had too much uneven engine work, and consequently lacked the necessary clockwork precision. The same thing occurred in the case of the submarine, which likewise requires work of the best quality. For the first time in Germany we obtained this workmanship, upon which serviceability in time of war depends, in the torpedo arm, and even the English did not quite reach the high level of our torpedo firing. When I gave a demonstration of the Whitehead torpedoes before the Crown Prince in 1879, in spite of many weeks' preparation, it was still a toss-up whether they would reach the target or ricochet wildly. Fortune smiled upon us, but I afterwards said to Stosch that now we must get to work on our own standard of precision.

The Admiralty next approached the German factory of Schwartzkopf, which had been advertising so widely the merits of their bronze torpedoes that the Admiralty wanted to give it a monopoly. I opposed this; in the first place because a share-holding company which has a monopoly easily pays too much attention to its annual dividends, and not enough to the development of the product; secondly, because I was convinced in this case of the advantages of steel over bronze; again, because in the tendency towards home-production that was growing in the bigger foreign navies, no foreign money would have come to Germany as a compensation for us; and finally, because the most important experimental work on the water could not be done by the firm, but was our own special prerogative. Thus I succeeded in calling into being State torpedo-workshops; the progress of the torpedo arm is indicated by the increase in its range, which only amounted to 400 yards at the time of its general introduction to the navy, but rose to 12,000 yards by the winter of 1915-1916. The nationalization of torpedo-production did not affect the opinion I held that State workshops are only suited for special and limited purposes, and that repairs are generally carried out better, and certainly more cheaply, in State workshops than in private concerns.

In order to avoid as far as possible the accumulation of expensive war supplies, I followed the principle when I was Secretary of State of keeping private industry, and contractors generally, prepared for the event of war. At that time I gave out our contracts, including those for provisions, clothing, coal, etc., on the condition that the contracting private firm made arrangements to proceed forthwith to an increased output in the event of mobilization. For these preparations for mobilization we had to pay rather higher prices in some cases. I have often been attacked for acting on this principle, but it was only by so doing that we were able to help out the army with 2,000,000 kilos of gunpowder up to the beginning of 1915. The army was supported far more than we were by State workshops, but it was not prepared for the enormous requirements of the world-war—and at that time it had almost emptied its magazines,[1] and was saved by the navy from the gravest danger.

In spite of the military advantage of a recognized, uninterrupted mobilization, the navy system of supply had possessed the great economic advantage that we were able to keep the unused stores quite low in times of peace and consequently lay out to productive ends the small amount of money which Germany could spare us; and further, if it came to the worst, we could only rely on carefully considered peace-time arrangements, and were thus relieved of the danger of over-hasty war-contracts.

I have often been attacked in the Reichstag because of my attitude to private enterprise and contractors generally. Parliament begrudged the private firms the big orders, and, with one eye on the State-socialism of the future, inclined more to the principle of State factories. Even in future wars any overstraining of the State-mechanism or any check upon private industry would lead to the most dangerous crises.

II

I mention here a small matter which I would not broach if the Revolution did not threaten to change so fundamentally our old conditions.

Schwartzkopf had explained to me the advantage

[1] The competent officer at G.H.Q. told me as early as in October, 1914, that Verdun was not attacked any more on account of the shortage of ammunition, since it was not desired to expose the Crown Prince's army to a reverse.

which would accrue from the purchase of some of his shares which, as was to be expected, had trebled their value in consequence of the naval contracts. Naturally I did not buy any shares, and would have dismissed any official who acted otherwise. Our State always premises in its servants that nobility of feeling by which it had risen to greatness under the Prussian kings. I am reminded of the Finance Minister who arranged the purchase of the Prussian railways, and on resignation left his own office in the most unsatisfactory condition. The salaries in certain high offices were not in just proportion to their importance and the expenses they incurred. When I was Secretary of State I had to draw on my own income at first in order to meet the calls my office made upon me. It goes without saying that our officials worked for the honour of the thing. With a minimum of expenditure we performed a maximum of creative work. Thus the State administration in the old Prussia-Germany was cheaper and cleaner than anywhere else in the world. After the expenditure of State money, and the creation of innumerable sinecures, which are bestowed upon persons more for their politics than for their fitness for the posts, it is to be feared that the new State will not be like the old. The old German State has been weakened and broken by a period of mediocrity at a time of the greatest danger; but the German nation will never be lost so long as it does not lose the clean character of the old administration. The corrupt German is worse than the corrupt Italian or Frenchman, who at least never betrays his Fatherland.

The German cannot afford to abandon that uprightness which was the palladium of his old civil service, for he lacks the other political qualities which help to render almost all other foreign nations immune from the poison of corruption. Even during the last generation one could notice the harmful influence of the materialism which was penetrating into the upper classes of Germany, in the shape of a weakening of character, a diminution of that positive idealism which the German nation will always have to exert in the interests of its own self-preservation. For it is only by proud, unselfish devotion to the State that it can counterbalance the deficiencies of its geographical position, its bad frontiers, its limited area, its jealous neighbours, its religious differences, and its too young and too uncertain national sentiment.

As then chance gave me for my first important task the development of the torpedo *arm,* and was so kind to me that we were able to overtake the performances of other navies in the same province, I was able to obtain at the same time an insight into the workings of the mind of a factory director. But I was glad when the torpedo *boat* brought me back to my natural field of activity, viz. tactics. In my whole progress the line of development from the technical to the organizing side by way of tactics has been repeated again and again.

Stosch opposed the torpedo boat, which had already

been constructed in England. But when I was working out the first manœuvres at his orders in 1882,
things went so well with our experimental boats, which
were bad in those days, that Stosch began to take an
interest in torpedo boats. Then Caprivi, who recognized in the torpedo boat a means which corresponded
to his strategic ideas, commissioned me to develop the
torpedo-boat section. There was a great variety of
opinions on the subject. Some wanted small coastal
boats. I demanded sea-going vessels which could fight
in the North Sea, and the struggle between the ad-
vocates of sea-going ships and those who supported
the coast-defence scheme continued through all my
activities down to the building of the submarines.

Even before the pattern boats, which had been ordered from various German and English firms, were
completed, Caprivi asked me to devise suitable tactics
with the older boats in the summer of 1884. Thus,
the growth of tactics preceded the development of the
more cumbrous technical side, just as it did later in
the case of tactical work with the big ships in the
nineties.[1]

In the meantime the boats which we had ordered
arrived, the Admiralty having wrongly left to the dis-
cretion of the different firms a number of important
considerations, such as sea-worthiness, cheapness, size,

---

[1] Cf. Chap. VI. For the rest, I never shared this infatuation
for torpedo boats, and pointed out to Caprivi that this auxiliary
arm, which (like the submarine later) was bound by its very
nature to become obsolete, could never be a substitute for a
battle fleet which was our real need.

and so on. The firms were therefore obliged to act without any military knowledge and to rely on their own methods; one aimed at cheapness, and the other at speed, and so on. But every warship is a compromise of different desires which can never all be fulfilled at one and the same time within the limits of the finished article. A certain armament, fuel storage, accommodation, buoyancy, armour plating, speed, are all wanted with a given displacement; then there is a fight in the committees over a matter of 25 or 50 tons; and if one wanted to satisfy everybody, one would soon have a 100,000-ton ship without having settled anything at all. Thus it is the strategic idea of the ship which must be firmly determined before anything else; in the nature of things, however, only the supreme naval command, and not the firm, can decide this.

The new boats proved to be either unsuitable or undeveloped; we were involved in some danger with them in a storm off Norway. Caprivi discovered a way out of the conflict between the Admiralty engineers and myself, on the subject of the type of torpedo boat, by instituting in 1886 a Torpedo Inspection Board, which he handed over to me, and which covered all branches of the torpedo section. We elaborated the sea-going boat armed with artillery. The fleet training, the dockyards, and the workshops were now controlled by one hand, which had its advantages at this stage.

III

A's Inspector of Torpedoes I had to report myself, along with other officers, to the old Emperor. He spoke with each individual in such a friendly and fatherly manner that everybody was deeply touched. Then he stepped into the middle of the circle, assuming quite naturally a kingly attitude, and reminded us in earnest words of our duty. It was all so simple that one's heart was moved; one felt the mind of this man, who had the State before his eyes in everything that he did. One would have suffered oneself to be torn in pieces for him.

In 1887 Prince William, afterwards Emperor, went to England to attend the Jubilee of his grandmother, where he was coldly received, probably on account of the medical controversy regarding his father (*wohl schon wegen des Aerztestreits um seinen Vater*). I commanded the torpedo flotilla which accompanied the Prince, and which was to be paraded quite unnecessarily before the English. It was at this time that I got to know the Prince, who plunged with a passionate interest into everything connected with the technical side of the navy.

The next year Caprivi handed over the Admiralty to Count Monts. The latter had an undisguised dislike of torpedo boats, which was indeed shared by almost all the older officers of that time, partly owing to a natural distrust of everything new, and partly because younger officers were appointed to independent commands in the torpedo section at an age which they considered was not sufficiently ripe. At any rate, at his first inspection of the flotilla, Count Monts declared that the whole thing was mere show, which would be useless in battle.

Thereupon I asked the leader of the Naval Cabinet for a command at sea, and further, that some restraint should be imposed upon Count Monts lest he should prejudice the torpedo arm.

CHAPTER V

THE NEW COURSE

1. Caprivi leaves the Admiralty. The fatal division of naval authority. The chaos. Memoranda. An "imposition."

WILLIAM II had sketched some types of ships when he was still a prince, and, as he did not come to the Admiralty, he had had a shipbuilder brought from the fleet for this favourite pastime of his. As soon as he had ascended the throne he summoned the chief of the shipbuilding section to him. This disregard of the Minister was contrary to the old Prussian traditions, and gave Caprivi the formal ground for handing in his resignation. Caprivi wrote to me that he would not have suited the young Emperor for long; that the Emperor did not like him, and only made him Imperial Chancellor later because it was thought that some strong man was needed against the Bismarck *fronde*. The deep-seated reason for Caprivi's departure was, however, that the Emperor wanted to divide the powers of the Admiralty, in order to be able the better to intervene himself. Bismarck, who had been discomfited in his collisions with Stosch by the powers united in the hands of the latter, unfortunately favoured this splitting up of the naval administration (1888), which had a harmful effect in peace-time, and was almost fatal in war.

In 1859 the naval leadership was split for the first time, and the executive command was separated from the administration. The several conflicts which resulted from this division ended in reversion to the old system under Stosch in 1871. And now in spite of those previous experiences, the executive command and the Admiralty were once more separated in 1888; in addition, a special Naval Cabinet was established and attached to the Monarch, and all three authorities were granted direct access to the Sovereign. The field was now open for play and counter-play, for three or four different naval policies.

There now appeared upon the scene a kind of Cabinet Government which had once before dug itself into Prussian history. If the Cabinet had restricted itself to advising the Emperor on the selection of the highest officials, and had left the responsibility together with liberty of action to the latter, then there would have been no objection to a Cabinet that was provided with some knowledge of human kind and character. As this condition of a triple responsibility developed, it was only in August 1918, when almost everything was lost, that the Admiralty and the supreme Naval Staff reunited in practice to form a supreme Naval Command, after they had been played off against one another for decades, and the intervention of the leader of the Cabinet was now abolished. The internal struggles and obstacles which hampered the practical work of the divided authorities during times of peace were naturally unknown to the general public.

If William II's burning desire to establish a navy had begun to be fulfilled in 1888, we might perhaps have attained our object before the grouping of the enemy Powers became so dangerous. The ten years lost between 1888 and 1897 compelled us either to inscribe a permanent " too late " on the aims which Germany's sea-power was striving for, or else to cross a political danger zone by proceeding with the building of the fleet.

In 1888, however, it was difficult for the Emperor to find suitably trained officers for the leading posts. Perhaps the navy was not yet old enough, and the success of Caprivi's efforts to exert an educated influence on the officers' corps could only bear fruit later.

After the short periods of office of Count Monts and Admiral Heussner, Admiral Hollmann came to the Admiralty in 1890, a high-minded man who was, however, never quite clear as to the direction to be followed. Caprivi had worked according to a principle which was only half correct from the navy's point of view, but now there began a period in which decisions were taken which were absolutely devoid of principle and adapted only to the needs of the moment. It was the tendency during this period to bring forward demands in the Reichstag which were based not so much upon requirements as upon the

probability of their being granted. Every fraction
of a cruiser was disputed in the Reichstag, and the
catchwords "zigzag courses" and "boundless plans,"
with which Eugen Richter worked against the navy
in the Reichstag, were difficult to refute. Worse than
this, every authority in the navy wanted and proposed
something different. The aimlessness of it all was
felt everywhere, and produced a chronic crisis. The
confusion of opinions displayed itself, for instance,
in the heterogeneous collection of vessels, from which
one could not confidently expect any mutual co-operation in the event of war. In justice one must add that
no navies at that time were at all clear as to how a
modern naval war would develop.

After I had commanded the *Preussen*, and then the
Württemberg, in the Mediterranean from 1889 to
1890, I was to have been made Director of Dockyards, but as the result of a remark made by Chancellor *v.* Caprivi to the effect that I should be kept
in a position which would better prepare me for responsible commands, I was appointed by the Emperor
to be Chief of Staff of the Baltic Station in the autumn
of 1890. There I had ample opportunity of observing
the conflicts between the Executive Command and
the Admiralty, both of whom were working equally
badly.

In the spring of 1891 the Emperor was once sitting
with us officers after dinner in Kiel Castle; the old
Moltke was there too. At the Emperor's suggestion
a discussion took place as to how the navy should

be developed. The most varied views were expressed
in the usual fashion, and without throwing any real
light on the subject. Being a junior captain, I kept
out of the discussion. Finally, the Emperor said,
" Here I have been listening to you arguing for hours
that we must put an end to all this mess, and yet not
one of you has made a really positive suggestion."
The Chief of the Naval Cabinet, von Senden-Bibran,
who had read one of my memoranda, nudged me
encouragingly; I took the hint, for it was painful
for me to hear the Emperor make this drastic criticism in front of the old general. So I described how
I conceived the development of the navy, and as I
had been continually jotting down my ideas on the
subject, I was able to give a pretty complete picture
without any difficulty.

The next day the Emperor got up early and walked
for some hours with the Chief of the Cabinet, talking
excitedly all the time, and drawing up a kind of
" imposition " to be done by all naval officers who
had taken part in the conversation.

CHAPTER VI

TACTICAL WORK

1. Commissioned to develop the tactics of the High Sea Fleet. My preparatory school for this in the study of torpedo-boat tactics. The "black company."—2. Training the High Sea Fleet. Line tactics. The squadron principle. The English in arrears.

I

WHEN I was appointed Chief of Staff to the Executive Command in January 1892, and was personally commissioned by the Emperor to develop the strategy of the High Sea Fleet, I had behind me a more thorough schooling in tactics and strategy than any officer in the navy. I was always attracted by historical studies; I was soon conversant with the ancient and modern history of naval warfare, and, as a matter of fact, the insipidity of modern accounts generally sent me back to the original writings for my information. I also continued to study the history of land warfare, not from mere inclination, but in order to obtain, a deeper psychological knowledge of my own subject. I should think I have read everything of any importance that has been written upon Frederick the Great, and the Wars of Liberation of 1866 and 1870.

When I was a young gunnery-officer on board H.M.

ships in the seventies I was fully alive to the changes
wrought in our service by engineering. I was all the
time striving to get at the fighting values of it all,
and I remember the joy which the first recognition
of my independent working methods gave me, as for
example, when a French captain gravely remarked
on inspecting my battery: " Je vous vois travailler
pour le but final." The task which had been set me
in 1877 of elaborating the torpedo arm had banished
me, as I have already said, to a purely technical field
of work, and the difficult and painfully exact task
of developing inanimate material was less congenial to
me, although, like mathematics, it trained me to
methodical procedure. I perceived, however, that the
new submarine weapon, whose laws had to be discovered, opened up prospects for the militant qualities of the German nation to rival the larger navies
of older and richer states. The precise methods of
work which my mechanical experience had taught me
soon stood me in good stead in my tactical experiments.

The special courses which I had arranged for the
training of officers and ratings of torpedo craft during the winter months led us to consider the problem
of single combats between ships. Very little methodical work had been given to this subject at that time.
We also sought to develop the art of manœuvring
vessels independently. I had excellent officers at my
disposal, who transmitted all that they had learnt
from us—and particularly our methods of work—to

the other vessels of the navy. One special object of my manœuvring course was to teach the naval officers to act on their own initiative much more than had been customary, owing to fear of collision. Before my time the single ship had hardly been given any training in independent manœuvres, but had been straightway worked in squadron formations, in which one ship is bound by the others. It was my principle now to train the individual hoplites before forming the phalanx. This secured a high certainty of movement, which attracted much notice when I was able to proceed with apparent daring as commander of the *Preussen* and *Württemberg* in the first operations with heavy ships in squadron formation; in reality my ability to do so was due to practice, but it was often wanting in the other ships owing to the weakness of their individual training.

Besides training the single ship for the duel, I was also working upon the complicated co-operation of several units, when I was commissioned to work out tactics and organization for the new torpedo craft. The great risk of collision had made not only us, but foreign navies, too, nervous of real battle practice with torpedo boats. Those countries which are parliamentarily governed have found by experience that it is almost impossible to hold naval manœuvres which really reproduce war conditions. But we overcame the nervousness of public opinion most effectually, and gained thereby an advantage in preparedness for war. In all the mishaps that occurred to our ships during

manœuvres I supported on principle the officer concerned, but I also demanded the most stringent sailor-
like precautions at sea.

Whilst working out these fighting formations, I
endeavoured to impress upon the officers that we were
able by these means to find out practically everything
that was wrong, but we were not certain to discover
what was absolutely right for war; we could not therefore lay down any dogmatic rules. In view of all
the incalculable possibilities of battle, the supreme tactical principle for torpedo boats was "Close up, and
fire at the centre"; in other words, when the moment
had come for attack, to stake everything on the safest
shot; the torpedo that hit the enemy was the best
protection against his artillery. The second principle
was more general; it bordered on strategy and ran as
follows, "Act according to circumstances." This
sounds simple, and a matter of course; but most persons in such situations prefer to act according to orders, instead of following their own responsible decision. If the officers in the higher commands believe
that they themselves can ensure success by their own
directions, then this tendency, which has its drawbacks in a crisis, always leads to a flood of regula-
tions and battle orders. There were times in the
years leading up to the world-war when assurance of
victory was far too prevalent in our navy, and this
always has the dangerous result of leading to spec-
tacular fighting formations and showy manœuvres.
After I was detached more and more from the fleet,

To my great sorrow, in 1897 I had no opportunity of effectively combatting these growing dangers, although my own earlier work convinced me that I saw quite plainly the results of these methods. This weakness for the decorative side, and the drilling and polishing that it entails, tend to quench the living spirit by mere routine.

Our work with the torpedo boats had helped considerably, even in Caprivi's time, to determine the development of the navy from the coastal-defence idea to the High Sea Fleet.

A special arm like torpedo boats must be allowed, if it is to produce its best, a special status and comparative independence in the main body of the fleet. Later on, the torpedo boats were included in the fleet of somewhat too arbitrary a fashion, and a cruiser was put in command of them; and this had more drawbacks than advantages, at least as regards the use of torpedo boats at night.

I spent the eleven best years of my life in the torpedo section among " our black comrades, of the wild and daring chase." We were bound to our incomparable crews by ardour and mutual comradeship in orm and danger. We officers of the torpedo section instituted a corps within a corps, the united spirit which was everywhere recognized, but also envied and opposed. When I became Chief of Staff I took ever the whole of the " torpedo crowd " with me, and so I had a trained body of workmen at my immediate disposal. I tried to do the same later at the Admiralty, but there my wishes as regards *personnel* met with opposition in the Naval Cabinet.

II

When I joined the Executive Command in Berlin in 1892 the necessity for improving the fleet training to meet the demands of active service was perfectly clear to me. To this end a corresponding organization had to be created for the fleet before anything else, and the short-dated commissioning of ships in the summer had to be done away with, in favour of keeping ships permanently in commission. At that time the Admiralty was at work unwisely arranging the whole navy on the lines of the army, in such a way as to transfer the centre of gravity of the navy to the land.[1] I prevented this, for it was only possible to give the fleet any tactical training by means of permanent formations which manœuvred and were composed in peace-time as they would be in war.

Soon after taking up my new duties I went to see the Naval Secretary of State, and told him that I would regard him as my leader in every way, but that he must give me a free hand with regard to the intellectual training of the navy. We parted good

[1] On mobilization, each vessel was to give up half its crew for newly commissioned ships, and to make up its complement with recruits. This would have meant the break-up of the whole internal organization of the ship, and consequently the squadron formation which had been trained with so much trouble; and our readiness for war would have been destroyed. We should have had a crowd of ships with men on board, but no fleet.

friends, but Hollmann did not go into my request in detail, and expressed the view that the Executive Command would have to make itself scarce. At this stage of our tactical proficiency this opinion could only be vindicated if the Secretary of State himself took the tactical training of the navy in hand, as Caprivi had done when Chief of the Admiralty. Hollman, however, had no intention of doing so, for he was completely absorbed by parliamentary difficulties. On the other hand, the draft of a series of exercises evolved by a commission was made official and given binding force. But this new regulation contained nothing but evolutions, *i.e.* merely the movements of ships, so to speak, in empty space, the transitions from one " quadrille " to another. The real fighting value had no place there, nor could it have, since people were not clear as to how they intended to fight, whether in the manner of Nelson or Tegetthoff. They exhausted their imaginations in discovering and manœuvring in theory as many formations as possible, from which the Admiral was then to make his choice.

I replaced these " roundabouts " (*karussel reiten*) by the principle of first making it clear to ourselves how we had to fight in battle. The next autumn manœuvres in 1892, which were arranged to this end, resulted in a new quarrel between the Admiralty and the Command, in the course of which the new regulation was replaced by one that I had evolved myself. To begin with, we improved the individual training of the ships, and then proceeded step by step.

It was only human that this intervention from above was not appreciated by the commanders and the squadron chiefs, and I was given the nickname " M ter." Towards autumn we collected all the ships that we had in home waters, and formed a manœuvr of fleet which operated under the personal direction of the Executive Command. As we arranged them in fighting units, regardless of the class of vessel, we combined numbers of ships which had hitherto never worked in company. It could be said that men fought here, and not ships. For the navy was so small that we could only establish large battle-formations and manœuvre them one against the other by scraping together all the training ships, mine-sweepers, and other simulacra that we possessed.

It was then that we began operations in large formation, and without more ado we dropped a number of practice formations which had been highly esteemed until then, including the wedge and square Between 1892 and 1894 we discovered our line tactics. The main feature of this was to keep the enemy at the centre of our line, no matter how he manœuvred. In addition we discovered our squadron principle. Until then there had been no theory of naval warfare and no certainty as to what number of vessels constituted the most effective squadron unit. Helped by the nature of our line tactics on the one hand and the success of our intensive training on the other, we fixed upon eight ships as the most favourable number for formations fighting in a line; in the event of most vessels being at liberty, more squadrons were formed which were to fight in a series of lines. Thus there arose out of our tactics a new organization which exerted a determining influence upon the Navy Bill. On the basis of our results I also reintroduced the old designation " Ship of the Line " into the navy.

I cannot avoid the impression that the real meaning of the squadron principle is at times not fully appreciated. The perfectly natural tendency of the Commander-in-Chief to lead the whole fleet as a tactical unit only meets the case in certain situations. On the other hand, it is usually only a certain independence on the part of the squadron commanders that can produce the highest effort on the part of the fleet. The larger the fleet, the more difficult it is to handle when concentrated. Its manœuvrings become clumsier, and the commander is easily prevented by smoke, rain, and particularly powder-smoke, from reviewing the position of the various sections. This is the most important reason why we decided upon the squadron as the tactical unit, and thus gave the squadron commanders and the equivalent leaders of flotillas the right to act "according to circumstances." The full realization of this idea is also connected with the endeavour permanently to adjust the organization and method of the navy to the training of men who possess the gift of leadership.

Soon after us all navies proceeded to adopt some kind of line tactics and our squadron principle. Thus it may seem strange to people to-day that no navy in the world had yet formulated any definite principles at the beginning of the nineties, and that the " wedge and square " question, for example, still played a considerable part in the specialist literature of those days; whilst even the Athenian Phormio had overcome by his line the Spartans, who clung to their land ideas and formed a square at sea under Brasidas. Whilst we were discovering these things quite empirically on the " small practice-ground " by Kiel Bay, the American Admiral Mahan was simultaneously evolving them theoretically from history, and when I made the acquaintance of his book later, I drew his attention to this extraordinary coincidence.

The English seemed to me to be very behindhand in their tactics at the time, a fact which was illustrated by the Tryon trial following upon the sinking of the *Victoria.* The truth of the matter was that the English had no need for tactics. The Battle of Trafalgar had removed all competition in sea-power, and from that day onwards the theoretical as well as the practical development of naval warfare came to a standstill, whilst the balancing of the Powers kept the science of war active enough on land. The British navy, with its overwhelming superiority, could more or less shoot any opponent to pieces. We were not in such a position. By our example, however, the English were once more compelled to work and to apply their minds again to naval warfare. At first the English troubled very little about the small German navy.

Their attention was drawn to our work by means of official memoranda which were either stolen or acquired from a sunken torpedo boat. About 1896 the British navy began to have the feeling that we were competitors, and since they began to regard us in that light, they have studied us and followed similar lines in their own manœuvres. They will never confess that they learned from us in this way. It is so, however, and we were quite aware, even at that time, that the British navy received the new spirit of its development from us. The fact that a navy which had practically no ships at all should lead the way in method, reflected Germany's position in the world. We had either to build ships or else give our ideas to foreigners. We built the ships, and in soundness and tactical achievement, but not in numbers, they were actually superior to the English during the world-war, although England had long since recovered from her place of tactical torpor and hazy manœuvres.

Those years saw my greatest achievement, the infusion of a militant spirit into the navy. But like everything else, the tactical and strategical work of my life lacks the stamp of final success. The unfounded prestige of the British navy robbed Germany's leaders of their courage at the beginning of the war, when the German navy had the best prospect of giving them victory. The Battle of Jutland, interrupted as it was by darkness, was not fought to a finish. If it had been, there would in my opinion have been a prospect of putting quite a different face upon the history of the world. The bitterest fate awaited the German fleet, and I was denied sailing out with it.

CHAPTER VII

NAVAL SCHEMES

1. Service publications. Sea-fight or cruiser warfare?—2. The necessity of a fleet for Germany. Correspondence with Stosch. Attitude towards England.—3. My 1895 plan of operations. Acquisition of Heligoland.

I

OUR tactical discoveries resulted of their own accord in a definite and desirable concentration of *matériel*. The activities of the Executive Command which had been put down in " official memoranda " consolidated into concrete proposals for the construction of a High Sea Fleet. When I returned from Eastern Asia later to take over the Secretaryship of State, I replied to the question, " What is going to be brought into the Reichstag? " with, " All that is contained in the ninth memorandum."

In spite of the tactical results of these official memoranda and their recognition by the Emperor, the Admiralty under Hollmann was still working for a cruiser war; it even urged the Emperor in this direction and represented the same views in the Reichstag, without any system at all, so that the Reichstag was just as unable as ever to understand what the navy was out after.

In the winter of 1894-5, a number of Reichstag deputies were to attend a naval conference in the Potsdam Palais; at first it was intended that I should report to them, but later the Emperor decided to address
them himself. I learned that the Emperor intended
to speak unreservedly in favour of a cruiser war, and
to influence the ⁸Reichstag in this direction. It happened that I had to report to the Emperor for the
Executive Command the day before, and I seized the
opportunity to inform the Emperor of the contents
of that memorandum, which represented the *battle*
to be the object and the centre of gravity of our
tactical organizing development. The Emperor was
vexed, probably because it meant disturbing the scheme
of his address, and he asked me, " Why was Nelson
then always calling for frigates? " I replied, " Because he *had* a battle fleet." At any rate the outcome
of my representation was that the Emperor spoke
about both cruiser war and battle fleet to the deputies
the next day, with the result that they had less idea
than ever of what was really intended. One portion
of the Reichstag observed a distrustful and hostile
attitude towards " personal naval whims "; Herr von
Leipziger, reporter to the commission on navy matters,
groaned aloud to me that evening in Potsdam and
said, " If only we knew which way they really want
to go! "

In the autumn of 1895 I asked to be relieved of
my office on account of new conflicts with the Admiralty. My successor was Admiral von Diederichs,

and Admiral von Knorr took over the Executive Command, without bringing, however, any relaxation in the conflicts and chaos of these years. In December, 1895, the Command handed in a memorandum on the necessary naval construction; I was commanded by the Emperor to give my opinion on this scheme, which I did both in writing and by word of mouth during the New Year (1895-6).

II

Two lines of thought were emerging at that time: the *tactical* necessity for a *battle* fleet, *if* we were striving for sea-power and wanted to build ships to some purpose; and the *political* necessity of establishing a protecting navy for Germany's maritime interests which were growing at such an irresistible pace. The navy never seemed to me to be an end in itself, but always a function of these maritime interests. Without sea-power Germany's position in the world resembled a mollusc without a shell. The flag had to follow trade, as other older states had realized long before it began to dawn upon us. As *The Fortnightly Review* put it, both tersely and correctly, in 1893: "Commerce either engenders a navy which is strong enough to protect it, or else it passes into the hands of foreign merchants, who already enjoy such protection."

A certain freedom from care and misgiving, the predominance of internal economic and social matters, still obscured this necessity from the mass of the Ger-

man people. The Emperor had realized it, and had
been enabled to do so by his frequent visits to England, where both he and his family soon felt quite
at home. The tendency of the Emperor to interfere
too prematurely and too noisily in world-politics, and
his inability to move in a world of realties—a difficulty
which was felt quite clearly by his people—hampered
his efforts to arouse in them an enthusiasm for the
expansion of the navy. Indeed the idea of a navy
was received with much suspicion among the people.
The Germans were pampered by the good fortune
which Bismarck's creation of the Empire and the
sudden stirring of our long-repressed economic abili-
ties had brought us, and they did not realize that our
development on the broad back of British Free Trade
and the British world-empire would continue only
until it was stopped. We owed the growth of our
physical and material strength to the growth of our
industry. We increased our population by a million
human beings every year, which means that we acquired annually the equivalent of a province within
the unalterable and narrow limits of native soil; and
all this depended upon the maintenance of our export trade, which for lack of our sea-power depended
solely upon the favour of foreigners, *i.e.* our own competitors. It was as Bismarck said: we had " to export either goods or people." In the long run the decision to form a power at sea was only an attempt
to keep a population German that was not increasing
in its own colonial settlements, but in the workshops

at home. The question was whether we were not too late for the partition of the world, which was then almost complete; whether indeed that expansion to which we owed our place among the Great Powers was not artificially and permanently untenable; whether this swift rise would not be followed by a terrible downfall. The "Open Door," which could easily be closed, was to us what their broad plains and inexhaustible natural wealth were to the other Powers. This, combined with our hemmed-in and dangerous continental position, strengthened me in my conviction that no time was to be lost in beginning the attempt to constitute ourselves a sea-power. For only a fleet which represented alliance-value to other great Powers, in other words a competent battle fleet, could put into the hands of our diplomats the tool which, if used to good purpose, could supplement our power on the continent. The object in view had to be the institution of a constellation of Powers at sea, which would remove the possibility of any injury to or attacks upon our economic prosperity, and would transform the brilliant semblance of our world-policy into a really independent position in the world. In order to bring this home to the German nation, I considered that a process of enlightenment on a large scale was required, to be executed with the reticence which foreign jealousy demanded. The question was whether this should be taken in hand by the naval administration itself, failing my other more suitable organization.

I should like to elucidate the train of my ideas in

those days, by reproducing a correspondence that I
had with my old master Stosch.

"KIEL, 21. xii, 1895,
"SCHWANENWEG 25.

"YOUR EXCELLENCY,

"I have the honour to request you most dutifully
to inform me whether the following argument agrees
with the views and the long experience of Your Excellency.

"It deals in the main with the question as to whether
a larger concentration of the maritime interests of
the Empire is to be attempted than heretofore, and
whether the Admiralty (*Reichs-Marine-Amt*) is to
be selected as the centre of crystallization. If I estimate correctly the policy that Your Excellency pursued in this matter as Chief of the Admiralty, then
Your Excellency proceeded on the above lines. Regarded from the historical point of view, it is the
standpoint adopted by Colbert and Richelieu in their
day, when they were engaged in extending the power
and economic sphere of France in this direction. If
this object were obtained for Germany, then the growth
of individual interests would lead again to disintegration. Up to 1866 our maritime interests were completely prostrated: sea-trade, export industry, trans-
Atlantic colonies, sea-fisheries, Germanism abroad, the
navy. All that survived of these had the character of
a 'parasitic existence.' A great deal of this issue still
remains. In my view Germany will swiftly sink from
her position as a great Power in the coming century
if these maritime interests are not brought to the fore-
front energetically, systematically, and without loss
of time. In no small degree also because there lies
in this new great national task, and the economic

gain which is bound up with it, a strong palliative against educated and uneducated Social-democrats.

"We cannot allow these interests to develop 'with a free hand' (Manchester-fashion), because there is no time left for such methods. Neither must our carefully planned procedure be in any way bureaucratic. The aforementioned interests can only be placed upon a sound basis by power, and indeed sea-power. Otherwise we shall lack the courage to draw cheques on the future. The 'parasite' must be changed on principle for *civis Germanus sum*. One particular difficulty lies in the fact that the expenditure on military sea-power must be made opportunely and in full realization of the economic advantages that will accrue. Narrowmindedness and the shop-keeping spirit—which only considers the personal gain of the moment—must be added to this.

"In spite of all this I believe that there is a growing current of opinion in Germany that is favourable to this idea. It will be the particular duty of the central authority to strengthen this comprehensively and persistently. If the Admiralty is chosen for this task, there is the advantage of being able to begin with an official body which contains in itself greater maritime interests than any other single Government department, and, moreover, an authority whose greatness and right to existence depends primarily upon the maritime interests, *as the navy is only a function of these latter.*

"The question would then be: will such an amalgamation as this contain the danger that the other nonmilitary maritime interests will be treated too much as secondary interests? or *vice versa,* that the exclusively naval interests will suffer owing to the activity and advertisement of the former?

"Further, as a fundamentally opposite standpoint

has been adopted since 1883, and as the other interests
have secured good treatment (which, incidentally, was
sometimes bad) from other Government departments
(Foreign Office, Home Office, Posts, the various Federal State Governments), is there still time and opportunity to strike out for this greater concentration, and
its resultant greater development of the maritime interests?"

A short time afterwards Stosch wrote to me as follows:

> "Haus Stosch,
> "Oestrich im Rheingau,
> "*Februaray 12, 1896.*

"My dear Admiral,

"I am sending you a question to-day. The anger
of the English with us, as shown on the occasion of
the Transvaal telegram, 1896, has its root in German
competition in the world-market. As foreign policy
in England is dictated solely by trade interests, we
have to reckon with the opposition of this island nation. This will crystallize as soon as these gentlemen
succeed in assuring themselves of the antipathy of
France and Russia, and we are beginning to feel uncomfortable again.

"All the English articles that I have read lately
take the view that they would knock out Germany
with one blow. I have also put to myself the question as to how we could conduct a naval war with
England with any success, and I now turn to you
and ask you to answer this for me. I may add that
I have drawn up a plan of campaign of my own, but
as I attach value to your naval judgment, I am very
eager to hear what you would propose. I hear from
Berlin that your departure to Eastern Asia (as Squad-

ron Commander) has been delayed; they are thinking after all of reducing our naval forces there in the interests of those at home. So you have had time to busy yourself with big questions.

"Be so kind as to fulfill my request. Good-bye.

"Yours,
"VON STOSCH."

I replied to this from Kiel on February 13th, 1896:

"YOUR EXCELLENCY,

"I have received your kind letter of the 12th inst., and hasten to reply to it. . . . Very urgent and unexpected business took up my whole time in Berlin. I should like to inform Your Excellency in confidence, and only for Your Excellency's immediate ear, that I have had an opportunity of vindicating in the highest quarter Your Excellency's views on the necessary expansion of the navy, and there is hope that the thread will be taken up once more where it was broken off in 1883. Perhaps I shall be able to give Your Excellency fuller details later. My appointment to Asia has become very doubtful, as your Excellency must have heard. For my own part I am very distressed about it. It was my burning desire to go out there, and it would also have been good for my nerves to have got away from this exhausting mental strain for a time, and to be right away from Madrid. I must now wait and see what fate has in store for me.

"With regard to the Transvaal question, I take the opposite view from the public and our political leaders, and consider that we have acted wrongly.[1] England puts up with a slight from America because the latter is a source of some anxiety to her, and more than any-

---

[1] By sending the Krüger telegram.

thing else because America is an unpleasant opponent, and Germany pays the bill because at the moment she has no sea-power of any weight. At the present time our policy is building on the army alone as a material basis; but the army is only effective on our land frontiers, and, in addition, only directly so through the pressure exerted from within. Our policy does not understand that Germany's alliance-value, even from the point of view of European States, does not lie altogether in our army, but in our fleet. For example; suppose Russia and France are standing together in some matter against England. The assistance of our present fleet would be too small a factor to be of any importance. But if England formulates her policy on the model of Pitt, she will prefer our hostility to our strict neutrality. We are an extremely valuable asset in any circumstances, and in the event of our remaining neutral we should gain in the most extraordinary way by being England's competitor. England knows this very well too. *Up to the present our policy has failed completely to grasp the political importance of sea-power.* If we intend to go out into the world and strengthen ourselves commercially by means of the sea, then, if we do not provide ourselves simultaneously with a certain measure of sea-power, we shall be erecting a perfectly hollow structure. When we go out into the world we shall come across interests everywhere that are either already established or to be developed in the future. This means conflict of interests. How then does the most skilful policy think to attain anything without a real power which corresponds to the many-sidedness of these interests, now that the prestige of 1870 has faded? Sea-power alone comprehends the many-sidedness of world-policy. Even if it does not come to war, therefore, we shall always come off worst politically.

It must also be taken into account that England has lost some of her belief that we should send our army to fight for her against Russia. On the other hand England can make Russia very considerable concessions, in Eastern Asia for example, if Germany comes off worst. In this last fact lies the danger, if we become involved at the present time in a conflict which affects Russia, France, and England. Also even if we propose to say that we were not going to war for trans-Atlantic interests, the other three States would not say the same, so we are continually working at a political disadvantage. A great deal more could be said on this point. But I just wanted to show that I did not arrive at my conclusions about the Transvaal question of the moment without some reflection. As a matter of fact, I conceived this opinion the moment I had read the telegram to President Krüger in the newspapers.

"This telegram was not even skilfully worded, for since England possesses the right of sanctioning this State's conventions with foreign countries—a fact which we cannot deny—we were not in the position to offer the Transvaal *our* help.

"This incident may, however, have its good side, and I should think that a much bigger row would have been actually useful to us, in the sense that it would have opened the eyes of our Parliament; firstly, to put a definite stop to the Anglomania of certain circles, and secondly *to arouse our nation to build a fleet* on the lines of memorandum 9. This estimate is actually to be included in the next Budget. The Government and the leaders of the Reichstag, to be sure, see no prospect of success. By representing unreservedly the military and political value of our present fleet, the Admiralty has at least discharged its obligation, and history will have to call other people to account.

" My policy is therefore to create within the next
twelve years a fleet which is in keeping with the requirements of the same, and whose strength shall not
be far removed in essentials from that laid down in
Your Excellency's first memorandum of 1872. . . ."

Jameson's raid upon the Boer Republic and the
Krüger telegram had blundered into the middle of this
correspondence.   The outbreak of hatred, envy, and
anger which the Krüger telegram let loose in England
upon Germany contributed more than anything else
to open the eyes of wide sections of the German people
to our economic position and the necessity for a fleet.

But whilst German public opinion hailed the Krüger
telegram with joy and vented itself in repeated philip-
pics against England during the next few years, I
considered the Krüger telegram itself, and all the ensuing challenges to England, to be both regrettable and
dangerous.   They betrayed a widespread ignorance of
England, of her power and of our impotence.   The attempt to form a sea-power, which was difficult enough
in itself because it was undertaken so late, was further
endangered thereby, although England's isolation at
that time and her difficulties with the Boers obscured
from the eyes of the people the danger zone which we
had to pass through in building a fleet.

I still maintain to-day that the attempt to work our
way through to real world-political freedom by the
construction of a fleet could not be left untried.   The
German people will not lack occasion during the years
following the world-war to test the truth of this, and

to feel what it means to be left to the mercy of the Anglo-Saxons. Any person who is convinced that we were altogether unsuited to become a sea-power in consequence of our historical backwardness, and that we ought to have accepted the guardianship of Great Britain from the outset, must naturally condemn the workings of my mind in those days. If I had not had faith in the great future of the German nation upon the earth, I should never have possessed the strength to build it a fleet. So far I may have been deceived, although I am convinced that this attempt to attain world-political freedom would have succeeded if our policy had observed greater caution in the one direction and greater energy in the other. With other leadership we had well-founded prospects of asserting ourselves in the world-war. But if people had *not* wanted to build the fleet, but to go the way of renunciation from the nineties onward, then we should have been compelled to slacken trade and industry of our own accord; we should have been compelled to re-start emigration, and to have allowed our foreign interests abroad to go to rack and ruin. Then, as Lichnowsky says, we should have had to leave the field to the " Anglo-Saxons and the sons of Jehovah," and to have contented ourselves with our old reputation of being the salt of the earth, the fertilizer of mankind. It was, and is, an illusion, however, to think that the English would have treated us any better, and have allowed our economic growth to have proceeded unchecked if we had had no fleet. They would have

certainly told us to stop much sooner. Anybody who
knows the English could have no doubt of this. The
threatening outcry in English journalism of the 'nineties is not by any means the only sign that the irk-
some but impotent German competitor would be struck
down at the first safe opportunity. The German considered it his *bonâ fide* right to spread himself peaceably over the world and outflank English influence
everywhere, and in general he did not sufficiently appreciate the feelings of the man in possession who
looked upon him as an intruder. Moreover, people in
Germany had a wholly inadequate conception of the
peculiar composition of English power and of its
ability to encircle Germanism with mental and material forces, until the world-war revealed the truth.

III

The plan of a German battle fleet was evolved without any idea of a war with England. It would have
seemed perfectly crazy both politically and strategically to have waived the possibility of a later attack
upon England. Before 1896—that is, under Caprivi
—the popular idea was, as I said, to regard England
as the naval complement of the Triple Alliance against
France and Russia. There was also no reason at that
time to draw up defensive measures against England.
The plan of operations which I drew up in 1895 has
the " two-front " war in view, and reckons in all its
details upon a neutral England. I started on the assumption that we were to open the war against France

not as a cruiser war, but with an engagement at sea. This is the origin of our construction of a battle fleet, but the unexpected demonstrations on the part of the British navy at the beginning of 1896, as well as the trade jealousy which was breaking out more and more undisguisedly, were naturally bound soon to add an English front to the French one. After the Krüger telegram the English put a flying squadron in commission against us. This brought a new point of view into our shipbuilding deliberations, and caused Stosch to draw up the plan of operations for defence against England which he had discussed privately with me. The first official plan of operations against England was not drawn up by the Naval Staff until the beginning of the twentieth century.

How wide of the mark was this charge that England made against our navy, and how fully we were occupied in our work on the "two-front" war, is shown by our attitude towards the treaty which gave us Heligoland in exchange for Zanzibar in 1890. As a matter of fact I had wanted Heligoland as far back as 1870, and had said so in a letter to my father which contained a kind of first navy scheme, but the possibility of anchoring there, which was open to a French squadron in 1870, was now no longer to be feared since we had torpedoes. We never thought of the value of Heligoland, however, in a war with England. The island's importancé for naval warfare did not really arise until I decided, daringly enough from the engineering point of view, to make a harbour out of the

island, which would make its cliffs a base for our
naval forces and would render more difficult a close
blockade of our coast.

Caprivi's reason for acquiring Heligoland was therefore not so much its military importance, which we
hardly took into account, as the desire to put us on
good terms with England.[1] The considerable concessions which he made in Africa for the correction of
a "beauty spot" on the German coast aroused some
indignation in Germany at the time. Personally I
never put the value of Zanzibar very high in 1890,
because the successful development of German East
Africa must necessarily attract trade past the island to
the mainland.

I had already been chosen for the Secretaryship of
State at the time of that correspondence with Stosch.
But when Hollmann obtained a vote of confidence in
the Reichstag, Prince Hohenlohe hesitated to make a
change of *personnel*. At Easter, 1896, I received my
appointment as Chief of the Eastern Asiatic Cruiser
Division, and incidentally the good fortune to obtain
one more glimpse of Germany's interests overseas before I took over the Admiralty and began building the
fleet. I took with me from Berlin the commission to
seek out a place on the Chinese coast where Germany
could construct a military and economic base.

---

[1] As a matter of fact the navy greeted the new possession
with mixed feelings as the fortification of the island deprived
the navy of sums which were excessive for those times.

CHAPTER VIII

I

GERMANY took a leading part in the opening up of
China to the world's trade, but she could never depend
upon the Manchu Government to understand the fact
that Germany had a friendly interest in the preservation of China's independence. Apart from everything
else, the lack of a base hampered us, because the sole
factor of power which protected German labour and
made any impression upon the hostile authorities was
our flying squadron, and the existence of this depended upon the Hong-Kong docks and consequently
upon the favour of Britain. If German trade was
ever to cease being a go-between for English and
Chinese products, and to begin putting German wares
on the Asiatic market, it needed its own Hong-Kong
just as our squadron did.

The three places suggested to me were Amoy, a

thickly populated little island with a treaty-port north-east of Hong-Kong, the desolate Samsah Bay farther to the north, and the Chusan Islands on the eastern tip of China near Shanghai. Tsingtao (Kiauchow), of which there had once been some talk owing to Richtofen's recommendation of it, had been " dropped," I was told, because it lay too far north and off the great trade-route; moreover my predecessor in office had declared Tsingtao useless. Besides this, the Foreign Office and the Admiralty were influenced by political reasons in their preference for Amoy; they feared Russia would object to an establishment in the north, and the British had a right of pre-emption in the Chusan Islands.

The statements of numerous engineers and merchants, as well as my own reading, led me to the conclusion, even before I had seen them, that all the three places suggested to me were unsuitable and that, apart from treaty-ports and Chusan, there was only one place for the German who had once more arrived too late, since the British had searched out the whole coast as far back as the 'forties, and that was the unset pearl Tsingtao. A base must be useful to the fleet, it must promise economic prosperity and offer possibilities of defence. My chief demand was capacity for economic development; it did not seem advisable to me to establish a purely military base.

When I inspected Samsah Bay some time later, I found a narrow entrance with a dangerously strong eddying current; green islands which lay in the gigantic bay turned into steep cliffs when the tide was on the ebb. The desolate expanse of water was surrounded by mountains which could only be crossed with pack-mules. How was the fever- and typhus-ridden bay ever to compete with Fuchow with its half-million people which absorbed the trade on the River Min, not far off on the other side of the mountain!

The Chusan Islands were as little suited for defence as Samsah Bay or Amoy. Above all, however, they lay off Shanghai, just like Heligoland off Hamburg. Trade passed by them. There was the probability of complications with England, moreover, if we went for them.

Amoy, an English settlement, which we had no right to take, promised but slight economic advantages. It was still an export-harbour for coolies to Manila; its tea trade was falling off; its important geographical situation with regard to the monsoons, which had been so important for sailing ships, had depreciated more and more through the introduction of steamships; the whole place was on the down grade.

In Tsingtao there was a possibility of building fortifications. There was an enclosed bay; the northern climate was in its favour. The absence of a waterway and the presence of a poor, over-populated province as its hinterland did not deter us, as there were overwhelming signs of unusual scope for development. All information pointed in the same direction. In short, if Tsingtao was not to be included in the number, I saw myself faced with an impossible choice.

One day during a walk on the beach at Chifu I met
Lieutenant-Commander Braun, my old flag-lieutenant,
who was in command of the *Iltis*. He and I had
worked together for eleven years, and he had been
my right-hand man on the Baltic Station. We were
thoroughly attuned to one another, and he understood
me immediately; he looked over my preliminary plans,
and the next day he came on board saying that he
felt as though scales had fallen from his eyes. I was
glad of his opinion, for it was the only reliable one
that I could get on the matter. I told him that
I would write out an order for him to go to
Tsingtao to carry out researches there and report on
them.

He went, and on that occasion was caught by the
typhoon and sank with the *Iltis*. I was now compelled
to send the sailing-orders to Berlin which had contained the order for Braun to inspect the Bay of Kiauchow. I now said to myself that I must go one step
farther, and, although I would have preferred not to
have aroused attention in view of the European rivalry,
I proceeded myself to Kiauchow with the flagship
Kaiser.

Previous to this I met the new ambassador, Herr
von Heyking, who was on the same mission as myself, in Chifu with his wife. I asked him for a private
interview on official business, and soon noticed that
I had made a mistake, because his clever wife, afterwards author of *Letters Which Did not Reach Him*
was the chief assistant. Heyking reported that the

Kaiser told him at Potsdam that now he had sent out
his best ambassador and his best admiral, surely the
pair of them would come to some conclusion, and had
asked him what he was aiming at; whereupon Heyking
had replied, "At Amoy." I asked the Ambassador,
"How could you mention a place which you don't
know?" and he answered, "But I could not leave his
Majesty without a positive answer."

Thereupon we agreed not to make for any definite
place without inner conviction, and I wrote down the
points upon which we were agreed. Each of us was
to examine the different localities with his apparatus,
and we were to come to a mutual decision after I had
had my ships overhauled in the Hong-Kong dockyard
in December (this dock had always to be booked nine
months ahead), in order to be ready to take possession.
I then proceeded to investigate Tsingtao, and
thence went to Vladivostock to let my crews recuperate
in the north. Here I met an old friend from Fiume,
the Finn Virenius, who was commander of the Russian flagship. Whenever I met him he always took
me to lonely places, which my German mind did not
at first understand; but once, when Admiral Alexiev,
who was afterwards Governor-General of Manchuria,
was visiting me and I happened to treat Virenius as a
friend, the Admiral asked in a strange tone, "What,
old friends!" whereupon Virenius turned pale and
from that moment he ostensibly kept away from me.
So Alexiev distrusted his own flag-captain! On another occasion I had invited the international society

and the *élite* of Vladivostock to dinner on board, when I received news from Berlin that the Czar had been made a German Admiral. I raised my glass and tcasted the Czar; the French Admiral, who was present, and his suite remained cold, but the Russians were forced to take it in a friendly way.

Alexiev was a pronounced Francophile. In spite of this fact I should have exposed myself to ridicule as a naval officer if I had not frankly admitted in conversation the need for a German naval station. Alexiev tried to divert me to the Chusan Islands, which was quite comprehensible from his point of view, for then we should have been permanently thrown into the balance against England out there. I received reliable information that the Russian navy had considered the acquisition of Tsingtao, but had abandoned the idea as superfluous and even inconvenient for Russian interests. I learnt the same from Peking, but also that the Russian ambassador there was meditating claims to Tsingtao in spite of this refusal by his navy. Heyking and the Berlin officials were continually feeling about for the line of least resistance, and expected to find it in either Amoy or Samsah. The Executive Command even returned once more to the idea of the Chusan Islands, and for one moment the exchange of the Cameroons or Samoa for this group was under consideration. I warned against a Chinese repetition of the Anglo-Indian Transvaal friction in the event of our settling in the neighbourhood of Shanghai, and I reported on Tsingtao as being the only place in question if we were bent on acquiring a base in China.

At the end of November I received orders from Berlin to remain off Amoy, to cancel the dock, to keep the detachment with me, and to be prepared for action. In reply to my astounded inquiry, Heyking wired back that Berlin had asked whether an understanding had been reached between him and me; he had replied, " Yes, Amoy "; China's declinatory attitude on railway questions gave us a free hand for taking action.

I refused all responsibility for this choice. Apart from everything else, my action would have had to be undertaken with ships that were not in the best trim. We should easily have overcome the miserable Chinese fortifications of Amoy with their Krupp guns and a garrison of a few thousand men; the taking of the populous town was a more serious matter; but above all if political ill-feeling arose between us and England, we could be refused the use of the dockyard, and then we should be left helpless, with ships which needed repairs and upon which Germany's reputation rested in this part of the world.

Days passed, and at last the order came that I was to go into dock when I thought fit. Amoy was never mentioned again. The report, with which I had to reveal the whole situation after the sinking of the *Iltis*, had burst in upon the conflict of opinion in Berlin; the Emperor had summoned to him a man who knew the place and who corroborated all that I had said. Later, the technical information of the hydraulic engineers, whom I asked for to be sent to Tsingtao, was regarded by the public as the starting-point for the acquisition of Kiauchow. When my successor, Admiral von Diedrichs, hoisted the German flag there at the end of 1897, the Russians brought forward their legendary right of " first anchoring " (on the ground of which England could claim not only Tsingtao, but the whole world, because Englishmen had at one time or another anchored everywhere). The purpose of this was not to create serious difficulties for us, but to obtain sundry advantages for Russia by means of diplomatic protests screwed as high as they dared. It is obvious that the Russians would have preferred to push us farther south into the English sphere, and were not pleased at our establishing ourselves in the vicinity of Peking, where they played the principal rôle at that time. They gave way before the resolute attitude of the Emperor.

II

While I was in Eastern Asia I had already worked out the form of the lease, so that it looked as little as possible like forceful intervention, and allowed the Chinese to save their face; I drew up the lease-treaty in its final form with Herr von Holstein in Berlin. As Secretary of State for the Admiralty I had from now on (1898) to proceed to conquer our newly acquired possession from within and to justify our step by means of peaceful civilizing labour. The

main point was, with a moderate expenditure of capital, to discover values of which the Chinese themselves
did not suspect the presence, and with a big flourish
in this small compass to show what Germany was capable of doing. The sixteen years of our labours in
Tsingtao, which have remained a torso and have
been robbed of the far greater development that we
had in view, have left an indelible impression upon
the foreign half of the world. In comparison with
British Hong-Kong, which was fifty-five years older,
the development of this desolate fishing place to a
town of 60,000 inhabitants and an important sea-port,
in spite of strenuous competition, was almost tem-
pestuous, and yet it was in every way sound.

The size of the territory was defined exactly according to our needs. I recommended that only so much
should be taken as was necessary for future fortification and the expansion of settlements and factory sites.
The whole territory was expropriated by us. I had
had experience in Eastern Asia of the great disadvantages which had resulted from a boundless land
speculation in the European settlements out there.
This is a matter which is also worthy of study at
home. We had to make up our minds forthwith in
Tsingtao. I therefore bought the land from the people
at its then value, perhaps slightly dearer in order to
reconcile them; this was a detail in view of the prospective rise in values there. The people could remain
on the land by agreement as long as they wanted, if
we did not need it. In addition we had an extended

sphere around Tsingtao, the so-called neutral zone, through which we could march troops, and consequently we kept a hand on the surrounding neighbourhood during the disturbances in Shantung.

I insisted, on principle, that Tsingtao should not be put under the Colonial Office. If the matter was going to prosper it had to be left in the hands of one department. The navy had immediate military interests there such as a base demands—quarters, dockyard, harbour, etc. It was better to avoid friction with a special colonial administration. As we had assumed responsibility for this Eastern Asiatic base, it was my opinion that we were better suited to push on its economic development. In the same way I had declared in my letter to Stosch that the concentration of all maritime interests in the hands of the Admiralty was only desirable for a time until these interests had grown to their full strength, and I considered it possible that Tsingtao, once it was " ready," would detach itself from the Admiralty of its own accord. But the time had not come for this. The bureaucracy was not altogether friendly to our little empire. The Foreign Office showed a certain jealousy; the consul who was swiftly dispatched to Tsinanfu took care that our influence did not extend to Shantung.

I share in all essentials Carl Peters' criticism of our original colonial administration. Their initial failure is doubly regrettable because the German possesses in a high degree the stuff of which colonists are made.

He also knows how to keep the natives satisfied. I remember that Lettow-Vorbeck was greeted as a deliverer by the natives when he crossed into Portuguese territory. In any case our colonies would have developed much more favourably in many respects if they had been connected from the very beginning with the military authorities at home. This would naturally have been too great a burden for the navy itself. It was only when the Navy Bill had materialized that I wanted to leave my successer the task of getting to close grips with the construction of bases abroad. The Colonial Office did not take this into consideration, although they were a necessary condition for the development of a possible cruiser war, and above all for the linking up of Germandom abroad. But apart from this, how easily could something have been done for the defence of German East Africa if one had only troubled more about it in time of peace! The navy has indeed given both work and blood for the other colonies. For Tsingtao we could draw upon the navy for a large number of engineers and officials, whom we could send back again if they did not prove suitable, while the Colonial Office was only a bureaucratic head·piece. We were in a position to build the harbour and lay out the town. Our crews worked in all parts of the territory; we could maintain naval conscription, and all the troops we used there (one naval battalion) were adapted to naval conditions; we had doctors who were accustomed to the tropics, and who were experienced in constructing hospitals, etc. Thus we did not feel ourselves fettered at every step by the Imperial Treasury and the Reichstag, as would have been the case with the Colonial Office.

In earlier days there had been a steady trade in Kiauchow Bay, but this was paralysed by the silting-up of the harbour. Since we were able to make use of reefs for the construction of an inner harbour within the bay, which was itself protected against heavy seas, this project was carried out at a comparatively small cost. Quays and docks were then built which we could have extended at our pleasure. Tsing-tao began to be an import-harbour for the petroleum from the Sunda Islands which was urgently needed in China. A splendid impetus was provided by the Shan-tung coal, a much-coveted commodity in Eastern Asia. Our own coal deposit in the protected area was of fundamental importance. As soon as war broke out the smelting of the ores which were buried at Poshan was secured for Tsingtao. I effected this because Tsingtao was protected against local disturbances by our absolute rule. The iron-works which were to be erected with steel-mills and crushing-mills facilitated the settlement of industrial undertakings. No iron-works in the whole of Eastern Asia or Western America had such prospects; the iron and steel market there would have passed into our hands, and this increased economic importance on the part of Germany must necessarily have improved our political position, and have reacted upon all other branches of German export.

The increase of the value of Tsingtao was also to be expected because there was not a single natural harbour along the whole of the neighbouring coast, and the possibility of a favourable railway connection was bound to make Tsingtao the outlet for Peking, and indeed—a fact which I saw from the first—for the railway line to Moscow via Irkutsk, which was the best connection between Europe and Eastern Asia, together with Australia. The Shantung railway opened up the neglected hinterland of Tsingtao. Unbounded possibilities of economic prosperity lay before us.

The risings in China compelled us to carry out the so-called Boxer protection, the walling-in of the town area to an extent of 5 kilometres from water to water. Thus we avoided being in direct touch with China and prevented these disturbances from affecting us, to the great satisfaction of the rich Chinese who flocked to Tsingtao. In contrast to Hong-Kong the Chinese were settled in a special quarter, a concession to the Europeans which we might possibly have been unable to maintain in respect of the well-to-do Chinese. The natives soon had confidence in our jurisdiction, and their town, to which we had given a high degree of self-administration, prospered.

The climate was comparatively good; bathing became a great feature of life there. We combatted fever and typhus successfully by erecting waterworks, and the pestilences which devastate China from time to time were kept in check by the sanitary cordon along the Boxer wall. We also improved the health of the community by afforestation on a large scale. Our plantations became a model for the whole of China, where it had never been believed until then that cleared woodland could be afforested again. The Chinese had cleared the forests to the last twig, and the rains made great ravines in the land. We too found it very difficult to make our plantations grow at first on a soil that was devoid of humus. Their ultimate success however, encouraged the rise of other plantations. This protection of forests so impressed the Chinese that they began to study the subject quite zealously themselves. We established tree-nurseries and instructed the natives, with whom we thus got into closer touch. Round about in the neighbourhood we also taught the inoculation of fruit trees, which was still foreign to the Chinese; they came in crowds to get the grafting-twigs from us, and the fruit cultivation of Shantung increased. The first modern abattoir in Eastern Asia, which we erected in Tsingtao, started our meat export-trade.

We endeavoured to keep on good terms with the Chinese authorities. The more reasonable among them came more and more to the conclusion that the occupation of Tsingtao was a blessing for them. The Chinese recognized us and made a perceptible advance towards us. Perhaps they began to rate us higher than the Anglo-Saxon because theirs too was an old civilization. I am not of opinion that we were at all behind the Anglo-Saxons in actual achievements be-

fore the war, not even from a colonizing point of
view, or even in Africa, where perhaps the administration might have been carried out with a wider vision.
I do not like to assume that we ought to attribute
to the Anglo-Saxons some sort of world-mission, when
we could probably have done it better ourselves had
we only possessed the material means. The German had still something of the upstart about him;
he was not equal to the Anglo-Saxon in self-reliance.
But all that we did was so regular and substantial,
that in spite of the many orders from above which
were issued for the sake of appearances, our achievements even penetrated to spheres which the English
regarded as their domain (such as colonization), because we had German diligence behind us.

The rise of Tsingtao was at all events a steeple-
chase, particularly as it promised to progress at an
accelerated pace. The Germans in China gradually
began to settle in Tsingtao and to regard the town as
a centre for all that was German.

III

The navy had given its heart to Germandom abroad
ever since Stosch at the very beginning of his activities
established the aim for the fleet of getting to know the
world and particularly Germans abroad. How their
national pride had suffered during the period of our
powerlessness! During the war of 1870 only one
German, Herr Siebs, of the Siemssen firm, dared to
acknowledge his fatherland in English Hong-Kong;

most of them followed Herr Schwarzkopf's example, who changed himself to Mr. Blackhead. Outside Europe, Germandom has maintained itself by its own strength in the Latin States of South America only, although that much-mistaken rescript of von der Heydt in 1859 actually crippled emigration thither, in the interests of North America, with the intention of providing in fatherly fashion for the future welfare of the German emigrants, who were, however, lost to us henceforward. When Count Bülow proposed in the Ministry in 1900 to abolish this rescript, there were still some voices raised in favour of its preservation. Many millions of Germans who emigrated were lost to us both mentally and physically, and enriched those countries which were afterwards our worst enemies. Without past and present German labour the Entente would never have succeeded in inflicting upon us our present humiliation; one of the bitterest features of our position.

If the absorption by America was unavoidable in itself in view of the conditions which greeted our emigrants there, the manner and the speed with which this abandonment of nationality was accomplished was due to our poorly developed national sense. It was with sad feelings that I witnessed an enormous torchlight procession in New York of 14,000 German ex-soldiers, all in their prime, in honour of Prince Henry. If the question of nationality was ever broached with these people, the answer was generally: We think of Germany as our mother, but America is our wife and we must stand by her. Still less pleasant experiences were to be had over there. The ideals with which the home country had endowed them were quickly forgotten for the sake of the material advantages of American life. A professor belonging to a good German family, who had been a lecturer at a German University, was once taking me over Harvard University. He had only gone over to America a few years before, but he told me that he had already become an American citizen. The manner in which he said this did not make a pleasant impression on me, and I availed myself of an opportunity to attach myself to another American gentleman for the rest of the visit. Quite against my will the ex-German must have sensed the impression made upon me by his remark, for he said to the naval officer who was accompanying me: " Your chief seems to wonder at my becoming an American citizen so soon, but you will understand, for I have been made a professor here sooner than I should have been in Germany, and so I must be grateful." It was obvious that what this gentleman had brought with him from Germany no longer played any part in his mind. I mention such examples, and I can remember many of them, in order to characterize the lack of national pride, sentiment, and obligation which is fatally inherent in our people.

With these experiences and impressions of the German tendency in my mind, celebrations and the unveiling of monuments, of which there was no lack with us, always left me cold. In keeping with the national character which they brought with them from their homeland, the 10,000,000 North Americans of German origin have watched Germany go to her ruin, without lifting a finger. Like others, the Irish compel respect, and yet it cannot be maintained that Ireland has given her emigrating children more civilizing values than Germany. To my great grief I was fated to catch the sound of the Swabian dialect round about me in the Tabernacle of the city of the Mormons, and to listen to a missionary, who had been sent into the "land of the heathens" to get converts, describing certain parts of Germany as particularly fruitful for his labours. Almost all over the world one found oneself grieving for one's own nation in spite of its great achievements, and whilst Germans abroad were generally swayed by personal interests, every Englishman became an agent of the Foreign Office almost as a matter of course as soon as English interests were at stake. A beginning had been made, however, just before the war to turn to account the rich capital which we possessed in our Germans overseas. With the growing strength and dignity of the German Empire, and particularly with the rise of its sea-power, even Germandom abroad began to feel itself once more a qualified and pledged member of the great body of our State in blood and civilization.

The Germans who had gone overseas were scattered over the world in such a way that it was much more difficult to concentrate German interests abroad than was the case with the Anglo-Saxon, Spanish, or even the French emigrants; moreover our representatives never gave the matter anything but the most perfunctory attention. In many cases they failed to realize that even the most scattered members of a great nation should not abandon their nationality. I will not countenance the malicious saying, that many of our official representatives abroad feel the presence of other Germans to be a nuisance; but I must say of the navy that it was on the average much more zealous in linking up German sentiment and instilling into it pride of the homeland. Wherever there was a German colony we worked to strengthen the national associations across the sea. The most varied occasions were useful for holding Germans together: we passed over all class differences; this was much easier to do in Eastern Asia than anywhere else because there was no serving-class among the Germans there. Divine service brought us together. On the Emperor's birthday everybody who spoke German was invited; all possible kinds of people were to be seen on board ship that day. Out there language and blood have much more binding effect and all frontier lines disappear; the Austrians everywhere reckoned themselves among us, and even the Swiss too. Our merchant shipping, which was formerly only too ready to ingratiate itself with other merchant services, was also made more national by these endeavours on the part of the navy.

I should like to illustrate how the naval officers' corps conceived this service to Germandom by quoting from a letter written to me on my birthday, March,

1914, from South America by the Commander of the *Kaiser*.

". . . At any rate I am more convinced than ever that it is necessary to send the ships abroad, as much for the officers and men, as it is for the ships themselves; if this is not done the navy is bound to become more and more steretoyped—I can find no other expression for it. But bigger things are also at stake. There is so much German blood abroad which must be kept German and reinvigorated. Why should not the time come when this blood should pulsate again? not to form states that might be annexed, but to take effect in the development of the race and to establish natural markets for our mother country, without which we must ultimately stifle at home. Then we can also allow emigration to continue again. The Brazilian does not colonize, he has no labour, and leaves the land idle. The race will not develop there until the country is filled from without. Embassies and consulates, however, don't win back Germandon or quicken German blood, and schools even can only preserve it in cases where the family still feels German. This work can only be done by us, for it needs a strong patriotic voice and a striking symbol which can inspire them with enthusiasm."

And again the same correspondent writes to me in 1915 from the midst of the tragic inactivity of the navy, as follows:

". . . Only the navy can bring to a conclusion the great work of restoring the essential character and nature of the German to their rightful place in the world. The navy is made to carry out into the world the national strength which reposes at home upon our monarchy and our strong army; it was born for the people out of this idea; I read it in all letters which I still receive now and again from South America; the joy over the growing German spirit and over the concentration of everything that is German even where it seemed already lost. And behind it all is the thought that when peace has come again, our ships shall return to tie inextricably the knot of German sentiment."

In this way that which I had endeavoured to plant in the navy began to take root, and it became more and more effective as a pioneer of Germandom, the less the fleet was compelled to squander all its youthful strength in home waters. When war broke out I saw that the immeasurable prospects of our world power, and consequently our fate at home, depended on our coming out of the war with a strong position against the Anglo-Saxons. Those values abroad which have been destroyed by the fact of the war could only indeed be fully replaced by victory. But even if we succumbed with dignity to superior forces and fell in honour, the German name could preserve its respect in the world. The future of Germany overseas, and our whole artificial and yet so indispensable , position in the world, depended upon whether people could remain proud of the fact that they were Germans. Nothing was more fruitful to the commercial prosperity of the Japanese in our time, or of the Germans after 1870, than proved strength and valour.

The world still had room for many Germans who would make their way as such, and not as hired slaves or deserters to foreign nations, so long as their national honour was too dear for them to sell it. A longer state of peace, or even an end of the war which left us as a whole nation, would have made up for our coming so late on the scene. If we had become a nation, respected as an equal by the rest of the world, of which there was a chance, and if the home country had then become so full of people that we were compelled to send some away, they would have remained German across the seas and would have been an addition instead of a loss of blood.

The bulk of those politicians who directed the Empire's policy at the fateful hour had not been trained to look beyond the range of European diplomacy, and never felt the stir that was going through the still plastic mass of Germandom.

They scarcely understood what was at stake in the war, and how much depended for all of us, but particularly for our workmen, on German prestige being raised and not lowered in all corners of the earth.

IV

It would have been of the greatest value to us if we could have advanced the German language in China—a very difficult task, because it is inferior to English in many respects as a business language. One means by which England has spread her language over the whole world is the sea-chart. England fulfilled a great civilizing task when she surveyed nearly the whole of the ocean. In the last century practically every ship that sailed the sea used English charts;

others were only used within narrow local limits. Our merchant shipping used to sail by English charts, even when German charts were to be had. I proceeded therefore systematically to produce a German series of charts. We already possessed charts of our own waters which were executed with greater thoroughness and exactness than the English, but they had several peculiarities to which our sailors were not accustomed. So I got into touch with our seafaring world, ascertained their likings in all details, even as to the form and the kind of paper, and we succeeded ultimately in producing a series of charts which was not only adequate, but also superior to the English. Then we tried to provide charts for big stretches of ocean running into hundreds of miles; one of them was the voyage from Germany to Eastern Asia. I wanted to do something for the dissemination of our language and the strengthening of Germandom, and this was one of my reasons for beginning this.

Guided by the principle of giving the Chinese the benefits of civilization, we erected a high school in Tsingtao; we also had in mind that it would pay from the economic point of view if we introduced our civilization to them. I was no stranger to the idealist standpoint that it was our duty to disseminate knowledge, but my real motive in all this was to set up for us more sounding-boards in the Far East by this extension of our labours. The high school was provided with a middle school for Chinese as a sort of understructure. We had to get to work quickly, as otherwise the English would begin to compete with us. On this account we decided swiftly and opened the high school before the middle school could have had time to train the students sufficiently. That was a secondary matter, however; we had to go ahead. It was not the Foreign Office, but Professor Otto Franke, the Chinese expert, who at my instigation conducted the negotiations with the Government at Peking, and he arranged in ideal fashion that Chinese Government Commissaries should co-operate in our examinations. By this means our examinees obtained the right to an appointment in China just as though they had passed a state examination. In this way we should have directed a stream of young people towards China who spoke perfect German, knew our institutions, and were acquainted with our products. We paid particular attention to the science of medicine, which, as it is above all competition, is more qualified than anything else to do national pioneer work for Germany.

Our colony became more and more a depository for the German import-trade. We began to construct a model exhibition of German products, a first-class advertisement which we could never have erected in an English settlement. Standing as we did on the threshold of China, we afforded an insight into our own economic and other achievements, yet we respected the character of the country, accepted and offered hospitality, and returned trust with trust like a " royal merchant."

V

We had everything, except a policy which enabled
us to turn this experiment, this trial of Germany's
worth, into permanency. I did not see Tsingtao
again after 1896, but I built into it so much anxiety and
affection that the loss of it moved me almost as much
as physical pain. With a garrison of only 3,000 or
4,000 men, the place as we had fortified it could have
been held for any time against the Chinese and a long
time against the French, the Russians, and even against
the English. But even with great expenditure of
capital we could not have built a fortress to resist
the attack of a Japanese army. There is no cure for
the fact that one cannot hold out against the whole
world.

The idea of procuring a strong base in Eastern Asia,
to which Germans could gravitate, was right in itself;
but a necessary condition was that we should be on
good terms with Japan. In spite of our protest against
the Peace of Shimonoseki in 1895, there was no dangerous shadow between us and Japan, so long as
Russia kept us, as it were, in the neutral zone. Even
after the collapse of the Russian Eastern policy in
1905, there was no reason for a discerning Japanese
policy to wish us out of China. But after 1905 we
ought to have done everything in our power to have
corrected the mistake of Shimonoseki.[1]

So far as I had any influence in this direction—and

[1] Chapter XIV.

it was not much—I have contsantly worked for a good understanding with Tokio. As far as I knew, the German Government never made any serious attempt to obtain assurances from Japan with regard to the neutralization of Eastern Asia. I was not really surprised by the Japanese ultimatum. But I assumed that Japan must really desire our presence in China on account of her grave opposition to America, which must become acute sooner or later. As Tsingtao had been declared a free port from the beginning according to my own desire, because I thought that we as the owner of the place would never come off worst, Japan did not do a bad business there; the only thing that could make our presence seriously unpleasant to her with all this free trade was her hunger for coal.

The Japanese ultimatum arrived on August 15th, 1914, and its brusque wording is said to have been very similar to that of our Shimonoseki Note of 1895. Upon the advice of our ambassador in Tokio, Count Rex, Bethmann was inclined to accept the ultimatum. I succeeded in preventing the reply from being sent. If we had given up Tsingtao without a fight, we should have lost it in any circumstances; the alliance with Japan, which we should have striven for, was only imaginable, however, if we preserved our honour in Eastern Asia. Even now it will stand us in good stead that we upheld the idea of "the fulfilment of duty to the utmost" right until the enforced end of our Chinese colonial experiment. The unconditional surrender of Tsingtao would have seriously depressed public feeling in our national struggle for existence. Japan has not done us any more harm as our enemy than the swallowing of the insult would have done us. Besides, in August, 1914, no one could say how long the war would last; at that time indeed the army was full of confidence in victory. We had to take the chance of holding Tsingtao in the event of a speedy end to the war. An attempt to hand over Tsingtao to America, in exchange perhaps for the Philippines, was bound to break down.

We had developed the Boxer line into a solid rampart which only included a few works, with trenches and barbed-wire entanglements, and the sea-front was fortified with a few Krupp cannon which we had taken from the Taku forts for use against insurgents. The last shell was fired when Tsingtao surrendered. When 30,000 of the enemy began the general assault, which there was no artillery to ward off, it was only a question as to whether the remainder of our garrison would allow themselves to be slaughtered in the unfortified town by the attackers. The governor acted correctly in capitulating. In the streets of the captured town the Japanese searched a long time for the 12,000 Germans that they expected to find there. But there were only 2,000, with perhaps 1,500 more conscripts and volunteers who had faithfully found their way thither from the German official and commercial circles in all the settlements in China.

CHAPTER IX

I

WHEN I was recalled from Eastern Asia in the spring
of 1897, and was travelling home across America, I
was informed by inquisitive American journalists in
Salt Lake City that Eugen Richter had already begun
a campaign against me in the press as the future Secretary of State. At that time I was not sufficiently
versed in parliamentary ways to play off against my
inexorable opponent the fact that he attacked me before he knew anything about me. I relinquished my
command with a heavy heart, for I had told the Emperor in 1895 that in my opinion the construction
of the fleet could only succeed by way of legislation,
and that universal experience showed that, to get this
through the Reichstag, a "gift of the gab" was
needed, which I did not possess, together with a
knowledge of political routine which had not been
included hitherto in my purely military career. When
I arrived in Potsdam in June, 1897, the Emperor told
me that everything was ready for the navy campaign;

I only needed to give my consent. During my absence the Emperor had had a draft-bill drawn up
by a committee, but in my opinion this was of no
use. I have never seen anything constructive done
by committees. They are more adapted for criticism.
Their sense of responsibility evaporates, and they are
not fully alive to the enormous difference between
an idea and its materialization. In this instance, however, the Emperor was very much impressed by the
work of his committee. I asked for a few days to
think it over.

The fundamental idea of this draft centred round *a
foreign-service fleet*. Now there were only a few
States left in the world at that time, such as Hayti,
etc., in which any infringement of our rights could
be corrected by foreign-service cruisers without giving rise to a serious conflict. States like the Argen-
tine already had modern warships at their disposal,
so that every foreign-service cruiser would have to
be supported by a naval force in home waters, if it
was to fulfil its purpose as an outpost. Moreover we
had not one single foreign base. Throughout my
whole career I have always had to oppose two ideas,
especially beloved of the lay mind—the idea of a
special coastal defence,[1] and that of a cruiser fleet.
The world-war has proved that the best *coastal de-*

[1] Even a soldier of the rank of Field-Marshal von der Goltz,
when Inspector-General of the Engineering Corps, brought forward plans for the fortification of the coast, and I was given
the trouble of rejecting a proposal to dot the coast with armoured towers, which were altogether unnecessary both militarily and politically, owing to the existence of a battle fleet.

fence is a *battle fleet*.   As to the cruiser war, I replied
to the Emperor at the time somewhat on the following
lines: As a thorough-going cruiser war and a war
on the high seas against England and other great
States is altogether excluded by our lack of foreign
bases and by Germany's geographical situation—the
foreign Admiralties know this quite well—what we
need is a battle fleet which can be stationed between
Heligoland and the Thames.

I had just had occasion to see in Eastern Asia the
artificial props of our position in the world.   I had
heard from many sides of the difficulties which the
English were putting in the way of everything German, and of the progress of the " made in Germany "
boycott, and the anti-German agitation aroused by
the Krüger telegram.   Germans were being pushed
out of the administration of Europeans' settlements,
in which they had hitherto taken part, and also out
of the English companies and wharves.   I had experienced myself how our Eastern Asiatic squadron could
be rendered incapable at the slightest provocation by
the refusal of the dockyards.   In those days, the middle of the 'nineties, one noticed how the world was
beginning to go more quickly.   German trade, the
" Open Door," could no longer be protected by flying
squadrons; we had to increase in general power all
round, *i.e.* to qualify ourselves for an alliance with
the Great Powers.   But alliance-value could only be
achieved by a battle fleet.   One single ally at sea
would have sufficed in the Great War to have enabled

us to fight with the most favourable prospects for the freedom of the seas.

The first thing therefore was to create for ourselves a fleet which would give us alliance-value; and the second was a corresponding policy of alliance, and the avoidance of all political friction before this end was achieved. These were the two objects for which we had to strive amid the aggravated conditions of the times. I viewed with anxiety the rash provocations in which German public opinion was indulging against England at that time. I also viewed with anxiety the advice dictated by the recklessness of the Naval Executive Command to the Emperor during the Transvaal crisis. In the same report therefore in which I presented my navy scheme, I asked to be consulted in the use of foreign-service vessels, on account of the political nature of such actions. The Emperor and the Executive Command granted this; but they did not act up to it afterwards. The Emperor agreed immediately to my navy scheme, with a change of mind that surprised me, and in June, 1897, there disappeared finally from the draft scheme that foreign-service fleet, which would certainly have had a short life in the war. I must say that I did not myself regard the prospective battle fleet as a panacea without an alliance with another secondary sea-power; but it was the necessary step towards our qualification for alliance, and consequently, the only tangible way of attaining that independence with regard to England which was unanimously and justly demanded in Ger-

many at that time, but which was unfortunately too
often taken for granted in a way which was not com-
patible with the real-political way of thinking.

II

My predecessor, Hollmann, used to read all the documents relating to his office personally, and he was
consequently inundated with the material. I restricted
myself to the preparation of the Navy Bill, and left
the current business to my deputy. In Ems and St.
Blasien, where the bronchitis which I had brought
with me from the tropics was to be cured, I gathered
round me the men whom I had chosen to work out
the Navy Bill with me. The older parliamentary experience of von Capelle, his critical mind, his logical
style, were a happy balance to my disposition, which
was more given to working by intuition. He was
less a fighter than a master of finance; together with Dähnhardt, who carried on urbane intercourse with the Reichstag deputies, he controlled the
financial side of affairs, which, in view of the poor
state of the revenue, was a tricky art in itself. While
I generally went straight for the goal, von Capelle
espied the difficulties and objections as well as the
different ways of overcoming them; he was always
the first to find the weak points to which our opponents could hitch on, but he was not perhaps so good
with the *imponderabilia*. He was just as indispensable
to me for the parliamentary side of the work as the
fiery von Heeringen was for arousing the people; von

Heeringen conducted the mental mobilization of the masses in a very tactful way.

My method of work always had Nelson's " We are a band of brothers " for its motto. Ever since my first commands, I have had to deal with things which needed to be regarded in perspective from many sides, and the man who does not feel like Napoleon, able to leave his personal stamp upon everything, is bound to make for himself a bundle of faggots which is more difficult to break than a single twig. If one is faced with a big piece of work, one must avoid trying to do everything oneself. I had noticed with Caprivi that he did too much of his own writing; once he had written something in his fine, even handwriting, it was difficult to make him change it; he was, so to speak, in love with his own thoughts. I have also noticed this danger in myself; I therefore kept myself in check all the more, so that I could face more dispassionately that which was right in itself.

One of the reasons with which it has been attempted to justify the breaking-up of the homogeneous—so to speak, sovereign—Admiralty, and its partition into different departments, was the assertion that the whole management of the navy was too much for one man. This assertion, which was at the back of the mistaken Imperial Command, thus put the reins into the hands of a monarch who was supposed to govern much more than the navy! But it is wrong to say that it would be difficult to set up a many-sided authority. The main thing is that one should have a sense for everything essential, and put all the rest upon reliable assistants. At all costs one must secure the assistants that one has chosen for oneself. I left time for what was essential, and should have liked to do much more.

There is nothing I have been so careful to avoid in organizing as taking a fundamentally false step. For, once a wrong course is taken, it is difficult to discover the original mistake; only the symptoms are evident, and precedent and interests are soon established on the mistake. Therefore, one should never lay organizations on the table of the House, but they should be allowed to crystallize round a given point. One must also leave open the possibility of dissolving the organization without any disturbance if any mistakes appear, for in general one only recognizes the advantages in radical changes beforehand, and seldom the disadvantages. In organization, formal logic is of less account than the goodness of the soil and of the seed. We therefore did not drive the Navy Bill tautly, but as slackly as possible.

Personal attendance in the Reichstag, in fact appearance in public at all, was not congenial to me. I felt that the less one spoke in the Reichstag, the better it was and the further one got, especially in a province so delicate as mine. I believe that I have never given any occasion of offence to any opponent either at home or abroad in this way. A certain shyness of the bustle of public life may have influenced me. It is true that the reproach was raised later against me, that the naval debates, both in full session and in committee, were either too "tedious" or too "glib," and that this was probably due to some secret arrangement behind the scenes. We certainly did have confidential talks with the party leaders. But our chief secret was the absolutely meticulous elaboration of every Bill, so that it convinced everybody and was unassailable. The success of this was due to the working methods which I had formed during my labours in the 'seventies, by which I first gave the idea, then consulted as many other people as I could, and then once more made an exhaustive examination of the final result. Capelle, as a rule, first wrote down the matters deliberated by us. Later on, the practical test of our technical and organizing work, quite apart from the careful elaboration of the Navy Bills, gave Parliament more and more confidence in us as time went on. Any other means than our thorough methods of work would never have won for us our successes in Parliament.

In the Prusso-German governmental system of my day the Ministers of State generally preferred to exhaust themselves with silent, often unrewarded, departmental work, rather than parade themselves in the public eye. The straitjacket of parliamentarism, which has been put on the German people by international theorists, who have no understanding of organic growth, and no regard for the judgment of history, will soon teach them to praise the old times as the good times. The new rulers will wonder at the ex-

pertness of the old Government, and at the amount of
loyal work achieved instead of empty talk.

Every word of the draft Bill was altered probably
a dozen times in our discussions at St. Blasien. I
used to "revolve" the matter, an expression about
which I was often teased. I always insisted upon the
principle of giving each collaborator the greatest possible independence. I used to urge my departmental
heads never to regard questions from their sectional
standpoints, alone; each of them was to criticize ruthlessly, just as though he were the king and had to
decide it all alone. There is always enough of the
detail work to do. Thus I demanded of the engineer
that he should learn to judge from the military standpoint as well as from his own, and *vice versa* from the
officer. There is nothing that I consider more unwise
than to stress the superior officer in discussion. There
always comes a point when one person must decide;
but I may say that it rarely came to the point of a
command at the Admiralty; we almost always came to
a mutual decision, in the course of which I as *primus
inter pares* spared my collaborators the feeling of being beaten by a majority of votes, and left them the
joy of their achievement, but at the same time I myself did better and more than if I had wanted to see
myself in everything. The transference of the brusque
word of command (which is necessary in face of the
enemy) from the ship to the office and to big undertakings, the working with mere creatures who obey
mechanically, the painful delimitation of departmental

views, cripple the sense of responsibility and the capacity for making decisions, which are the chief requirements in military authorities. When one knows oneself what one is out after, then one can get the best out of one's subordinates, and in modern organizations one can refrain from personally dragging the whole burden forward a few feet, and instead one can help all one's assistants to advance their own part of it an inch or two.

The field of my activities accustomed me to great versatility. The more complex an organization becomes, so much the more does the head take on differentiated functions, and if it is to keep itself clear it must not try to take on any of the work of the members. I gathered round me specialists, who had on the whole a good store of knowledge, and I gave my attention to the inter-connection, so that if necessary their different specialties could be brought to the fore. I always furthered the promotion of independent characters, but the longer my experience, the more definite was my peculiar discovery how scarce really creative minds are, and how characters which have proved themselves in secondary positions can fail completely in higher ones. In advancements one can hardly protect oneself from making a bad captain out of a good lieutenant.

III

I was assured at the Admiralty that we should never get the Bill passed as it was. Our most reliable friend in Parliament, the National-Liberal leader, von Bennigsen, was also of the same opinion, and he advised us to try yearly credits. I insisted upon this Bill, however, quite resolved to attempt what was said to be improbable, and to resign in the event of failure.

I needed a Bill which would protect the continuity of the construction of the fleet on different flanks. The circumstance that was most in the Bill's favour was that it intended to make the Reichstag abandon the temptation to interfere each year afresh in technical details, as they had hitherto done when every ship had become the "exercise for debates"; and the Admiralty had not demanded what was most important in reality, but that which they could get passed in the interplay of changing majorities. But with party coalitions which treated ships as objects of compensation, it was impossible to construct such a naval armament as was demanded by a generation of patient, uniform growth.

I could never discover, however, how to ward off the frequent interference of the *Emperor,* whose imagination, once it had fixed upon shipbuilding, was fed by all manner of impressions. Suggestions and proposals are cheap in the navy, and change like a kaleidoscope; if the Emperor had spoken with some senior lieutenant or had seen something abroad, he was full of new demands, constructing, reproaching me with backwardness and even thinking to rouse me by means of warnings. Apart from several threats to resign, I could only secure the continuity of development, which was the fundamental factor of success, by means of legislation. The third side from which chaos threatened and against which I needed a law was *the navy itself*. Whenever it is a question of special knowledge, opinions diverge. When I became Secretary of State, the German navy was a collection of experiments in shipbuilding, although not so varied as the Russian fleet under Nicholas II. Even the English navy is the same to a certain degree, but there money is of no importance; if they had built a class of ships wrongly, they just threw the whole lot into the corner and built another. But we could not permit ourselves that. Besides, in England they understood better that opinions change, whilst the doctrinaire German immediately declared that as he had built something wrong, *anathema sit*. The German more readily believes in a system if it is put before him as such. I was quite aware of the minor defects of the Bill, but I had no choice if we were going to make any progress under the present conditions.

The form of the Bill had the very great additional advantage that it enabled us to proceed in a more business-like fashion and arrange matters economically in many ways, since we were able to look a long way ahead. And economy, which entailed a great deal of previous calculation, was a bitter necessity for Germany's armaments.

At the beginning of 1897 I had a conversation with von Miquel, then Minister of Finance, mainly for the purpose of discussing the general political side of the

Navy Bill with him, and he gave me a few general assurances of support. An article in the *Norddeutsche Allgemeine Zeitung* (August 5th) came as a great surprise to me, therefore when inspired as it was by Miquel, it made out that the Bill, which was desirable in itself, was not feasible at the present time. Progressive development was required in the navy, but it had to be achieved without infringing the parliamentary rights of the Reichstag.

This publication was undoubtedly inadmissible, and dangerous to the Bill. But I avoided an open conflict. Miquel was against the Bill, as was indeed the whole Ministry, but he did not want to put up any open opposition to it on account of the Emperor; he was trying, therefore, to appease me, and yet to dissuade me from my plan by representing its difficulties. When he saw, however, that I was determined to stand firm, he became more friendly.

The general scepticism among the leaders and the indifference of the mass of the people made me think of canvassing for Bismarck's support.

CHAPTER X

1. The launching of the *Fürst Bismarck*. My first visit to Friedrichsruh. A fatal beginning. Bismarck on the balance of power at sea.—2. Drive through the Sachsenwald.—3. The last visit to Friedrichsruh.

I

In June, 1897, I had suggested to the Emperor that the next ship to leave the stocks should be given the name *Fürst Bismarck*. I knew that Prince Bismarck or his family cherished the wholly erroneous suspicion that a ship bearing his name had been intentionally struck off the list at the time of his resignation. By this means I hoped to soften the estrangement between Bismarck and the Government, and I wanted to take the invitation personally to Friedrichsruh in the autumn, and to seize the opportunity to obtain the old Prince's blessing for the Navy Bill.

The Emperor agreed after some hesitation, but later sent an official letter on his own account to Bismarck inviting him to the launching of a ship, without, however, giving the name with which it was to be christened. He anticipated by this act of grace, as he generally did, the pleasure which such occasions always gave him, and intended to give the Prince a surprise. Bismarck's reply was to the effect that he was too old for such things. Then I received the command to straighten up the situation, which had got into a pretty muddle.

I wrote to the Prince requesting an audience of him, in order to report on the intended procedure on the part of the navy. The letter came back unopened, with a note to the effect that the Prince did not receive any letters which did not contain the sender's name plainly written on the envelope. In reply to a second letter I was told that I could come.

It was the custom to arrive at Friedrichsruh about midday. I was met by Count Rantzau, whom I knew personally; I begged for his support. When I entered the house the family was already at table, the Prince sitting at the end. He got up, cold but polite, very much the *grand seigneur,* and remained standing until I had taken my seat. He was tormented by violent neuralgic pains, and kept holding india-rubber hot-water bottles to his cheek; he ate scraped meat, and could only speak with difficulty. After a bottle and a half of champagne he became more lively. When the simple lunch was finished, the Countess Wilhelm Bismarck lit his long pipe for him, and the ladies left the room. The atmosphere was sultry. Suddenly the great eyebrows contracted, he gave me an annihilating look and growled, "I am no tom-cat that gives off sparks when it is stroked." I am not generally very ready, but I could not remain silent in the face of these almost desperate prospects, and so I replied, "So far as I know, those are only black cats, your Highness." Count Rantzau put in eagerly, "The Admiral is right, only black cats do that." The atmosphere became less electric. I delivered my message, and he answered that he could not come to Kiel and put on his uniform and spurs, and that he did not wish to appear before the public as a ruin. In order to get something positive out of him, I suggested that perhaps one of his daughters-in-law could appear at the launching ceremony. He replied that I must ask them; he left it as a matter of form to their personal decision. Thereupon I brought out my chief reason for coming.

I set forth my plans and endeavoured to persuade the Prince that this was no mere whim on the part of the Monarch, although I had had many such to deal with in the course of recent years; and impressed upon him that it was our intention to carry out the Naval Programme approved by the Reichstag in 1867, but recast and brought up to date. We must have, I said, a certain measure of political sea-power in view of the new times that were coming. This had not been so necessary in the 'seventies because the immeasurable fame and brilliance of great names had helped us over any difficulties in those days. Now, on the other hand, a foundation of real power was necessary, for example, in view of our position in an Anglo-Russian war, which had to be seriously reckoned with. In conclusion, I added that I had come to obtain his blessing for the creation of a definite naval power which corresponded to our tactical experiences.

From Bismarck's first few words it was evident
that he did not want to hear anything of the military
side of the matter. He had no high opinion of big
ships, he said, and he agreed with his friend Roon
that a large number of little ships were needed which
could swarm like hornets round the big ships. I did
not succeed very well in making him see that the
heavy ship represented a concentration of force and
had the advantage in certain positions; he objected
that this would be already for a ranged battle, but he
stuck to his "hornets," and wanted to push on the
service abroad by the aid of a number of small ships
which could be sent all over the world. My admission that this would be important if we would get a
few bases abroad, led to an outburst against Caprivi.
He said that apart from his old friend Roon, who
represented a department of the Naval Ministry up till
1871, he had never agreed with any of the Naval Secretaries. Caprivi, he continued, had always come to
him in the Wilhelmstrasse, like a wooden ramrod;
and what else could one have expected from him?
While he, Caprivi, was a lieutenant in Berlin without
extra pay for twenty-two years he had seen the well-
to-do cavalry officers, whose fathers had landed estates;
and when he became Imperial Chancellor he thought
he could rub this into the landed proprietors. Moreover, the dissolution of the Insurance Treaty with
Russia was the most terrible disaster. In the event
of an Anglo-Russian conflict, Bismarck declared, our
political position was summed up in the phrase " Neu-

trality towards Russia "; Russia wanted this, and it was sufficient for him too.

The possibilities suggested by me that a new Pitt might not desire such a neutrality, and might prefer our hostility, and further that other constellations were just as conceivable, and that only a respectable naval force could qualify us for an alliance with Russia and other Powers, were thrust aside by Bismarck almost angrily. He said that taken as individuals the English were quite worthy people, but they were shop-keepers in politics. If they came, we should slay them with the butt ends of our rifles. He was totally incapable of understanding that a close blockade would overcome us.

The old Prince was obviously thinking of the agrarian Germany of 1870, and the political England of 1864; and he no longer understood the powerful position of the British world-empire in 1897. Altogether, he was following his own preconceived ideas rather than giving himself the trouble to take in a new scheme. In the main, however, he agreed with me: "There is no need for you to persuade me that we need a bigger navy." He confirmed his approval of my procedure in writing later.

The memoranda of the former French ambassador in Berlin, Baron de Courcel, show how responsive the Prince was, in his best days, to the idea that we ought to possess a certain definite value as an ally against England. When the colonial aspirations of Germany and France seemed to converge in 1884, the Prince sketched to the Ambassador the possibility of a naval covenant between the two continental neighbours. The Prince is said to have expressed himself as follows on that occasion [1]:

"What I am aiming at is the 'restoration of a certain balance of power at sea,' and France has a great part to play in this matter if she is ready to enter into our views. There was a great deal said at one time about the European balance of power, but this belongs to the eighteenth century. I do not believe, however, that it would be too old-fashioned to speak of 'a balance of power at sea.' I do not want a war against England, but I should like to make her realize that the navies of the other nations can establish a counterpoise to her at sea, and compel her to take other people's interests into account if they combine. But England has got to accustom herself to the idea that an alliance between Germany and France is not outside the bounds of possibility."

Bismarck himself would probably have been the only man who could have brought about a reconciliation with France. As this reconciliation, however, was not effected, the ageing man became alienated from these views. He no longer felt how strongly this diplomatic dependence on Russia, which he demanded (and the necessity of which was quite clear even to me), required as a foundation, in view of the altered international situation, a naval "balance of power" policy and the power of offering an alliance at sea. Owing to the British hostility towards us which had

[1] *Neue Preussische (Kreuz-) Zeitung,* August 20th, 1918.

revealed itself unsparingly since 1896, the question of power was now: How could we, huddled together as we were on our over-populated soil, preserve peace with England without capitulating to her trade-jealousy, or, if England resolved to bottle us up, how could we survive a war with her? Neither of these problems could be solved by our being without a fleet, or by our having a foreign-service fleet, but solely by means of a battle fleet, the military potentiality and alliance-value of which must make it difficult for the English to pick a quarrel with us. "A new epoch had begun," as the old Prince said at his last glimpse of Hamburg harbour, when, overwhelmed by the enormous activity which had developed there since the post-Bismarckian era, he thought of the easy-going old Hamburg of the days when it was controlled by the English.

II

After we had been sitting about two hours at table, he asked me to go for a drive with him through the Sachsenwald. He never rested in the afternoon. There were big bottles of beer right and left of us in the carriage, which were opened and drunk; it was not easy to keep pace with his powerful constitution. So that he could speak freely in the presence of the coachman, the Prince used a foreign language, and as his nature combined delicacy with forcefulness, he chose the English language, which he assumed would be most familiar to me as a sailor, and which he

himself spoke excellently. He was unsparing in his
criticism of the Emperor, but did not mind my object-
ing to his strong expressions, because as an officer I
had to take the Emperor's side. He told me how the
Empress Augusta had worked in 1848 for the abdica-
tion of the King, and the renunciation of the right of
succession by the Prince of Prussia; how as leader of
the Right in the Chamber he had replied to the deputy
von Vincke, who proposed—at the instigation of the
Princess—a Regency of the Princess Augusta for
Prince Friedrich Wilhelm, that, if such a motion was
introduced, he would formally propose that the mover
should be arrested; how the Princess then interviewed
him once more in Potsdam, violently slapping her
thighs meanwhile, and declared that she was only concerned for the interests of her son, and how the latter,
who was waiting in an alcove in the corridor, came
up to him weeping, with outstretched hands. He
spoke with affection about the Emperor Frederick,
who had always supported the Chancellor, even during his illness and in spite of the Empress Victoria.
He would like me to tell the Emperor that he only
wanted " to be let alone " and to die in peace. His
work was done, and there was no more future and no
more hope for him.

We drove for two hours without a covering in spite
of showers from time to time; the Prince smoked his
pipe. He talked about his earlier passion for hunting;
how he could once go a hundred miles to shoot one
stag, and how, now that he was a broken man, he

still liked to see the game although he could not longer bring himself to put a hole into the shining coat of the beautiful animal. He talked about his dead wife, who had been his support in life; tears came into his eyes; the way in which he described his condition was very moving. He also talked of his English relationships, and how he had generally liked the sailors, but not the admirals. . . .

I took care to show him the honours due to royalty; one felt that one could not do otherwise. When I got out I stood at the salute; a small crowd had collected in front of the house. We went in to supper and again I sat next to Bismarck. Here I must relate an incident which showed his tactfulness. I should have liked very much to ask him for a photograph with his signature, but I knew how unpleasant it was to be pressed for such a thing; and when I accompanied Prince Henry in Italy I had been disgusted at the struggles which had taken place on both sides to secure decorations and photographs. On the other hand I was sorry that I had not ventured to ask the old Moltke for a souvenir when I was showing him over the torpedo section in Kiel, in Stosch's time, and had had occasion to feel the ascendancy of his great fine spirit. Bismarck now spared me making the request by professing to remember my old father when in the top form of the Grey Friars School, and handed me his own portrait for my old father, who was still living then.

III

I visited the old gentleman twice after this; the last time when in the suite of the Emperor, who announced himself with the whole company rather suddenly in Friedrichsruh, after the ceremonial departure of Prince Henry for Tsingtao. Bismarck received the Emperor in his wheeled-chair at the modest entrance to his country house. We went straight to table. Bismarck seated himself with some assistance, but after he had been sitting down some time he livened up again. My place was diagonally opposite the Prince, who was sitting next to the Emperor, and I had at my side von Moltke, the future general. The Prince tried to begin a political conversation on our relations with France, etc. To my great regret the Emperor did not follow up these openings, but carried on the anecdotal conversation which is so usual at the Imperial table. Whenever Bismarck began on politics the Emperor ignored it. Moltke whispered to me, " It is terrible "; we felt the lack of reverence for such a man. Then in some connection or other Bismarck said a few words, the prophetic weight of which impressed them deeply upon us: " Your Majesty, as long as you have this officers' corps, you can do everything you want; when this is no longer the case, matters will be quite different." The apparent nonchalance with which this came out, as if there were nothing in it at all, showed an extraordinary presence of mind; it revealed the master.

When we broke up, the Prince in his wheeled-chair

accompanied the Emperor as far as the door, and then we bade each other farewell. Bismarck parted in a friendly way from Bülow, Miquel, and others. Before me there was the Cabinet-chief, von Lucanus, who had had a share in Bismarck's dismissal in 1890. He offered his hand to the Prince and was on the point of bowing. Then a remarkable scene took place which produced a powerful effect. The Prince sat there like a statue, without moving a muscle; he gazed into space, with Lucanus fidgeting in front of him. The Prince's features were expressionless; there was no dislike there; his face was an immovable mask, until Lucanus understood and withdrew. Then came myself, and after me my faithful Captain von Heeringen, who was so carried away (he was a man of temperament) that he bent and kissed Bismarck's hand. I was glad of it: I had also tried to make the Prince feel as much as I could, but the action of Herr von Heeringen was stronger. Then the Prince took Heeringen's head between his hands, and kissed him on the brow.

This is my last memory of Bismarck.

CHAPTER XI

I

FROM now on the Bismarck press supported me. Further, I had personally asked all Princes of the Empire, including the Grand Dukes, for their support, and had sought to make them feel that they had a share in the decision by reporting to them on the subject. This succeeded particularly in the case of a Prince like King Albert of Saxony, who was a man of considerable business knowledge and who gave his serious attention to the matter; or like the Grand Duke of Oldenburg, whose own achievements had been of such great service to our naval interests; or like the Grand Duke Frederick of Baden, a man provided with all the qualities of an old-time ruler, whose personality was far above the average, which in my opinion has fallen throughout the whole of Germany during the last generation, both in the royal houses and among the leaders of the various professions. Of course I also paid attention to the Hanseatic towns; and further, to the Minister of the Federal States, my getting to know whom proved to be a good means of propaganda, particularly as this practice of touring the country was not usual at that time.

Then I considered it my privilege and my duty to bring home to the broader masses of the people the interests that were here at stake. It was a question of widening the limited horizon of the people, of awakening a sense of the civilizing influences bounds up with the sea, that had suffered or had been pushed on one side by our historical development; of deepening the conviction that this was the way imperatively assigned to us if, instead of resorting to emigration on a large scale, we wanted to maintain at home the crowded masses of Germans in that state of prosperity which they had enjoyed since Bismarck's tariff legislation. Heeringen organized the information department of the Admiralty. He went the round of the universities, where almost all the political economists, including Brentano, were ready to give splendid support. Schmoller, Wagner, Sering, Schumacher, and many others showed that the expenditure on the fleet would be a productive outlay, and illustrated Germany's position, the insecure politico-economic foundation of our whole civilization and power, and the danger that our superfluous population might become an intolerable burden instead of a source of wealth. They showed how our position in the world was built upon sand, and how Chamberlain's tariff reform schemes would condemn us to vegetate as a small nation, unless we had the power to throw a word in our own favour into the scales against the Powers overseas. Thus the discussion of national-political questions received an impetus which formed a healthy counterpoise to social-political Utopias.

There were none of the great historians left, who had guided public opinion in an earlier generation, after the death of Treitschke, that glorious man, whose lectures I had attended at the University after 1876, and who had also given me private advice as I sat at his side in Josty's, scribbling my questions on a tablet. I cannot understand why the spirit of Treitschke has disappeared from the teaching of German history. Without a sea-power to protect our industry, we should have ceased to be a European Great Power, and the argument that we were satisfied, which seemed to be indicated by the world-removed attitude of many savants, could only hold good in the question of German unity. After this question had been solved, however, the other, as to whether we were to mean anything at all to the human race, came to the front with all its force. Perhaps it was the novelty and the speedy development of this political problem that prevented the majority of historians from realizing it as clearly as the political economists.[1]

[1] Among the historians I received particular support from Dietrich Schaeffer. Mommsen was still alive and he was quite ready to give me ships, but not a Bill. In conversation with him I told him that his account of the second Punic War seemed to me to fail to realize that Hannibal was conquered by the Roman mastery of the sea. In the same way, the Seven Years War and the Napoleonic Era are generally interpreted in a far too one-sided fashion in Germany. If the traditional teaching of history in Germany had only accustomed us to think more

The army, with its continental traditions also, did not willingly keep up with the changes in the international situation. I soon had an illustration of this in the bungling preparations for the miserable China Expedition, in the execution of which the deficient *matériel* and defective mental qualifications of the army administration for tasks which were not connected with the "two-front" war, were only prevented from obtruding themselves upon public notice by the *savoir faire* of Count Waldersee. But I met with sympathy among prominent soldiers, such as Field-Marshal von der Goltz, with whom I used to speak just as I did with the savants, although laying much more stress on the politico-military point of view. We caused meetings and lectures to be held, and made special efforts to get into touch with the press on a large scale. We received every newspaper impartially, and gave them all positive information without indulging in polemics. They could do with it just what they liked; a certain gratitude for the material we had given them was always evident, and thus we progressed.

The traditional hospitality of the navy indicated

in terms of continents, Bethmann-Hollweg, the head-boy of Schulpforta, might have better understood the point on which the whole of the world-war turned. One very melancholy sign of the narrowness of our historical horizon to my mind was the slight regard that was paid to the books of A. v. Peez. I had them distributed in hundreds and also caused Admiral Mahan's work to be translated, in the well-founded hope that the rising generation of our naval officers would contribute by its education to the necessary expansion of the nation's historico-political horizon.

the way in which the public was to be handled. We did not want to put railings round ourselves, but wanted to have the fleet as a thing belonging to the German people. We instituted tours to the water-side and exhibited the ships and the wharves; we applied to the schools, and we called upon novelists to write for us: stacks of novels and pamphlets were the result. Prizes were to be given by the Ministry of Education to the schools. The Government, without whose consent a subordinate department like the Admiralty could not undertake anything at all, supported us under Bülow. But the propaganda would have been still more effective if the Ministry had taken it over. We were still outsiders. In Prussia, for example, we had no right to use the machinery of state; moreover, no budget grant could be reckoned on for the purpose of such propaganda. I was able, however, to carry out the whole of the campaign, so to speak, without cost to the State, by means of voluntary contributions. This also was a new procedure in Germany: the decisive thing was that the idea caught on; then the spark went farther afield of its own accord.

There revealed itself a certain need on the part of the nation for a goal, for a patriotic catch-word which would bring them all together. The nation was not yet satisfied. When a nation is satisfied it goes back. Inaction and decline are very much akin. This was not the case with us, and in a short time the fleet was recognized to be a vital question, a self-evident possession of the nation. To be sure, the politically naïve German suddenly thought in many cases that he was already *in possession* of a mighty fleet, while it was still a question of building the fleet. Exaggerations and incorrect comparisons with England, provocative statements and tactlessness in the press, parliament, and the public generally, were not wholly to be suppressed in spite of the warnings I issued.

The fact that the people were beginning to have an affection for the sea was a distinct advance. The German only sins in exuberance of national feeling, because he wavers, an incorrigible political illusionist, between the two extremes, the fear of power and the intoxication of power.[1]

II

On September 15th, 1897, I reported to the Imperial Chancellor, Prince Hohenlohe, for the first time on the Navy Bill. I made it especially clear that a postponement was not advisable; there would be Reichstag elections next year; so that if the Bill was rejected, a dissolution could be avoided, and the navy question would not make at all an unfavourable elec-

[1] The Admiralty did its best to give the public a sober estimate of its work. We also included information about foreign navies in the monthly periodical *Marinerundschau,* and in *Nauticus,* which we published annually as a kind of private handbook, as a means of expressing our opinion on naval matters and the practical issues more freely and without official weight. The sale of *Nauticus* rose from year to year. From the very outset it was of great assistance to us against the anti-navy pamphlets of Eugen Richter and others; and when we were celebrating the acceptance of the first Navy Bill with various Reichstag deputies at my house we laughingly toasted the great anonymous journalist, "Herr Nauticus."

tion issue. With its party funds exhausted by the elections the next Reichstag would be unwilling to face dissolution. The Ministry gave its consent on October 6th. The publication of the Bill took place early one Sunday morning, so that it had thirty-six hours in which to make an impression before Eugen Richter, who had been very unfriendly towards it, could write against it in Monday evening's press.

The opponents of a big navy in the Reichstag, and others besides, were offering resistance to the gagging of the Reichstag's right of sanction by this permanent grant. For a precedent, Eugen Richter pointed to the fate of the naval programme in 1865, which was rejected in spite of the warm feeling in the navy's favour because of its important and intimate connection with the Constitution question. But more dangerous than the implacability of Richter was the fact that even those circles which acknowledged in substance the essential and well-founded nature of our demands, considered a formal sanction by act of parliament as out of the question, try as I might to obtain it. In this matter my arguments were received with a doubtful shrug of the shoulders even by my best friends. Now, I was concerned above all with the principle of the Bill, as I have indicated above. I pointed out that the fourteen armoured vessels which had been acknowledged to be necessary in 1873 were not all sanctioned and built until twenty-one years afterwards; only a formal Act could guarantee the ships being built within a specified time, and it alone could pull the navy out of the confusion, weakness, and critical condition generally into which it had been thrown by its indifferent treatment by the Reichstag.

In order to establish this principle, *i.e.* that of a formal Act, I confined myself in substance to the absolutely essential. We asked for new taxes or subsidies, we voluntarily restricted our financial requirements to the minimum, binding ourselves to a period of seven (six if need be) years. For the present we only asked for a small "raiding fleet"—anything more than which was out of the question at that time as the technical preparations for building ships on a large scale had yet to be made. We therefore made it appear that by this first step we were not effecting anything more than Stosch's scheme for the foundation of a fleet. The whole procedure was not to appear as a break with the past. The coast-defence idea was mentioned, partly for the sake of its historical connection and partly to prevent ourselves being charged with offensive intentions. There was also the armoured coastal squadron, and this was simply included in the Bill. As provision was made at the same time for replacing these coast-defence vessels at a later date, but as nothing definite was said as to the class of substitute, this inclusion of the old types did not stand in the way of desirable development later.[1]

---

[1] In the second Navy Bill we rechristened the armoured coast-defence vessels which we possessed with the name "ships of the line," which cost nothing at all, but which definitely established the fact that the ships destined by the Act to replace

It was hoped to get the Bill through the Reichstag in consideration of its being firmly founded on long years of work, so that the scheme presented itself as a reasoned demand, which had not been born in a moment, but had evolved out of experience.

On Capelle's advice, I included a financial limit in the first Navy Bill. As the raising of money offered no difficulties—for, as I have already said, the necessary means were at hand without taxation, this financial limit made the Bill more palatable to the Reichstag; but it created difficulties for us afterwards in the administration of the Bill, because the value of money depreciated steadily.

In order to get into touch with influential Reichstag deputies, I arranged for interviews with my collaborators, and I myself joined in these discussions when I had myself sensed the general trend of feeling. It was impossible to approach Eugen Richter. But a section of the Progessives ranged themselves on our side. The National Liberals were our best friends. I did not need to trouble myself about the Conservatives, who were only lukewarm at first, as with the exception of free-lances they always voted on principle for military Bills, ever mindful as they were of the thorny past and threatened present of Prussian Germany. The balance in the scale was the Centrum.

this class were to be included in the High Sea fleet. The service afloat did not understand the real reason for the inclusion of these old vessels in the fleet as constituted by the Act, and thus this obsolescent class of vessel was given the name of "floating coffins."

Like the majority of politicians, Freiherr v. Hertling, who was a friend of our cause, doubted the possibility of our obtaining parliamentary sanction. He said that the previous lack of uniformity in the treatment of all naval questions had made it too easy for our opponents to arouse feeling against naval schemes; in addition, there were rumours of a *coup d' état*.

Our conversations with Dr. Lieber, the leader of the Centrum, who in spite of his personal sensitiveness proved in practice to be very amenable, finally secured the success of the Bill. The alteration of the time limit from seven years to six was made at the suggestion of Lieber himself.

Thus the leap was accomplished which was first necessary to establish our sea-power in legislation. The Reichstag renounced a portion of its right to interpose every year in the development of the navy. The national view-point superseded that of the parliamentary routine. We were ultimately able to convince the Reichstag, because we were ourselves convinced.

III

In the winter of 1898-9 I was still firmly resolved to keep to the six years' limit. It was, however, always quite clear to me, and I also expressed myself to this effect in the Reichstag, that the first Navy Bill would not create the fleet in its ultimate form. It was frankly stated that we would have to bring forward supplementary demands after the conclusion of the six years' limit.

After the nation had confirmed *on principle* in 1897 the right of existence of a strong fleet, but had imposed strict limitations upon its *matériel*, the time approached when we had to decide whether the political step towards real sea-power was to be ventured upon or whether the whole enterprise was to remain a systematic demonstration. Personally I was determined to proceed from the first step to the second, paying attention meanwhile to the political situation at home and abroad. I had in mind the idea of proceeding " in spurts," nursing the Reichstag as much as possible meanwhile. This nursing, however, proved to be very difficult; for after we had begun to build seriously, people's expectations exceeded the limits of possibility. Thus, I found myself relieved of the necessity of raising the financial limit much sooner than I had ever surmised, only to begin the preparation of a second Navy Bill.

Since the autumn of 1898 I had resolved to adopt the principle of arranging all the details of organization so that they would be adaptable to the future increase of the fleet. Since our measures were directed towards a distant goal, they were often misunderstood within the navy, and led to internal friction, which had to be patiently endured so as not to endanger the general scheme.

In the course of the summer of 1899, we realized that the supplementary estimates could not wait until the conclusion of the six years' limit (1904), and we decided to bring them in at the latest in 1901 or

1902, but to arrange the annual estimates for 1900 in such a manner as to open the way for the supplementary Bill and to announce at the same time that we intended to anticipate the latter by some years. The actual decision as to the contents and date of the supplementary Bill would not then take place until the spring of 1900, after all the details of the draft had been thoroughly elaborated, and the prevailing political conditions had been taken into consideration. I requested and received on September 28th, 1899, the Imperial consent to such a procedure. The Chief of the Naval Cabinet, who was present during the reading of my report to the Emperor, regarded as doubtful the prospects of the Bill in the Reichstag, whereupon the Emperor opined that the iron pitcher (the desire for a navy) would break the earthen one (the Opposition).

I was prompted to this decision by three reasons. The first was of a parliamentary nature. We could not manage with the financial limit fixed in 1898, for we had underestimated the increase in the price of ships. If the building of the new ships which were to be ordered was not to suffer from shortage of money, we would have to approach the Reichstag in 1900 or 1901 at the latest, but better still at once, with the request that we should be released from the money limit. If we did this, however, then it would be impossible to avoid further inquiries in the Reichstag as to our shipbuilding plans after the conclusion of the six years' limit. If we had then announced the supplementary Bill for 1904, we should have had a general debate in 1899 to no practical advantage. Thus, it was better to establish from the outset a positive object for this unavoidable parliamentary discussion, and to give the debate the character of a first reading.

The second, and still more important, reason in favour of the speeding-up of the supplementary Bill was of a technical and administrative nature. We had to try to build *as many ships as possible* every year; our military object and the means at our disposal suggested three big ships a year as our rate of construction. The best thing would have been a straightforward Bill providing for the annual construction of three ships, but the Reichstag would never have agreed to such an abandonment of its right of sanction. It only agreed to bind itself by the first Navy Bill in so far as the latter was based upon the necessities of *organization*—that is to say, by that organic navy scheme which contained, not single ships, but the *squadron formation,* which had been tested by us as a tactical unit and imitated by the whole world. If we made our demands in terms of squadrons, the Reichstag could cancel squadrons but not ships, because in the latter case it would have exceeded its authority and have interfered in matters of military organization. This squadron formation, which was recognized by the Reichstag, together with the average life of a ship, resulted in a rate of construction which changed from year to year. According to the first Navy Bill the rate of construction of three ships per year would continue until 1901; then we should have reduced it to one ship, and have risen again later to the three-ship rate—even exceeding it from time to time.

The Reichstag would scarcely have taken amiss the reduction to one ship, but it certainly would not have liked the spasmodic increases in the estimates when the rate rose again. Considerable creaking in the parliamentary machine was to be feared, like the complaints that I had in 1912. We should avoid this fluctuation in the rate of construction, however, if we presented a new Navy Bill so opportunely that the maintenance of the three-ship rate followed of its own accord.

The third, and most important, reason why the Foreign Office of those days under Bülow, and I personally, did not want to delay the new Navy Bill for some years was the altered international situation. Violence had been done to a few of our ships in Samoa by English and Americans. This humiliation, combined with the unfortunate Manila affair, had strengthened the feeling in favour of a more effective sea-power among the German public. Other signs of the times were the subjection of the French at Fashoda to the will of the mistress of the seas, England, and the war of the Spaniards against America, which was lost at sea and deprived Spain of her colonies. Finally, the Boer War was casting its shadow ahead. Enormously increased naval ship-building programmes on the part of nearly all the naval Powers pointed to a speeding-up in the world's development, which we had not been in a position to anticipate in 1897. Even in home politics things were developing. The dispute over the Central Canal seemed to be a prelude to the collision between the economic groups, which threatened in 1902 on the occasion of the revision of the commercial treaties, and if the navy question had become mixed up with this it would have run the risk of not being treated on its merits.

At the end of September, 1899, therefore, I was prepared, with the Emperor's consent, to include as many troublesome demands as possible in the estimates of 1900, to get in touch with the Reichstag deputies during the winter months of 1899-1900, and to draw up the form and contents of a new supplementary Bill in the Admiralty, the introduction of which was to be decided in the spring of 1900 according to the international situation and popular feeling.

IV

As I knew how difficult it was for a man of the Emperor's temperament to allow this matter to mature and to refrain from making it public, I sent a request to the Foreign Secretary on October 11th, asking him to bring his influence to bear on the Emperor to prevent the latter from making a premature statement on the navy question on the occasion of the forthcoming launching of H.M.S. *Karl der Grosse* in Hamburg. Count Bülow readily agreed to this and showed some concern on his own account at the possibility of any political utterances on this occasion.

The launching took place in Hamburg on October 18th, and produced a sensational speech from the Emperor, who, without consulting the Imperial Chancellor or the Foreign Secretary made a public statement, couched in his own phraseology, on our plans, which were still in the elementary stage. With his phrase, " We have bitter need of a strong German fleet," the Emperor took upon himself the initiative in the eyes of the people. Afterwards, the naval administration had to fight more than ever against the suspicion that their actions proceeded from " absolutist influences against which the Empire's constitution had to be protected."

Meanwhile, it was immediately clear to me, after the Emperor's speech, that I could not remain silent, but must either apply the brake or put on pressure. In the first case, all our prospects would be sacrificed. In the second, work must be hurried on at all speed, and now the order of march was changed. Yet there was no choice. But I wanted to wait at least until the Reichstag should assemble in order to discuss matters with the deputies.

The Emperor, on the other hand, demanded the immediate introduction of the supplementary Bill. The Civil Cabinet urged the same: " Bismarck would have made the whole Imperial constitution in twenty-four hours; why did I hesitate like this?" They wanted to distract public attention from the Prisons

Bill, and the navy therefore was to be made the subject of debate.

Thus, while we followed up the Emperor's speech,
the Admiralty was still in the first stages of its work.
The seizure of German Imperial packet steamers by
the English about the end of the year then introduced
an element of national feeling into the pro-Boer enthusiasm of the German public, already regrettably
high; this facilitated, however, the introduction of the
supplementary Bill at the beginning of 1900, to which
the Emperor was persistently and impetuously urging
me. Moreover, thanks to the co-operation of the political economists, public opinion was much stronger
in our favour than even we had hoped.

The supplementary Bill was welcomed by Russia,
and Prince Hohenlohe reckoned also on France's silent approval. The opposite was to be expected from
England, although the Emperor believed on his return from England at the end of November, 1899, that
he brought with him the congratulations of the British
Court and the English Ministers and Naval officials.

When working out the second Navy Bill, we hesitated for a long time whether or not to bring the idea
of the English menace into the preamble. I should
have preferred to leave England out of it altogether. But such an unusual demand as was presented here, namely, the doubling of our small naval
force, made it scarcely possible to avoid hinting at
least at the real reason for it. Our public could not
be taught to observe silence with regard to England,

for, conscious of its own peaceful harmlessness, it believed that it had a right to pour out its moral indignation over the antagonists of the Boers. As all our efforts to damp down the bluster against England were in vain, it was desirable to strike a more sober note in our own declarations on the occasion of the Navy debate. I decided, therefore, in the preamble to the Navy Bill, to give clear expression to the war aim of the fleet, *i.e.* that of an honest political defensive, and I pointed out in the Reichstag, in December, 1899, that the most difficult war situation must be taken as the basis for the size and composition of the German navy. This would occur if we were opposed to the greatest of our possible opponents at sea. To this end the fleet must be so constituted that its highest military achievement, in a war of defence, would lie in a naval battle in the North Sea.

The lay mind must distinguish here between tactical and political offensives. Every warship, and therefore every battle fleet too, is technically and tactically always an instrument of offence; even the spirit of its leadership, as Stosch said in his correspondence with me, must be " galvanized for the offensive." Politically speaking, however, the proposed German fleet offered the English every guarantee of peace, because the latter were two or three times stronger, and it would have been madness to have let loose a war with such slight prospects of overcoming the British fleet.

On the other hand, what we aimed at was to be so

strong that it would mean a certain risk even for the
English fleet, with its enormous superiority, to pick
a quarrel with us. Herein lay the *political defensive*
as well as the *tactical will to fight* in a war of defence.[1]

Thus, this idea of a *risk* which we hinted at was
brought home to the people in the shape of the formula
that our navy was not to be maintained on a bigger,
nor on a smaller, scale than would be necessary to
make an attack upon us seem a hazardous undertaking even to the greatest sea-power. The logical se-
quence of this idea would have been that a respectable
fleet would also increase our qualifications as an ally.
All that we said and thought quite unambiguously
about this risk applied only to its defensive aspect,
but it was systematically distorted by the English
press.

In the year 1900 it was universally felt that Germany was about to take the unavoidable step towards
a world-policy and to send her flag after her trade
at least as closely as possible. The fewer big words
that were used at such a moment, the fewer perspec-
tives that were opened up (according to the advice
given to me by Bismarck at Friedrichsruh), so much

---

[1] Roosevelt said of the American fleet in July 1908: "A first-
class battle fleet is the best pledge of peace; a purely defensive
fleet is worthless. To support a defensive fleet is practically
the same as the offer of a prize for fighting in which only
parrying is allowed. A fleet must be able to hammer at its
opponents until the latter throw up the sponge." In the latter
part of his speech the President proceeded to talk about the
political offensive in a way which, to be sure, was very remote
from our conception of the political risk involved by a large
fleet.

the better. Whilst I regretted that this will to world-power, which was based upon unintentional economic development and the natural shifting of forces, had created by the various statements in the course of the programme the false impression of its being the outcome of a conscious decision and action, I expressed my own conviction to the Emperor at Rominten under the following heads[1]:

"When our object is attained, your Majesty will have an effective force of thirty-eight ships of the line with their auxiliaries. England alone will be superior to this force. But our geographical position, military system, mobilization, torpedo boats, tactical training, the systematic construction of our organization, and our unity of command offer us undoubtedly good prospects even against England.

"Apart from fighting conditions, which are by no means hopeless for us, general political motives from the sober standpoint of the business man should destroy any inclination on the part of England to attack us, and lead her to concede to us such a measure of sea-power as would not threaten our justifiable interests overseas. Of the four world-powers, Russia, England, America, and Germany, only two are accessible by sea; it is on this account that political power at sea is coming more and more into the foreground.

"Salisbury's saying that the big States were getting bigger and stronger and the small ones smaller and weaker, represents the modern development towards a concentration of strength—towards the Trust system. As Germany is particularly behindhand in re-

' Cf. Chap. XV.

gard to sea-power, it is vital for us to make up for lost time. Germany's development to a world-power in trade and industry obviously includes the best means of keeping her superfluous population German. This development is as irresistible as a natural law. If one tried to dam it up, it would break down the dams. The points of contact and of conflict with other nations naturally increased during such a process of commercial and industrial development, and sea-power is therefore indispensable if Germany is not speedily to decline. This raises political considerations, affecting alliances, which are outside my authority."

In January, 1900, I pointed out to the Emperor that our navy programme would never be sufficient to threaten England with attack. The battle fleet, I said, was never intended for war on the high seas, but solely for the defence of home waters, and it would be a mistaken procedure to go ahead with the second section of the navy awaiting development, the foreign-service fleet, before the battle fleet had materialized.[1]

The foreign-service cruisers for which we had asked had actually been refused by the Reichstag, which had of course to make some reduction.[2] The military issue

[1] I made use of the occasion once again to recommend to the Emperor more reticence in his public statements.

[2] As we could not put down more than three big ships in the year, owing to the limitations of our technical arrangements as well as the difficulties of increasing the *personnel,* the six cruisers which were cancelled were not ordered until 1906. Thus the cancelling of them did not really amount to anything. On the occasion of their rejection, however, in 1900, I remarked that we would introduce a supplementary demand for them within the specified period. Hence the demand for these cruisers in

of the second Navy Bill was the doubling of the battle fleet. Further, the disappearance of a financial limit was of importance.

V

In the preliminary negotiations regarding the second Navy Bill, a prominent part was played by the Centrum deputy, Müller (Fulda), a somewhat "erratic" character, who afterwards was not so much to the fore, and who indeed generally worked behind the scenes. To our joy, he moved the abandonment of the financial limit, which he declared to be an undesirable restriction of the Budget. Thus, as we did without a financial limit this time, all our financial difficulties disappeared. The Reichstag's right of annual sanction was left untouched so far as money matters were concerned. The Reichstag showed its appreciation of the fact that it was much more firmly bound from a moral than from a financial point of view; for it had bound itself to a definite shipbuilding programme by the Bill. If ships became bigger and dearer, the Reichstag, which was now bound to sanction the ships as such by the provisions of the Bill, could not possibly limit their technical construction for financial reasons; it could never assume the responsibility for allowing the ships authorized by the Bill to be turned out either too small in size or defec-

1906. I preferred the *whole* of the foreign-service fleet to be cancelled in 1900; this left a sufficiently big item for the supplementary demand, and in addition one which to a certain extent enjoyed greater popularity than the building of a battle fleet.

tive in construction, owing to insufficient money grants.
By this *lex imperfecta* as represented by the second
Navy Bill, which was binding as regards *matériel*, but
allowed a free hand as regards finance, the Reichstag
surrendered the possibility of refusing money for the
new types of vessels, which were increasing in size
and cost, unless it was prepared to bring upon itself
the reproach of building inferior ships. Thus, in 1900
the Reichstag decided by legal enactment to carry out
the naval scheme which had been drawn up, and bound
itself morally to create no more financial difficulties
for us, as had so soon been the case with the first
Navy Bill.

The co-responsibility assumed by the Reichstag by
the form of the second Bill justified itself. When we
were later compelled by the English to take the giant's
stride to the Dreadnought class, the Reichstag itself
proposed the increase to me, although this meant doubling the fighting force of the navy again and the cost
as well, still, however, within the scope of the Bill
of 1900.

In order to lessen the opposition of the Centrum, I
had recommended the abandonment of paragraph 2
of the " Jesuit law," but on the advice of Lucanus,
supported by Bülow, the Emperor refused to do this.
Matters went off well even without that. Our majority was bigger than it had been in the case of the
last Army Bills. I have never met with unsur-
mountable obstacles in the Reichstag, but generally
with sympathy on the whole, even from the bourgeois

Left. Eugen Richter, it is true, accused me of breaking my word, because, in accordance with the general situation at the time, I had replied in the negative to a question in January, 1899, as to whether we intended to bring in any supplementary demands before the conclusion of the six years' limit. I may say that at all times the information that we have given the Reichstag has always been in strict accordance with the truth.

Thus, the second Navy Bill was brought into being, and I was quite aware that it was bound to have quite a different political significance from the first, particularly as regards a policy of alliance, because it gave the other navies of the world a chance of establishing a certain balance of power at sea by means of coalition with us.

CHAPTER XII

BUILDING THE FLEET

I

A MAN who has a great object in view is not always in a position to reveal his inmost thoughts. Political work too is based on the divination of certain factors; just as the sailor has to steer by dead reckoning, *i.e.* by calculation, when the sky is clouded over, or just as the place for which one is making will not betray its local colour from afar off. During the voyage the prospect often changes, and it is easy for those who are not taking part to find contradictions or dispute the existence of difficulties. They say: if you only talk properly to the Reichstag, the thing will do itself. Those who are working on some special detail readily cling to it; it is only the responsible leader who feels the welter of the conditions around him.

The Secretary of State was to carry out the great programme for the fulfilment of which he had pledged himself to the nation by means of an authority centralized in himself, which was taken for granted by everybody, but which no one really conceded to him. It was a question of justifying the confidence of the community by throwing all one's energy into the work and overcoming obstacles, the size and number of which exceeded all expectations.

We were immediately faced with a labyrinth of technical and organizing problems and differences of opinion. I found that the structure of our ships was particularly unfavourable. Years passed, however, before I could remedy this evil by setting up establishments in which the best build of ships for purposes of speed could be ascertained by the towing of models; hitherto our technical experts had not thought highly enough of them. We were restricted in the length and size of our ships by the locks at Wilhelmshaven. These two circumstances are largely responsible for the fact that particularly those ships built during the first period of the Navy Bill could not attain the speed of which their engine-power would have been capable. This was a chronic source of embarrassment until the third Wilhelmshaven entrance was built in 1910. Moreover, we were put at a great disadvantage in contrast to all other shipbuilding nations by the sand-bars in our North Sea estuaries, which prevented us giving our vessels the draught they needed. In a certain sense we were hampered by the restriction for which the Dutch had to pay dearly in the seventeenth century in their fight against the British. In all essentials, a naval battle is a fight

of one ship against another; the decisive technical
factor is rather the concentration of force in the individual ship than the actual number of ships. Because
the Dutch could not build their vessels very big, owing
to the courses of their rivers, as the English were
able to do, the latter obtained this local superiority.
We had thus to overcome these and many other obstacles within a few years, so that in spite of everything our ships surpassed the English in fighting value.

Generally speaking, the building of the fleet was
rendered difficult by the low standard of our technical
construction at that time. The administrative officials
at the Admiralty had been given too much power over
the technical side of the navy; the calling of a naval
architect was far from brilliant, both as regards pay
and social position. The silent struggle between lawyers and technical experts was one of the reasons
why we had to begin the construction of the fleet with
a *personnel* which was insufficient in numbers and
lacking in experience. The technical adviser-in-chief
to the Admiralty had fortified his position; he locked
up the only things worth knowing in his notebook
and would not suffer the existence of a rival. This
state of affairs could have brought us to ruin. Meanwhile, technical achievement could not develop slowly,
as the organization could, but it had to set to work
fully equipped from the outset on the construction of
the fleet and accomplish at once almost as much in
speed and output as it would be doing ten years later.
I began therefore from the very first to try to improve

the position of the technical branch, and to create a "nursery " for it; I tried to get to know the individual members, and picked out those who might develop into future shipbuilders, which comparatively few of them do.   The English appoint an engineer-in-chief with almost sovereign powers and press upon him a salary of £5,000.   Such "extravagance," which well becomes the magnificence of an old aristocracy, should have been proposed to the Treasury and the grudging democrats of our Parliament!   I formed a special fund for achievements in construction, and awarded those men who distinguished themselves bonuses up to the value of £200.   But although I sent them the money with a letter asking them to say nothing about it, the punctilious honesty of the German was too strong; the recipients themselves asked for an equal distribution of the fund because of the jealousy of the others!   Thus it was no wonder that private enterprise enticed many good engineers away from us; in many cases the men reported sick after a short time and went straight to some big firm or other.   In spite of these and innumerable other difficulties, which cannot be discussed here, we succeeded in course of time in beating the English in the quality of our naval shipbuilding, a state of affairs which also became evident in the case of private firms engaged in the construction of big passenger liners.

A year after I had taken office, there occurred a difficult period of transition, in which for lack of other talent an executive officer, Admiral Büchsel, had to

fill the breach as architect-in-chief. Among the other
shipbuilding officials whom I intended for higher
posts, and to whom I gave opportunities of preparing
themselves for the great object before them by sending them on voyages and seconding them for special
duties, especial merit is due to our later architect-in-
chief, Geheimrat Burkner. Personally, I considered
the way he co-operated with us, the executive officers,
in our mutual and indivisible task to be ideal. The
other members of the technical staff also contributed their full share to our constantly improving
and finally unrivalled naval construction. The nature
of our shipbuilding, and the sum total of the intellectual labour crystallized in it, may be made clear to the
lay mind by an example.

In naval warfare the main object is not territorial
gain, but the annihilation of the enemy; since the introduction of steam power and modern artillery this
is no longer effected by boarding the enemy, but only
by sinking him. So long as a ship is afloat, it retains
a certain fighting value and can afterwards be easily
repaired. Thus the deadly injury of that part of a
ship below the water line is the ultimate aim of the
weapon of attack, and the increasing of the buoyancy
of the vessel the main object of protective measures.
Up till 1906 our ships were but little protected against
attack below the water line, whilst the English ships
were badly protected even as late as this war. With
the old vessels, a hit by a torpedo invariably resulted
in the sinking of the ship, as is shown, for example,

by the successful fight of the U9 with three big English cruisers. As soon as the Navy Bill was settled I caused this question of buoyancy to be taken up with great thoroughness. We soon found out that we had to experiment with real explosions in order to gain sufficient experience. As we could not sacrifice modern ships, and could not learn enough from the older ones, we built a section of a modern ship by itself and carried out experimental explosions on it, with torpedo heads, carefully studying the result every time. We tested the possibility of weakening the force of the explosion by letting the explosive gases burst in empty compartments without meeting with any resistance. We ascertained the most suitable kind of steel for the different structural parts, and found further that the effect of the explosion was nullified if we compelled it to pulverize coal in any considerable quantity. This resulted in a special arrangement of a portion of the coal bunkers. We were then able to meet the force of the explosion, which had been weakened in this way, by a strong, carefully constructed, steel wall which finally secured the safety of the interior of the ship. This "torpedo bulkhead" was carried without interruption the whole length of the vital parts of the ship. These experiments, which were continued through many years, and on which we did not hesitate to expend millions, yielded moreover information concerning the most suitable use of material and the construction of the adjoining parts of the ship. In addition to this, the whole of the under-

water parts of the ship were designed for the event
of failure to localize the effects of the explosion, or
of several hits being made, and so forth; endless labour was expended upon details such as the pumping
system or the possibility of speedily restoring a listing
ship to a vertical position by flooding certain compartments. Finally, we completely abandoned the practice
of connecting the compartments below the water line
by doors, which had played such a fateful part in
the sinking of the *Titanic* and other ships too.

The buoyancy which was attained by our system
stood the test. In contrast to the British ships, ours
were well-nigh indestructible. The whole English fleet
went on hammering the little *Wiesbaden,* and yet the
poor ship would not sink. Although the *Mainz* was
almost shot to pieces and torpedoed, it could not be
brought under the water until an officer and a torpedo artificer, after everybody else had left the ship,
opened the torpedo tubes, submerged the ship and
sank with it. The distinguished commander of the
Emden put his ship at a coral reef under full steam,
and yet the inner structure stood firm. It was as-
tounding what our ships could stand in the way of
mines and torpedoes without sinking. During Admiral v. Rebeur's attack upon Imbros, the *Goeben*
was struck by three heavy mines, but she was still
able to return to the Bosphorus under her own steam,
whilst a modern English ship of the line, the *Auda-
cious,* sank in the Irish sea after striking one single
mine. It was only our older ships, like the *Pommern*

and the *Prinz Adalbert,* built at a time when our experiments on buoyancy had not been concluded, that showed less staying power.

The supreme quality of a ship is that it should remain afloat, and, by preserving its vertical position, continue to put up a fight; in this respect the English navy was so much behind ours that this difference in quality alone was able to decide the issue of a naval engagement. But our shipbuilding also aimed at the highest degree of fighting efficiency in every other direction. Inasmuch as we were aiming principally at qualities which only tell in battle, the excellence of our ships could not even be correctly estimated by all executive officers in times of peace, particularly as we had to abandon a number of well-known qualities and conveniences which are all right in peacetime, to the advantage of our effectiveness in battle. The complete absence of doors in those parts of the ship under the water line was most uncomfortable, for example; such a thing, however, could at the critical moment decide one's fate. In every naval engagement that is fought to a finish, there is the psychological moment, when the one side suddenly thinks " Good God, the enemy is sinking and we are not, they are on fire and we are not "; and from that moment this side will have no more losses, whilst the enemy loses everything. How our ships compared with the English vessels of the same years may be shown by a few figures. Quite apart from our better ammunition, etc., a most carefully conducted examination shows that our *Derfflinger* could pierce the heaviest armour of the British *Tiger* at a range of 11,700 metres, whilst the *Tiger* could not pierce that of the *Derfflinger* until it was within 7,800 metres' range. A similar superiority in armament and armour-plating, calculated to grip the imagination of any reflecting person, existed in the case of nearly all battleships of the same years.

While translating in shipbuilding our conception of warfare into terms of iron and steel, we were giving up other things which would have won immediate recognition and would have spared us the continual critical comparison of our ships with the advertisements of foreign firms. We had heavier displacements, owing to the thick and heavy armour-plating in the region of the water line, to our provisions against sinking and against fire, to the special measures taken to ensure the safety of the parts from which the ship was controlled, and so on.

We had secured the superiority in quality of our fleet over the English in the decisive years of Germany's development and thereby acquired an important counter-poise for our inferiority in numbers. Naturally few people in Germany knew anything definite about this superiority; many, but not all, trusted the creators of the fleet. Any ship afloat in time of peace did not exhibit its solid qualities and fighting value; it was a matter of indifference whether its armour-plating was thick or thin. On the other hand an opportunity was afforded, and eagerly grasped by fault-finders in Germany, when it was a question if our heavy guns were of a smaller calibre than the English; it was *not* seen that, apart from our more effective projectiles, we obtained in practice the same results in the matter of armour-piercing with our smaller calibre as the English with their greater, and besides, obtained other very important advantages. The conservatism of my working methods often seemed unnatural in many people's opinion, and was hated to death by those who liked to draw up lists of what they wanted from the foreign catalogues. If our ships, which were handed over to the enemy in such a shameful manner, are scientifically examined, the English will be amazed as they work through the whole, as well as through the hundred-and-one details, at the rivals they had in the Germans in their own particular province of shipbuilding. The English have not been nearly so conscientious and intelligent in their work as we have been. As the English are not Germans, however, they will only reluctantly admit that the foreign work is better than their own. It is difficult for me to refrain from insisting on this point. But if our nation is to learn anything from its fate, it must realize the suicidal tendency in its nature. For many did not understand the weapon that they possessed in the German fleet until after the Battle of Jutland. There was too much delay in drawing at the right moment the historical consequences from the possession of it.

When the German armies went to war in 1870 with

an inferior rifle, the troops were told: "The chasse-
pot is only superior at long range. So run in under
its range, and then you will have the superiority at
500 yards."

The German navy had only to be told the truth,
and they would have been able to go into battle in
August, 1914, with an unconquerable feeling of superiority. Instead of this, it was considered the thing
in the higher commands in the navy to criticize all
short-comings in detail. This introduced a trait into
the officers' corps that was dangerous in time of war;
there was more doubt than faith. It goes without
saying that we could have improved things here and
there. But the final result should be looked at. Our
Germany of 1914 was not able to do this. It acted
on the lines of the motto inscribed on the shooting
range at Meppen:

> You can score a hundred hits,
>   And people nod and go their way,
> But ne'er a puppy that forgets
>   If you score a miss one day.

At bottom the German nation had a great deal of
luck with the construction of its belated fleet, but as
it pursued it with a clear purpose in view, it completed this fleet at the right moment. But ultimate and
decisive good fortune was denied it, partly owing to the
tendency in Germany to find fault with things made
at home and to admire everything foreign. It was
also partly owing to this that the fleet was not thrown

into the scale at the right moment of the war, with the consequences that I shall deal with later.

II

Naval shipbuilding is applied tactics, but it is also at the same time a money question. If Germany was to have a useful fleet, we could not allow ourselves any large unnecessary expenditure at all. The success of the work of the interested naval officers and the extensive staff of loyal officials can only be duly honoured by those who take our financial restrictions into account. No foreign navy has ever produced such a maximum of achievement with such a minimum of means. As we purchased in 1898 the principle of the permanent maintenance of the supply of ships mainly by renouncing any new taxation, and disarmed the Reichstag by pointing to the financial resources already at hand, we were never afterwards able to burn the candle at both ends. In naval expenditure we were not only behind England, but far behind America at all times, and now and again even behind Russia and France; by a better allocation of our money, however, we succeeded in building the second strongest navy in the world. To be sure, there are patriots to-day who reckon it as one of the sins of the German navy that it accomplished so much with the means voted by the Reichstag.[1]

Economy requires exact work and business-like principles. The Admiralty acquired a certain repu-

[1] *Vide* Appendix.

tation for beating down prices, for making speculative purchases of land, and so forth. Never again will Germany acquire so cheaply such an admirable piece of work. This rich nation which did not need to count the milliards in time of war, in the time of its prosperity turned over anxiously in its hand the millions—and even the thousands—the giving of which to its army and navy might have secured the permanence of peace and its own continued welfare.

After the resignation of Prince Bülow, who gave the navy full sympathy, the latter fell a victim to chronic money hunger. I have had to fight for the most necessary grants until I was tired out, less with the Reichstag, which evinced growing insight, than with the Imperial Treasury and with the Imperial Chancellor, who, the one blinded by departmental fanaticism and the other by political dreams, suppressed a great deal that was desirable for Germany's armament during those years, because, as they said, Germany had no money to spare for this purpose. I put through at that time what could not be delayed; hoping, with a heavy heart and the feeling of being hindered in the development of our armed defences, to obtain the means to supplement the rest later. There was less room than ever for subsidiary matters; but in spite of this I applied all my energy to new developments, such as, for example, the construction of submarines, as soon as they could be used in war, so that even in this arm we were superior to all foreign navies at the outbreak of war.

The efforts of certain political circles to decry the achievements of the navy led during the war to a campaign of lies regarding my former official activities; this brought home to me in lively fashion the tendency of humankind, and particularly of Germans, to rate criticism higher than creation, and to regard what has been done as a matter of course, and what still remains to be done as an omission. Even in the time of my popularity I was always quite clear that the "Hosanna" of the moment is easily followed by the "Crucify" of the morrow. I do not regret on my own account, but for the nation's sake, that confidence in the navy was artificially shattered, but I do not want to waste the reader's time with these quarrels which will presumably soon fade. I refer to the appendix to this book, which has been added in order to prevent the field being left clear by ambiguous silence for those whose pleasure it has been to decry the loyal labours of a generation.

Even in time of peace I was accustomed to be reproached with backwardness, but I did not consider it correct, in view of foreign countries, to enlighten the public. My tried and trusty method of waiting to prove the military usefulness of a new invention before adopting it universally was proof against disappointments, and was the chief foundation of our successes, but of course it exposed me to the reproaches of the inventors and of impatient patriots. I will take two examples, the submarine and the airship. I refused to throw away money on submarines

so long as they could only cruise in home waters, and
therefore be of no use to us; as soon as sea-going
boats were built, however, I was the first to encourage
them on a large scale, and, in spite of the financial
restrictions imposed upon me, I went as far as the
limits of our technical production would permit.

The question as to how the submarines were to be
used could not be answered practically until the instrument itself was there. The immediate question, therefore, was to construct boats which could operate overseas, and, as soon as this was possible, build as many
of them as we could. This was done, and consequently
nothing was neglected.

What was to be done with the arm thus constructed could only be shown by the special necessities
of war. If the English had not thrown international
naval law overboard, wholly in their own interests,
the submarine war on merchant shipping could have
been regarded from a totally different point of view.
As soon as it was possible for submarines to operate
overseas, the war on merchant shipping was in the
air; no special father was needed for this idea. The
great hopes that had been centred in the High Sea
fleet, however, made submarines at first the auxiliary
organs of the Staff. Then when the transition took
place to the campaign against merchant shipping,
everything that could have been prepared for this purpose in time of peace was already done. To expect
the navy to have foreseen and considered all the developments of the war is the same as to demand that

the army should have prepared some defence against tanks in time of peace.[1]

As a naval officer who had got to know the force of the wind and the malice of squalls on sailing ships, I never promised myself much from the airships, and the war has proved me right in this. I set much greater expectations on the development of the aeroplane. During the Zeppelin craze which passed over Germany I kept myself in the background as much as possible, without appearing a wet blanket. As a proof of the urgent temptation to over-hasty adoptions all around me in this and many other provinces, I reproduce a letter together with my answer.

"BERLIN,
"*August 27th*, 1912.

" YOUR EXCELLENCY,

"Forgive my disturbing your holiday; but it is a question of an urgent and important matter!—the improvement of our airship construction. The new naval airship will represent an enormously big advance. To me the time seems to have come when we should proceed to the systematic building of an aerial fleet; for as things are at present we shall not turn our advantage to any account. The creator of the German fleet should also be the creator of the German aerial fleet. A definite building programme and all that this includes is necessary if we are to retain the lead, and in the circumstances a Bill to this effect. The cost will not be too great, for with 30,000,000 marks we can build in three years eighteen to twenty Zeppelin ships, together with nine or ten sheds each holding two ships, including, further,

[1] *Vide* Appendix.

the cost of commissioning the ships for from 250 to 300 days. This calculation is based on the following annual expenditure of 10,000,000 marks:

		Marks.	
1.	Building of six ships . . .	4.50	millions
2.	Building three sheds for above .	3.00	"
3.	Commissioning each ship, 800 marks per day—therefore six ships for 300 days . . .	1.44	"
4.	Other expenditure	1.06	"
		10.00	"

"Thus with 30,000,000 marks a very great deal could be done for peace and for our own safety. The money for this purpose exists, in the first place, in the surplus of 1911, of which all was not used by the Army Bill; 1912 is also going well and will certainly yield a surplus. A systematic procedure is to be recommended, otherwise it will be the same as with the navy before 1898. . . . I wish your Excellency a good recovery and with the most respectful greetings,

"I am,
"Your Excellency's devoted servant,
"M. Erzberger, M.d.R.
(Member of the Reichstag)."

"St. Blasien,
September 6th, 1912.

"Dear Herr Erzberger,

"I send you my best thanks for your letter of August 27th, which interested me greatly. From it I see with great pleasure that you take a warm interest in the utilization of airships for the defence of the Fatherland, just as you do in the army and navy. I am afraid that the new arm will not be pushed forward so speedily as your letter suggests. After settling the naval and military estimates of the last year, the Reichstag will not unjustly demand that the Zeppelins asked for should be first tested with regard to their use at sea and on the coast. If that was not necessary, a well-founded complaint could be brought against the Government on the score of its not having put forward in the military estimates of last year a larger allowance such as you outlined in your letter.   A thorough-going test combined with the selection and training of the necessary *personnel* is, I am firmly convinced, also absolutely essential if we are not to suffer severe disappointments. The use of airships on a large scale for military purposes will still give rise to many difficulties, although it will probably come to this, but not in a day as your patriotic heart desires and imagines.

" With kind regards,
" Yours faithfully,
"von Tirpitz."

III

Busy civilians, and business houses who were not concerned so much with the usefulness of their goods for war purposes as with the wholesale delivery of them, formed only the one wing of my critics; the other was composed of specialists.

To be just, I must say that the enormous leaps forward made in engineering while we were building our fleet had necessarily given rise to lively controversies among the experts, and had occasioned difficult compromises. It proved to be dangerous to make any definite arrangements a long way ahead. Every ship became obsolete by the time it was finished, and the critics did not always remember that, when building was begun, it could not be otherwise. Internal struggles are also to be found in the history of foreign navies as things begin to develop. Yet the partition of the Admiralty on the accession of William II was the cause of inter-departmental friction, which wore me out more in the course of years than either the Reichstag or the work I had in hand. I stood under fire from all sides.

After the Navy Bill had been passed, the Executive Command was annoyed, because the Bill with its battle fleet did not correspond with the draft of a foreign-service fleet drawn up with the co-operation of the Executive Command.[1] On the other hand, I had objections to the political activity of the Executive Command, which had used its influence in the Delagoa and Manila affairs; it was surely enough for two naval authorities, the Admiralty and the Cabinet, to have a hand in politics. The really natural promise which had been given to me when I took up my duties, that I should be consulted in the use of the foreign-service ships, had not been kept. I now demanded that the foreign-service ships should be put under the Admiralty, but I did not succeed in getting the Emperor's consent. In this quarrel the authority of

[1] For some time the teaching at the Naval Academy had been in favour of the cruiser war, and against the High Sea fleet until I intervened, for it was not fitting for our shipbuilding to be opposed by our highest training school.

the Supreme War Lord was played off against me, which, it was said, would be narrowed if the Secretary of State, who was responsible to the Reichstag, were to receive such extensive powers. I could hardly say anything in reply to this argument, and I had to make the best of it, in order to make progress. So I accomplished the break-up of the Executive Command in Berlin, in the course of which I had repeatedly to send in my resignation; I succeeded by strengthening the conviction of the Emperor that his own authority could scarcely bear the existence of an Executive Command on the one hand and the Admiralty on the other, in view of the powers which had hitherto been allotted to each. A portion of the powers of the Executive Command were now transferred to the Admiralty, and the rest were given partly to the naval stations in Kiel and Wilhelmshaven and partly to the newly formed " Admiral Staff."[1]

This partition was effected for lack of the better arrangement which was unattainable, the centralization of the navy in an Admiralty, such as always existed in England, and existed with us until 1888.

During Caprivi's latter term of office I dissuaded

[1] The Admiral Staff was formed on an analogous scheme to the General Staff. I do not know whether it was a fortunate thing for the army that the General Staff grew so consistently independent as an after-effect of Moltke's greatness. This perhaps led to the estrangement of the General Staff from technical matters and to the fact that the War Ministry had so little to do with war. In any case such a cleavage on the part of the Admiral Staff would not do for the navy; it was an idea of the doctrinaires which did not lead to the institution of a really energetic collective authority.

him from the partition of the Admiralty. Caprivi shared my views. In the next years of my tactical work I had placed too great hopes upon rearrangement of organization among the newly divided authorities, as I did not realize clearly enough at that time that the fact that the Admiralty was so little occupied with active-service problems was due more to persons than to organizations. Then when I took charge of the building of the fleet, it was clear to me and other officers of good judgment that the Admiralty needed other powers whilst the fleet was being constructed than during the period of inactivity. What unlimited powers did not the Americans give Goethals when he was to build the Panama Canal! As we had now to reckon with many heads in the navy, division of authority between many people was still more bearable than the dualism which existed between an Executive Command in Berlin, with authority over the whole navy, and the Admiralty. With all this fencing going on around me, I could not fail to be charged with tyranny and defection from the views I had held when in the Executive Command. The fact is that I had to protect myself from this confusion of forces with a different defence according to my position and the state of my work at the time, whereby the curse of this divided authority kept on appearing again and again in different places.

In the long run the success of organizations depends upon the men who work on them. A great creative work can only be accomplished by one who has in his own heart the conviction of the rightness of his own aims, and in the main finds the way himself to his goal, or, else makes it altogether the property of his own mind.   Advice and suggestion stream in, and nothing would be more wrong than not to give them full consideration.   But the decision must rest with those who feel the difficulties and responsibilities of execution.   The navy was an unusually finely adjusted organism.   The continual interchange of men, selected for the central authorities, between the Admiral Staff and the service afloat deprived the idea of its justification in fact, that the Admiral Staff could as a naval strategic authority judge questions of development better than the Admiralty.   Even between the naval authorities on land there was instituted in course of time a barely sufficient working relationship.   We also succeeded in keeping in check the natural demand of the North Sea and Baltic stations for coastal defence and coastal warfare, since this could only have been satisfied at the expense of the fleet, *i.e.* the politico-military importance of the navy. Relationships with the Command of the High Sea fleet were not so clear, for the former had gained in influence as the construction of the latter progressed, and was developing a tendency to unite under it all *matériel* afloat.

The French and English put the Commander-in-Chief of the fleet in command of a squadron and thus gave him a " private possession " of his own. We had retained the arrangement from the time of the Executive Command, however, of putting the Commander-in-Chief on a special fleet-flagship outside the squadron formations. We hesitated as to whether the foreign method which was supported by naval history, or our own arrangement corresponded better with modern conditions. I wanted to clear up the matter by tactical experiments. But I met with insurmountable resistance in this matter. The question of the flagship became a departmental intrigue. In this connection, I was given great anxiety by the position of the Commander-in-Chief of the fleet, which was becoming more and more a kind of monopoly; and after the retirement of Köster, a strict master after the fashion of Frederick William I, the Cabinet was not always guided by common-sense arguments, and certainly not by a great knowledge of human nature, in its choice of his successor. From my study of the French navy, which was more accessible than the British, I had seen that a change of Commander-in-Chief practically always led to a change of tactics, and to the loss of a large portion of previously gained experience. I had regarded the chief activity of the officials on shore belonging to the Admiralty Staff to be the collection and co-ordination of these experiences; but the active participation of the latter in the manœuvres of the fleet was restricted more and more by the power of the Commander-in-Chief. Further, whereas the juxtaposition of the numerous corps leaders led to a useful rivalry in the army, the views of the leader of the High

Sea fleet soon hardened into dogma in view of his incontrovertible position, although there was a great need here also for useful clash of opinion. In order to keep alive constructive criticism, for which our Imperial manœuvres did not suffice, and in order to facilitate the rise of independent characters endowed with the gift of leadership, as well as to revive the search for truth in contrast to the drill and the fine fighting formations, I proposed—though in vain—to leave the various sections of the fleet much more independence and to gather them together only for the purpose of the big manœuvres; moreover, I also suggested that these manœuvres should not be actually in the charge of the Commander-in-Chief, but of different leaders from time to time, irrespective of their length of service.

When I am reproached with not having concentrated the navy in the hands of one person in time of peace, my power is being over-estimated. What with the jealousy of different heads, and the Emperor's nature, I was only able to smooth over, instead of putting an end to, the harmful friction which arose from the division of the naval organism into so many sections. There was only one way open to me, and that was not to give any of the authorities with immediate access to the Emperor any predominant influence, to leave the Emperor the feeling that his prerogative was not being encroached upon, and to cherish the hope that in the event of war the monarch would create a Supreme Naval Command which would combine everything in the hands of one man. The nation, which had no idea of the half-measures of the authorities and the compromises which were hampering production, ascribed all the responsibility to the Secretary of State, a fact which I felt very deeply. But owing to the lack of a unified Admiralty I often had to negotiate between the various sections instead of taking action.

The most difficult part of the situation for me was when the Chief of the Naval Cabinet, von Senden, in spite of his chivalrous nature and his warm-hearted interest in the advancement of the navy, began to pursue from time to time a very arbitrary policy in questions affecting my department. To give a picture at random of my feelings amidst the changing factions and coteries which hardly gave me any rest at all owing to the extraordinary activity of the Emperor in naval matters, I may quote from an old letter of mine to Prince Henry:

" With regard to the question of battle cruisers, I have not succeeded in convincing His Majesty that any procedure in the sense desired by him means the collapse of our Navy Bill. . . . Most of the gentlemen who have no responsibility but a big say in this matter do not see the whole situation. . . . It would really be selling a birthright for a mess of pottage if we were to try to modify the fundamental principles of the Navy Bill in the one cruiser which still remains to be finished. A Chief of Cabinet probably could think so, but not a Secretary of State who is watching His Majesty's true interest and feels himself responsible therefor. While nothing did us so much harm formerly in our demands on the Reichstag as a certain restlessness and eternal changing of views and plans, we have now actually collected together a certain fund of confidence in this direction, which stands our demands in good stead. If we give the Opposition an opportunity of talking again about the changeable art of war, the zig-zag course, etc., we shall be putting a very sharp weapon into its hands.

" Will your Royal Highness be pleased to take it in good part if I have allowed my pen to run away with me when discussing these worries, but I am very near to despair when I think of the difficult and dangerous position of our State, which is naturally exerting its influence upon the Admiralty, on the eve of a supplementary Bill; and when I see on the other hand how irresponsible advisers are aggravating the difficulty in almost stupendous fashion, and consequently to the ultimate detriment of His Majesty's interests. . . ."

IV

The Reichstag did not give me so much trouble. What had to be passed was absolutely indispensable; but the confidence of the Reichstag in the official handling of armament questions was certainly becoming stronger. By means of information from all quarters and personal inspection of ships, dockyards, etc., the Deputies had convinced themselves as to the way the work was being carried out. This led to the disappearance of all conflicts between the Reichstag and the Government. My comparative independence of the Reichstag enabled me on the whole to let all captious criticism exhaust itself. Under a purely

parliamentary system of Government, on the other
hand, progressive officials are almost bound to be
stifled by the national vices of pettiness, party jealousy,
and unbounded capacity for illusion. It is specially
difficult for parliamentarism to build a fleet, even if
it spends a great deal on it as in France. The English
succeed because the qualities of the nation and its
great historical tradition have constructed a firm foundation. Even in my time parliamentary bodies had to
be kept in a good humour; a good deal of work was
needed to keep them quiet, and a great deal of fruitless haggling; they needed, as somebody said, "a ball
with which they could play." Thus, in order to be
able to stand firm on the main issues, I sometimes had
to sacrifice unimportant things to the Reichstag. Once
this affected the personal affairs of the officers' corps,
to my great regret, as for example in the reduction
of mess allowances; the officers concerned were dis-
satisfied and mobilized their forces against the Secretary of State, who was dependent upon Parliament. I
have, however, always endeavoured to support the
personnel of all categories.

In the same measure as the squadrons increased and
spread the realm of the navy along the coast, and as
land was won back from the sea by building dykes,
villages expropriated, and whole towns and mighty
workshops founded and constructed, the many-mem-
bered family of the navy grew far and wide. We were
the only Imperial institution which drew the hundreds
of thousands from a provincial way of looking at

things to a common horizon. The navy became the
melting-pot of Germanism. Before the inactivity of
the High Sea fleet during the war killed the life which
was coursing through it, the growing strength of
Germany could be felt in its pulse-beat. No navy in
the world had such an excellent *personnel* as we had
in our coastal population, in the merchant seamen
who gradually cast off their former international character owing to their service in the navy, and in the
fishermen who, particularly indispensable for the man-
ning of our small ships, returned to their villages, after
serving in the navy, with a widened mental horizon
and professional ambition. When our Old Prussian
people on the shores of the Baltic with their handiness,
and our North Sea folk with their heavy strength,
were no longer sufficient for the growing needs of our
personnel, we went inland for recruits; service on
modern ships did not make the same demands on seamanship as in the old days of sailing vessels. The
South Germans, and among them the Alsatians, distinguished themselves in the navy. Under the leadership of an excellent engineering corps, service in the
navy afforded a very good schooling for the technical
personnel; the industries fought for our stokers.[1] The
best of our youth joined the officers' corps—think

[1] As the modern ships demanded a big increase of the engineering *personnel* which is recruited from the industrial dis-
tricts, and since the latter remained practically shut up in the
dockyards, this formed a favourable soil for Socialist agitation,
the more so since the workmen in the dockyards came most
in touch with the engineering *personnel* of the navy. In time
of peace no obvious harm had come from this.

of our submarine commanders—and indeed all the more gladly as the magnitude of our task seemed to increase. The outsider can hardly imagine the hard work that was done in the navy. Never has the State been served more joyously and more devotedly. We felt ourselves to be the outposts of a great people which, thanks to its State, was about to acquire freedom and equality among the nations of the world.

Soon therefore the worst was over, and we were able to extend our aims. With a greater separation of the fleet from barracks and home coasts the navy would have grown more and more into the nation, which needed something like this; for it does not know even to-day what a treasure it possessed in the officers' corps alone.

The purely destructive fools who are now exulting over the dissolution of the old Germany as over a great deed ought for once to create an organism which could equal only this one of our old Imperial institutions in solid strength and devotion to the ideals of the whole. The view-points of world-policy were concentrated most strongly in the navy; therefore we were bound to become a power in the nation. Since circumstances and persons, which I will discuss later, squandered the peace which was secured by the fleet, and let slip the victory which the fleet promised, the nation has sunk so low that it is ashamed of its one-time strength and takes pleasure in abusing that which has been its pride and joy so long.

In my proposals to keep the organization alive, and generally in my inclination to follow up the constantly changing conditions of naval efficiency, I often had to contend with circumstances and the special departments. Many admirals stamped me after 1897 as the Director of Administration and the supplier of *matériel* to the navy, although my own line of development and my own inclination was in the direction of naval tactics. As a consequence I had to see a great deal of which I did not approve, without being able to interfere in any way.

The united spirit which had animated the whole navy in the 'eighties and the first half of the 'nineties was to a certain degree lost. The men who were put in command at the beginning of the war would hardly have yielded in such fatal manner to the political leaders' fear of giving battle if the specializing departmental policy which was the fashion had allowed the capital of our previous tactical labours to be drawn upon to the full. When I was acquainted with the operation order of the Admiralty Staff on July 30th, 1914, I was terrified by the theoretical speculation which in certain quarters had over-ridden the spirit of resolute initiative, owing to the subdivided treatment of the main questions. In spite of this the navy was good; it had worked tremendously hard, even though not always in the most appropriate direction. And so it only needed the right command to bring out all its qualities and to lead the fleet, such as it was, to victory.

It is with a bleeding heart that one thinks of the circumstances which have hurled the German nation back into the darkness when it was so near its highest perfection.

To the astonishment of Europe, the Prussia of the eighteenth century had grown in a few years from an indifferent member of the impotent German people to a great power, thanks to the development and good leadership of her military strength by the Hohenzollern kings. It looked as though the German Empire was going to be able to retrieve its belated development to a world-power just as speedily and successfully by the swift creation of its sea-power, assisted as it was in this by many favourable circumstances. The apparent unreadiness of the nation as a whole to understand the grave necessity for this undertaking in every detail likewise resembled the position of Prussia in the eighteenth century, which had been still less comprehended by the whole nation. But imagine what would have happened to Prusso-German history, if, instead of a Frederick William I and a Frederick the Great, a much-divided military authority had had to make decisions under a highly commendable War Council! What we lacked most of all was the unification of the Admiralty.

V

The reproach which is levelled at me from time to time of having pursued a one-sided and obtuse battle-fleet policy, is based upon an error. In comparison with the historical progress of our empire, we were late in going out into the world and upon the sea. In the bustle of the world, however, we had to expect conflicts of interests. It was important that we should avoid such things, and indeed impose no restrictions upon our activity so long as the understructure of our power was not secure. Until this was strengthened by our fleet and by political support, we could not move with any freedom upon the seas of the world and demand equal rights. Our, and particularly my, personal task therefore lay primarily in the creation of this sea-power, and this could only be done by the institution of the battle fleet. Moreover, we were compelled by the threats of the British in the first decade of this century to concentrate our fleet in force in home waters. Under these conditions trans-Atlantic expeditions, such as the China campaign, the action against Venezuela or the Agadir affair seemed to me altogether undesirable, quite apart from their particular disadvantages, for they only gave rise to jealousy of a State which could not yet be regarded as an equal at sea. During the last few years before the war, however, I saw the time approaching in which England's inclination to attack us would cease, and give place to an attitude which would invite trade on an equal footing. This opened up a prospect of greater liberty of movement, which I also considered advisable for reasons affecting the service. The Prussian military spirit on which the whole national existence and the higher economic life of our people was founded, and will also have to be founded in the future, has one weak spot; the tendency to routine. It needs great personalities and keen judges of human nature like Moltke, Roon, and the old Emperor, to keep the live spirit going in the machine. The Prussian must have his pig-tail cut from time to time or else it will grow too long. Thus a certain rigidity in diligent, correct but subordinate work threatened to deprive the over-strained officers of the navy of any width of horizon. Particularly owing to the short period of service in our military organization, the life of our battle fleet in home waters ran the danger of losing through continual drill its enlivening contact with peoples and countries overseas. I not only wanted to train the officers in navy routine, but I also wanted to enable them to feel at home in Berlin society and the great world. The training of squadron commanders in particular to a more liberal and universal way of thinking can scarcely be effected without their appearing as independent individuals in the great world. Further, as I have said before, the gathering together of Germanism over the whole world required the support of the fleet more strongly than ever. Finally it was in my view our fleet's mission to react fruitfully upon the narrow horizon of many Germans at home by means of the experiences which it had collected abroad. In conjunction with Germans abroad, who were to be bound more closely to the home country, the fleet was to deepen the understanding for our national existence, which, in consequence of the increasing population and industry, was no longer confined between the Rhine and the Vistula, but had to sink its roots more and more in activities overseas.

Thus the second item in the development of the navy, the foreign service, gradually came into the foreground again side by side with the first, its striking power. As we had not enough station cruisers for this purpose, I proposed so to organize the home fleet that whole squadrons would be used across the Atlantic for lengthy periods, without their training suffering at all thereby. This was to be effected by a different plan of distributing recruits so that one of the squadrons would be practically manned by men of the third year. My proposal met with the opposition of the Commander-in-Chief, who, supported by the Chief of the Cabinet, evinced a strong inclination to sit tight upon his eggs, and even opposed an attempt to begin my scheme with only two ships. In order to show the practical effect of the appearance of our newest big ships in countries abroad, I succeeded in the summer of 1913 in securing the Emperor's consent to the voyage of two ships of the *Kaiser* class to the States of South America. The peaceful mission of our ships brought off such a striking success that a larger number of voyages on the part of our battle fleet could not have been prevented for long. As a modern battleship is at the same time the best possible industrial exhibition on a small scale, I was also justified in assuming that new connections would be secured for our manufacturing classes in this way. Such a development of our fleet would have led of its own accord to the establishment of suitable places in the colonies as bases for our cruisers. Apart from Tsingtao I had refrained from obtaining any more bases, as the time was not yet ripe and the money for the fleet must not be divided.

CHAPTER XIII

UNDER THE KAISER

1. Suggestions. A constructive amateur.—2. Cabinet mischief. Marginal notes. Lack of character.

I

WITH the almost immeasurable wealth of love, reverence, and constitutional power which William I had bequeathed to his grandson, the Emperor was the deciding personality on whom the success of the great attempt depended, to win for Germany both intellectually and materially an independent position of her own by the side of Anglo-Saxondom, which was embracing the whold world like a polypus. William II had realized the necessity for this effort even at the time of his father's illness, as I could see when crossing to the Jubilee of the English queen. Even in those days his thoughts embraced all the vital conditions of Germany's existence connected with the sea. But whilst the manner of doing business under our unforgettable old Emperor had been characterized by clearness and resolution, that of William II was characterized more by impulse. With his swift comprehension, his imagination, which was easily distracted by individual impressions, and his self-consciousness, there was the danger that irresponsible influences would release impulses which would either be impossible to carry out or would not be in harmony with the whole course of action. For a man in a high position it will always be a difficult task in life to separate the momentary success from the permanent. For the merely decorative is always insinuating itself treacherously, and never quite distinctly, in the essentials:

> "Der Schein, was ist er, dem das Wesen fehlt?
> Das Wesen, wär' es, wenn es nicht erschiene?"

Now a sense for the facts was the principal condition for the success of the great effort, and as the Emperor had selected me as his assistant, it became my personal duty to keep the constancy of the course we were steering. This was quite in keeping with my nature. It will perhaps be understood, however, that this duty was not always easy to fulfil in the circumstances. The Monarch's character was the opposite of mine. In the course of time many people had their moral backbones broken. I was able to save myself from that. The Emperor probably believed that he would not be able to do without my organizing experience; but I was an awkward subordinate, and as such I have gone through all the stages of favour and disfavour. An acquaintance once said to me that in such situations as mine the " state of slight disfavour " was the most desirable. Of course I had to give the Emperor his due. I always endeavoured to satisfy the wishes of the Monarch that were capable of fulfilment, even such as were more capricious, so long, that is to say, as I could be financially responsible for them. I was less successful in damming back the flood of decorative celebrations and speeches, festivities like Kiel Week and the baptism of ships, because the Emperor considered that they were useful for the German public, whilst I had in my mind their effect in foreign countries.

In all essential points affecting the construction of the fleet I had to stand firm. I have not always been able to say everything I thought, but I only poured out pure wine for the Emperor.

Among the questions for which the Emperor made suggestions—and these were very many, to be sure —a prominent part was taken by technical structures, buildings and coastal forts, but the most prominent part was taken by the ships themselves. The problem of how they would fit in with the whole fleet and the money-question then disappeared into the background. The Emperor knew the foreign navies quite well, and with the eyes of a German he inclined to see more strongly their advantages than their disadvantages. Anybody who bore to him some suggestion of distrust in the quality of our own *matériel* always found a willing ear. He drew sketches of ships with great talent and zeal, had them reduplicated and distributed them liberally, as is well known even to the Reichstag, which received them with mixed feelings.

The fact that a body of officials like the Admiralty, provided as it was with scientists and practical experts, had at its disposal more abundant means for the formation of an objective judgment than any individual human being, was not readily recognized, and a certain measure of distrust was expressed in our officials. Nor could one demand from the Emperor the judgment of a trained expert in technical matters. Thus I once had to receive the inventor of a *perpetuum mobile* who had been recommended to the Emperor by that original old man, Admiral Reinhold Werner; I had to allow his " engine " to be demonstrated, until Emil Rathenau, who had also been invited by the Emperor, was able to deprive the miracle-man of his nimbus.

Without the Emperor, Germany's estrangement from the sea, and the interests and tasks bound up with the latter, would never have been overcome. That is his historic merit. His suggestions have also been of use in other ways. His drawbacks, with regard to foreign countries, were the great stress he laid upon our aims and successes, and, with regard to home affairs, the ever-recurring clash of personal impulses with the real tasks of the land authorities and the navy. In addition to its excess of work, the Admiralty very often had to elaborate preliminary constructions for the Emperor's plans, which often suffered from internal contradictions. For example, during the last few years before the war the Emperor heard how difficult the improvement of shooting at sea, and the great range of modern guns, made it for the torpedo boats to approach the enemy in battle by day. The Emperor immediately became enthusiastic about an ideal ship which would be heavily armoured, swift, and armed with many torpedo tubes, and would relieve the torpedo boats of their task. Apart from the fact that speed and heavy armour plating compete against one another on a big ship, the torpedo armament which was to be put below the water line would have taken up the greater part of the engine- and boiler-space. We set to work, however, to comply with the command we had received, and, in view of the impossibility of coming to any useful results, the department gave this project the name of Homunculus. Then, when I had an opportunity of presenting and explaining the draft plans, the Emperor abandoned his idea and accepted my explanation. As a reward I received permission to shoot a stag, so that I was able to telegraph this clearing of the atmosphere to my Chief of the Central Department, who was anxiously waiting in Berlin, with the words " Stag and Homunculus dead."

It became the custom that I should go to Rominten every year during the last days of September to make my report. The air of the forest and comparative quiet suited the Emperor well. He was calmer and more collected there than was possible for him to be in the bustle of the world or on journeys. In Rominten I found that the Emperor was always ready to hear me and to weigh reasons; there were no sudden outbreaks of nervous excitement such as occurred elsewhere, announcing themselves by a certain restlessness in his eyes. On the appearance of such symptoms I used to put all the important decisions silently under

the table. This was, however, not always practicable
with questions which required haste. I came to the
conclusion that the Emperor's constitution was not
equal to the pressure of responsibility. At any rate,
both at the outbreak of war and during its course,
the Emperor was frequently faced with nervous
breakdowns which gave the doctors much anxiety.
Perhaps there is also some connection between this
and the fact that as he increased in years he inclined
more and more to yield to the weaker natures in his
circle of advisers.

II

One had to speak to the Emperor *tête-à-tête*, because
if there were a third person present his own real
opinion was easily influenced by his strong impulse to
act the Emperor in every decision. The power of the
Cabinets was rooted in this fact.

The Chief of the Cabinet attended the official reports of the responsible Secretary of State, and it was
natural that after the latter's withdrawal the Monarch
should discuss the matters with him in private. The
Chiefs of Cabinets therefore only needed to wait for
the right moment and to adapt themselves to the imagination and temperament of the Sovereign in order
to carry their own views. There are very few people
who would be able to confine themselves to their own
proper province in such a situation. Caprivi told me
that he only knew of one Chief of Cabinet who proceeded strictly according to this principle, and that

was General von Albedyll. To be sure, our old Emperor had a strong liking for transacting business through departments. The interference of Chiefs of Cabinets in matters that were outside their province led to proposals which were not so carefully considered as those of the responsible departments which have to bear the brunt in the event of failure, and cause the matter to be worked out by their apparatus before it is brought to the Emperor. That the Chiefs of Cabinets remained in office too long was due to the Emperor's fear of changing his immediate circle, but it estranged a man from active-service conditions as he got more and more into the habits of court life. In the navy at least a feeling predominated that the many mistakes of the Cabinet in its own province, the selection of *personnel,* were due to the fact that Admiral von Müller became more and more a court politician, and less and less a sailor.

Any attempt on the part of men in responsible positions to check the encroachments of the Cabinets came to an abrupt end; for as the Chiefs of Cabinets skilfully adapted themselves to His Majesty, the Emperor looked upon them as his clerks, whose main duty was to put his will into form of command. The Emperor has several times stressed this fact in conversation with me. I often thought of 1806. In war-time particularly, the extremely slight power of judgment that emanated from the Cabinets once more became a source of evil to the nation. Whilst I found a natural and constitutional support under Hohenlohe and Bü-

low against the encroachment of the Cabinet, the opposite was the case under Herr von Bethmann.

It was strange to me that neither the democratic
wing of the Reichstag nor that section which is hon-
estly concerned about the Monarchy have ever com-
bated the most essential error of the old *régime,* namely
the excessive influence of the Cabinets.   When it was
a question in October, 1918, of depriving the Emperor
and the Chancellor of their power, the Reichstag, putting aside the order of the day, proceeded with raging
haste.   But during the long years before this, democracy had never troubled to protect the Constitution.
As a matter of fact the best that we had, namely the
work of the Government offices, which was created by
positive national sentiment and which every nation in
the world envied us, was most effectively ground to
pieces between democracy and the Cabinets.

Officious and unproductive forces of the most varied
political colouring have always united in Germany to
hinder the creative energies of the State.

It is to be feared that many people who did not
fulfil during the period of the previous Government
their duty of combating the influence of the Cabinets
will now apply themselves with so much greater zeal
to damning the whole of the old Government system.
It is to be assumed that the Emperor's marginal notes
will play a part here; their number is unlimited, as
the Emperor readily adopted the marginal style of
his predecessors.   To ascertain the historical value or
worthlessness of these and similar expressions of the

moment, it is necessary to have known the Emperor very well. He himself said: " You must not bind me to my marginal notes." He was very much astonished therefore when I once considered it my duty to tender my resignation on the ground of one such marginal remark. On a similar occasion the Emperor said that he used to tell his other Ministers things without their taking them literally. The fact was that the Emperor took it for granted that his responsible advisers examined his statements and that they were able to distinguish what was of permanent importance from what was the outcome of a mood. In general the Emperor also listened to well-founded objections.

Unfortunately the Cabinets helped to give the Emperor's marginal notes an exaggerated appearance of importance. Every one of these notes, even those which were interpreted by the Government offices as suggestions for their consideration, were fixed by chemical means in the Cabinet, in the same way as the pencil sketches of an artist. By this means there was preserved for future writers of history, who are no longer eye-witnesses of the conditions they are describing, an amount of material which if turned to wrong account seems calculated to give a very distorted picture of the Emperor's personality, and also of the kind of Government under him.

When I spoke to the Emperor alone I restricted myself on principle to my department. This meant that my influence on his character was limited, and I lost it completely when during the war I was deprived of the possibility of private conversation with him.

My predecessor in office, Admiral Hollmann, was a frequent guest at Rominten, and he and the Chief of the Cabinet participated at the reading of my official reports there. His quietness, his practical knowledge, and his personal detachment had a beneficial effect, as the Emperor rightly regarded him as a friend who was watching his interests. If the Emperor did not always regard his official assistants in such a light, even though they were not wanting in real loyalty, it was because, I have been told by men who knew something about the youth of William II, that his tutor Hinzpeter systematically taught him to distrust his future advisers. If this is correct, then Hinzpeter was not doing justice to the Prusso-German conditions of the time, even though it is necessary to teach a future ruler to be a judge of men. I have always found in my smaller field of activity that it works better and brings out good qualities more strongly to give a subordinate unreserved confidence after a certain period of trial, although by so doing one may have an occasional bitter disappointment.

At his hunting lodge at Rominten the Emperor's household was more in the bourgeois style; the fare was homely and the tables were decked with leaves. In the evenings the company often read to one another. Among the regular visitors was the colonel of the nearest Russian frontier garrison who was jokingly requested to spare the deer and the heath if ever he were to advance against Germany. As a matter of fact the Czar gave an order at the beginning of the war that Rominten was not to be laid waste. The " Supreme Hunting Lord " expected good sport from the navy. It was many years, however, before he gave me the green hunting dress of the Court. I was often taken deer-stalking on Rominten heath in all its autumn glory; but during my official report no stag was allowed to roar, my good friends the keepers saw to that.

The Empress, whose regular attendance gave a special colour to the Rominten world, refused on principle to take part in political questions. If she believed, however, that she ought to interfere now and again in the real interests of her husband, she did so with character and generally with success. I think of this noble lady with true reverence. Her nature was felt to be a blessing for the country by all those who had the good fortune to know her more intimately. When the Emperor suddenly went from the west to the east in the spring of 1915, after a difference of opinion had arisen between him and Field-Marshal Hindenburg, the Empress coming from Berlin caused her carriage to be attached to the Imperial train at Halle and surprised her husband next morning. The well-known picture which represents the Emperor and Hindenburg together in Posen was taken by her.

Perhaps it is incorrect to say that there was a scarcity of independent character in post-Bismarckian Germany. Yet Haldane rightly characterized the tragedy which hung over our work, when he said after his visit in 1912, as I have been told: " I am struck by the lack of outstanding characters in Berlin as against my previous experience. The almost religious monarchic devotion that William I inspired allowed a freedom of opinion and activity of character to exist which later gave way more and more to an insistence on strict obedience under the influence of the Cabinets. The manly vigour which was brought to the surface in 1866 and 1870, and even in 1848, did not seem to exist in the same measure during the great trial of our day, or else it was not brought into play.

CHAPTER XIV

ADMIRALTY AND FOREIGN POLICY

I

THE public not infrequently conceives an incorrect picture of the business procedure of the Government. Bismarck's Imperial Constitution did not create an Imperial Ministry. In the Prussian Ministry of State of which I was a member, foreign political questions were hardly ever discussed. The Empire, however, was led by a single man to whom the heads of Ministries were placed in the position of subordinates and not colleagues. The Imperial Chancellor could even issue orders concerning the navy over the head of the Chief of the Admiralty, nor indeed, against the will of the latter, although the Admiralty had a right to a portion of the Imperial authority. The remedy of sending in one's resignation was not applicable in every political situation. In spite of the Civil Servants Law, the Emperor could make resignation very difficult for the head of a department who was at the same time an officer, and the threat to bring about the fall of a Cabinet gets threadbare if used too often.

Now it rested with the Chancellor whether he intended to consult his "deputies," the Secretaries of State, or whether he would leave them in the dark as to the main lines of his policy. The monarchical constitution of the office of Chancellor, as fashioned by Bismarck to suit himself, contained the inestimable advantage of enabling a dominating personality to take effective action. But in the case of a less unique personality as Chancellor, it would have been easier for a Ministry to avoid making mistakes or losing its head if it could have arrived at fundamental decisions in council. Any alteration of procedure required either a more friendly attitude on the part of the Reichstag and the Federal States to the suggestion put forward by the Ministry, or a perhaps unprecedented measure of self-denial in the man who, after the Emperor, enjoyed plenary powers. The public in general presupposed a more profound sense of responsibility and a more active exchange of ideas between the different Ministers than actually existed in fact, and it would have been astonished to discover how unreliable and disconnected the information was which was given to such a highly political department as the Admiralty in the grave years before the war. Prince Bülow's Government had, it is true, instilled into me quite a different feeling of security than did his suspicious and sensitive successor with his inexperience in foreign politics. The monarchical constitution of the Chancellorship became absolutely grotesque during the war, when without consulting the naval authorities the Chancellor induced the Emperor to issue naval orders which were practically incapable of fulfilment.

In these circumstances, the number of political moves with which I had to deal was not great. I had no share, for example, in the Samoa business (1899), in the negotiations with England about the beginning of the century, or the intervention in Morocco. I have already mentioned how I was passed over in the dispatch of the squadron to Manila (1898). On the occasion of the China Expedition I opposed the sending of Waldersee and the 24,000 men, as the sending of a whole army was liable to misinterpretation, and the marines which were already on the way out were enough for the real purpose. In the highest quarter, however, the word was "the Potsdam drill-ground must now decide."

In so far as I was asked to give my political opinion I advised: (1) that peace should be maintained on principle, for we gained thereby every year, whilst a war would bring us in very little and on the other hand could rob us of everything; and consequently (2) that all incidents which resulted from attempts at intrusion, which the English in particular would not stand, or from challenging acts, should be avoided; further, (3) that I could only see the assuring of our young world-power by means of a policy of balance of power at sea. I therefore regretted our forming too close a union for better or worse with Austria-Hungary, who counted for nothing at sea; and moreover I had no doubts about our Balkan and Eastern policy because it contained the danger of romantic entanglement in interests of secondary importance. I was strengthened in this conviction by the fact that England kept on warmly recommending us to seek expansion by these back-stairs. On the contrary we had to collect all our strength to keep open for ourselves the front staircase to the world, the Atlantic Ocean; a preliminary condition of our so doing was an assured continental peace, but our relations with France were unfortunately a permanent difficulty here. While our policy was burdened by our world-wide economic rivalry with England I did not consider we were strong enough to carry on Bagdad diplomacy, in which the interests of the nation as a whole did not promise to prosper so well as in individual economic enterprises. With a policy which was not altogether concentrated upon essentials, I was afraid above all of the loss of the confidence of those Powers which I was convinced provided the key of the situation: Russia and Japan.

II

In my opinion one of the first essentials of successful policy was the timely development of the Bismarckian principles with regard to our relationship with *Russia*. It was necessary to become quite clear on those issues which involved vital Russian interests, but not vital German interests, and to meet Russia on those points. I do not know whether any energetic effort was made in this direction before the world-war. I shall speak later of a *démarche* which was made during the Russo-Japanese war, but which promised little success from the outset. Our approaches consisted mainly of meetings of monarchs which were indeed valuable for the maintenance of the old dynastic traditions. But other methods, the press for example, were neglected. The land-greed of the Russian Empire was bound to clash with British Imperial interests, even after the conclusion of the Entente. We went and wedged ourselves in along the line of Berlin-Constantinople-Bagdad in the most unhappy fashion. The cancellation of the Reinsurance Treaty by us in 1890 was followed by the Franco-Russian dual alliance. Pan-Slavism was growing, and was pointing its weapon towards Austria and us. In spite of this, however, there still existed many and varied Russo-German traditions and strong mutual interests. Czardom in particular was a strong support for us.

As the situation developed after the cancellation of the Reinsurance Treaty, I first began to believe in the possibility of inducing Russia to enter upon a real alliance when this was rendered possible by way of Japan. During the Russo-Japanese war I attended a meeting in the Chancellor's house on October 31st, 1904, at which Herr von Holstein, at the instigation of the Emperor, suggested that an alliance should be offered to Russia. According to Holstein, the combined forces of Russia and Germany ought to prevail upon the French to join the continental coalition which was so desirable in itself. Count Schlieffen, who was

present, took up the purely military standpoint. He
estimated that the Russians would probably be able
to mobilize some army corps in the event of a march
against France. I noticed both then and in the discussion of the China Expedition a certain neglect of
non-military factors in the distinguished and laconic
strategist, who was so prominent in his profession;
and for the rest, I considered Holstein's psychological
calculations to be quite wrong, as did also Freiherr von
Richthofen, the Foreign Secretary. I doubted whether
an alliance with France, with a pistol pointed at her
head, would ever mobilize French forces for us. Simi-
larly, I did not consider that the cold douche which
Kiderlen-Wächter gave Paris in 1911 was at all opportune. At that conference in 1904 I also expressed
a doubt as to whether the reinforcement of our army
by a few Russian corps would really strengthen us,
and I laid particular stress upon the fact that an alliance with Russia would increase the existing danger
of war instead of producing the hoped-for success of
securing us against English lust for war by way of
Paris. In the event of a war with England, we should
with our fleet in its then undeveloped state—it would
in addition have had to dispense with the support of
the Russian Baltic fleet—have had to pay the bill with
our foreign trade and our colonies, in which case it
would be difficult to patch up a bearable peace with
England. Herr von Holstein backed his plan very
strongly. The next day I wrote the following letter
to Richthofen:

" I have been turning over in my mind the difficult question which occupied us yesterday at the Chancellor's, and it has become still clearer to me that not only, as I said yesterday, is the military importance of an alliance with Russia absolutely nil for us in a naval war, but that it does not materially affect the balance in a land war with Englnd. For even if in the most favourable circumstances the Russians were to rise to the height of giving us a few army corps for use in France, the advantage of a hundred—even two hundred—thousand men seems to me to be slight in a war in which millions will be opposed to one another, if not cancelled altogether by the difficulty which would be experienced in the functioning of our military apparatus by the addition of the Russian element. The passive advantage which such an alliance would give us is, however, in my opinion already attained, even without the alliance, by the present condition of Russia. This fact will stand out more clearly every additional month that the Japanese war lasts. Even after the war, Russia will be so crippled for a year and more, as far as an offensive in the west is concerned, that to my mind we can in high policy regard our eastern frontier as not actually threatened. For the time being we should be able to manage with Landwehr formations on the eastern frontier. In this I am not taking into consideration the fact that the personality of the Czar would make an intervention by Russia in a war by Germany on England and France in itself improbable, and I also leave open the question whether we could not obtain such an assurance of security from the Czar on the basis of our previous friendly relations and without an alliance.

" The main fact remains that a real, *i.e.* military advantage does not accrue for us from an alliance with Russia.

" On the other hand, there can be no doubt that a Russian alliance would create for us the danger of an armed conflict with England. After the Dogger Bank affair only a few more episodes of a like nature are required during the voyage of the Russian argonauts. In order to measure the increased danger of it all for us, imagine the publication of the news of a Russo-German alliance at the moment! Would not the whole rage of public opinion in England vent itself solely upon us? The idea of an alliance with Russia is only based on the hope of bringing such pressure to bear upon France that she will do everything to keep England from making war upon us. In this, Russia's share consists solely in the value of a treaty drawn up with other premises, a sheet of paper therefore; it does not consist in real values. In reality, the desired ' pressure ' can only be exerted upon France by Germany's threat of war. For such a threat, however, no alliance with Russia is necessary to-day. We are strong and free enough to be able to do this at any moment. It is not therefore absolutely necessary for us to increase the danger of a conflict with England that would ensue from the alliance.

" Finally it is doubtful whether the intervention of France would at all restrain those in power in England from moving against us if they really wanted war with us, quite apart from the fact that there would be no real soul in France's mediation. Should this be the case, however, and should England abandon the idea of war with us, she would only incite Japan all the more brutally and ruthlessly against us; and if I understand the draft of the Treaty correctly, the *casus foederis* for Russia would not occur if we alone oppose Japan after the end of the war. We could not carry on such a war with a hostile England behind us without powerful friends at sea. Therefore in this case too an alliance with Russia brings us no real help. Lastly, if we take the most interesting instance from our point of view: if England declares war on us alone, and Russia is then compelled to come in on our side, then the existing dual alliance between France and Russia which is directed against us will cripple our decision with regard to France, whilst the help from Russia is of no account to us. The chances of peace could only have been positively influenced by a really clear defensive alliance between Germany, France, and Russia against England, and this is not to be effected by the procedure under consideration at this time.

" After these reflections, which only sketch the main points, I should like to define my own view as follows: While maintaining our friendship with Russia in the most practicable manner, especially by means of the relations between the two Emperors, we should not undertake the conclusion of a political treaty for the present, but await events. On the whole, our most important political object is to gain time and to build our fleet.

" As high policy is *your* domain and my position in the matter is only of secondary importance, I am addressing these lines to you with the request that you should inform the Chancellor as to my standpoint."

The offer of an alliance was sent off. As Holstein informed me later, Russia gave us the cold shoulder. I suspect also that the Russian Ministers made use of the German offer in their dealings with the Western Powers at the time and turned it to good

Nicholas II himself was well-disposed towards Germany. The German public had a false picture of the Czar, as indeed it had of many political circumstances and personalities. He was an honest and personally fearless man, with muscles of steel; his instinctive autocratic dignity was coupled with a correct habit of straightway referring all political business to the authorities concerned. His inmost longing was to disappear into the quiet of bourgeois life. This was why he loved Wolfsgarten in Hesse, where he liked nothing better than to be spared visitors. For this reason also he liked to mix with the German fleet, where, released from the restraint of his position, he felt a man among men, and conducted himself in a frank and agreeable manner towards us.

Among his own people the Czar seemed half a prisoner. When we sailed to meet him on the occasion of the Swinemünde meeting in 1907 (contrary to the arrangement by which we were to lie at anchor and the Czar was to sail through the lines on his yacht, the Emperor pressed to go and meet the Czar) we sighted him off Kolberg. In spite of the high sea running, the Emperor caused the boat to be got ready and went over to the Russian Imperial yacht, a thing which the Russians had not considered possible. The yacht, however, kept close to the wind so that it pitched heavily. We could not understand why, for the elementary help that a ship can give to a boat at sea consists in the ship heaving to, so as to form a protection (lee). Whilst we were passing round the stern of the ship the Emperor shouted to the Czar: "Niki, won't you make a lee?" We could see the Czar, still in undress, trying to make preparations. As we came alongside we noticed that a parade was being held on deck. But the accommodation ladder by which the Emperor should have ascended with the usual grand ceremonial was not let down. Nothing remained but to go forward where a sea-ladder for the use of sailors was hanging. The Emperor was beside himself. We saw the Czar also in a state of great excitement rush forward, whilst the gigantic fellows stood stiffly in immovable ranks; the Russian grandees, Lambsdorff, Benckendorff, Fredericks, and others collected round the accommodation ladder that was not let down. The mounting of the forward ladder was difficult and not without danger for the Emperor. Not even a rope was thrown down to us. The Czar came to meet the Emperor alone; all the others stood as stiff as corpses, for parade was in progress, our arrival unexpected, and neither of the commanders, of whom curiously enough there were two on board, assumed responsibility, in spite of the pleading of our naval attaché, of giving the command which the situation required, and which with us the officer of the watch would have given of his own accord.

This scene put the Czar out of humour for the rest of the day. Whenever he met the Emperor in Russian surroundings he looked oppressed, perhaps because the Emperor immediately became the natural centre of the circle, and when wearing Russian uni-

form moved quite like a Russian in Russian society
Then the Czar, in whose nature there was a genuine
Russian force of passive resistance, with little initia·
tive, soon felt himself outshone. The social and po·
litical initiative always proceeded from us. So far as
opportunity allowed, I have always supported the Em·
peror's efforts, which were very active in their way, to
arrive at a good relationship with Russia, and I was
able to enjoy the good-will of the Czar although his
nature always imposed a considerable measure of ret·
icence.

In 1903 the Emperor sent me to St. Petersburg to
see the Czar on a very delicate mission, which I kept
to myself, in the first place because the Anglophile
Czarina never left her husband alone with me. My
conduct eventually proved to be right. I cannot judge
whether this beautiful woman was gifted intellectually; in any case, so far as I could see, she had not
much love left for her German Fatherland. On this
occasion I warned the Czar about the Far Eastern
danger, which I estimated very gravely in view of the
merely decorative nature of the Russian Asiatic fleet,
which was well known to me. Nicholas II, who personally, could not bear the Japanese, replied to me
that he considered the danger was past, for he was now
too strong for the Japanese to do any more. I regretted the Russo-Japanese war on our own account,
and even on September 2nd, 1904, when the victory
of the Russian troops was still universally reckoned
on, I elaborated to the Chancellor the danger which

would arise if, in the event of a Russian defeat, we were left as outposts in Tsingtao.

We could not imitate the cool way in which the English helped the Japanese in the war, although we did the Russian fleet more service with our help and advice within the bounds of neutrality than the French did. When Admiral Roshdiestvensky asked that the German naval attaché, von Hintze, might accompany him when he sailed with the Russian Baltic fleet, the Emperor refused permission on the ground that such an action infringed neutrality. On the other hand, however, English *personnel* took over to Japan after the outbreak of war the Japanese cruisers *Kasuga* and *Nishin* which had been built in Italy, and English officers played a very active and important pàrt in Admiral Togo's staff both at Port Arthur and in the Tchusima Straits. In the sea-fight off Port Arthur, Togo wanted to break off the engagement under the impression that he had little prospect of success, but the Englishman on his staff urged him to keep on, and shortly afterwards the Russian Admiral's flagship *Cesarevitch* received the decisive blow. After the feat, for which the Russians had to thank the English just as much as the Japanese, the trend of Russian policy began to turn away from Germany towards England. On his return from Japanese captivity, Roshdiestvensky explained this to Hintze in words thoroughly characteristic of the Russian people: " The Russian gives a kick to anybody who helps him and is kind to him, for he regards such a person as his lackey; but he will kiss the hem of the robe of anyone who thrashes him." In spite of the fact that Russia accepted the settlement with England after 1907, I retained the conviction that Czardom did not seriously threaten our future.

The navy was not blind, however, to the increasing agitation for war in Russian circles. Herr von Hintze had skilfully contrived to make for himself a place of more importance at the St. Petersburg Court than our Ambassador there, and shortly after the Japanese war he had reported anti-German tendencies in the Russian army, thereby bringing himself into disfavour at Potsdam. But in spite of this the dangerousness of the Russian war party, of the Grand Dukes and their Paris lady friends, and of pan-Slavism, ought not to have been over-estimated, but on the other hand no opportunity of combating them by all possible means should have been neglected. Our Balkan policy between 1908 and 1914, particularly the sending of a military mission to Constantinople, seemed to me fraught with danger.

Nicholas II, who said to me in one of the last conversations I had with him, " I give you my assurance that I shall never make war on Germany," did not want war with us even in 1914. I will not enter upon a discussion as to what extent we should have been able to stem the influence of the St. Petersburg war party by a more correct treatment of the Czar and the Serbian question in July, 1914.

The war with Russia was the cardinal mistake of

our policy, and a speedy conclusion of peace with the Czar was the essential object of a diplomacy which was working for victory. This conclusion of peace was undeniably rendered more difficult by Turkey coming in on our side, and the non-fulfilment of the Hindenburg plan of campaign of 1915. In spite of this an acceptable peace could have been concluded in 1916, when the Czar began to feel his throne unsafe and appointed Stürmer to make peace with us.

It is in keeping with Bethmann-Hollweg's effort to put his political mistakes on the military departments that the most incomprehensible of these mistakes, the proclamation to Poland of November, 1916, has been cast upon General Ludendorff in the most plausible fashion by the Wilhelmstrasse. This is contradicted, however, by the fact that Bethmann described in a Ministerial Council during the winter of 1915-1916 such a solution of the Polish question as the most appropriate one.

After the meeting I proposed to a colleague that if such a procedure were really to take place, the Ministry would certainly have to oppose it. After my resignation I called upon Governor-General von Bessler shortly before the decision regarding Poland, and expressed to him in private my view of the inappropriateness and fatal danger of such a step. It was clear to me that this would not only procure a new enemy for Germany, but it would also cut off one of the last possibilities of a separate peace. As a matter of fact, in consequence of the intensification of the war spirit that it produced, there could have been no more unsuitable overture to our peace offer of December, 1916, than the Polish Proclamation, which the Czar is said to have described as " a smack in the face for me," and which, in Stürmer's words, "killed the peace." In the middle of July, 1914, I wrote to my Berlin deputy from Tarasp, expressing my fear in view of the impending ultimatum to Serbia that Bethmann-Hollweg's ignorance of English policy might cause an irreparable breach between Russia and us. Without looking into the details of Bethmann's diplomacy at that time, I wrote: " It is only necessary to imagine what sort of policy an English Bismarck would pursue against Russia and Germany. The Chancellor is wholly entangled, bewitched by his idea of courting the favour of perfidious Albion. It is the whole fate of the German people that is in question. *Coûte que coûte* we must come to an agreement with Russia and set the Whale against the Bear. All sentimental promptings must be silenced."

Bethmann himself probably could not have obtained a separate peace with Russia before the Polish Proclamation, because Russia was bound to think that he would surely sell her to the English. It was a catastrophe that the Emperor did not find the strength to effect a change of front in our policy in 1916 and to this end appoint a new Chancellor at that time.

The sympathy of our intellectuals for the Western civilization is also partly to blame for this misfortune. In itself it is one-sided because we have long ago assimilated the old civilization of the West, and its glib utilitarian-capitalistic mass-civilization of to-day is probably less profitable to the German character than the perverse idealism of the Russians in the East. It was not a matter of civilization here; it was a question of policy. In order to strengthen and spread German civilization, our political independence with regard to the Western Powers was essential above everything else. This independence, however, could not be secured by any border-state policy nearly so well as by the most practicable peace between Germany and the great non-Anglo-Saxon Powers of the East.

Contrary to all historical wisdom, but amidst the jubilation of the intractable democracy of Germany, Bethmann bound round his brow the laurels of the liberator of the Poles. I leave open the question whether he was influenced in this more by his incorrect judgment of English policy or his desire for some success or other, combined with the skill of the Poles in flattering German weaknesses.[1] I did not see that Germany's future was threatened even if the Russian Empire were to be restored to its full power. I only saw it threatened if we were cut off from our overseas trade on which almost a third of the German people lived, and if we were condemned to horrible poverty owing to the impossibility of our regaining our position in the world's commerce. There was no compen-

---

[1] Cf. also on the elder Bethmann-Hollweg: Bismarck, *Gedanken und Erinnerungen*, i., 110 *et seq.*; ii, 13 and 97.

sation for the expulsion of Germany from the seas, which England intended, even if Bethmann's assumptions were correct and we could achieve by military means a penetration of the East. I should have tried to come to any arrangement whatsoever with the Russian statesmen, even Kerensky, and I should have been prepared to make big concessions to them which really left our hands free in another direction. I doubt whether history contains a greater instance of self-deception than that practised by the Germans and Russians in annihilating one another to the greater glory of the Anglo-Saxons.

We ought not to have thrown in our lot with the Poles, at any rate without demanding some return from them. What are not the other nations of the world obliged to do in return for the kindness of the Anglo-Saxons in ruling them? and yet we did not demand a single thing in return for liberating the Poles.

Up to 1887 there existed between the Russian navy and our own a mutual confidence which was almost that of brothers-in-arms. When it was no longer possible to exchange valuable pieces of information in consequence of the coolness which had sprung up between the two countries in their political relations, I maintained our good personal relations with the Russian navy, in spite of the prevalence of the idea of the "two-front" war, by showing them kindnesses which did us no harm. For instance, I referred all the inventions which were proffered to us, and which did not wholly convince me of their usefulness, to St. Petersburg, where everything new was devoured with ravenous hunger. The authorities there built on the principle of finding the white light out of all the colours of the rainbow. The ardent *verve* with which the Russian Admiralty produced a fleet that was a conglomeration of inventions was not to its advantage. I also gave the Czar various hints which culminated in the following piece of advice: " Do not listen to too many people, your Majesty, but choose a man whom you can leave to do everything alone, or else you will never get any system in all this business." The high degree of personal confidence which the Czar placed in German officers, particularly in Hintze, was valuable political capital, which we did not apply, however, with the understanding of a Stein or a Bismarck. For example, the position of trust which the old custom of attaching a Prussian *aide-de-camp* to a Czar placed at our disposal was never used to its full extent after the recall of Hintze.

A'fter her victory over Russia, Japan found herself in the greatest financial difficulties, because the personal obstinacy of the Czar and the mediation of America, behind which English diplomacy skilfully concealed itself, had deprived this otherwise poor empire of its hoped-for war-indemnity. I have heard from different sides that between 1905 and 1914 it would several times have been possible for Germany to come to an agreement with Japan by granting her a loan. According to my own impressions of those Japanese statesmen with whom I was on friendly terms, I am bound to consider this possibility as probable, and I am convinced that Japan put out feelers towards us which our diplomats did not understand or did not dare to grasp through fear of the Anglo-Saxons. ' It is in any case difficult to understand the political soul of Japan. If instead of playing the part of " Jack of all trades," we had felt all the real factors of power upon which the politics of the world are based, we should perhaps have been able, with the help of Japan, to secure ourselves altogether against the possibility of a world-war. In 1915—and even in 1916—Japan could have ended the war with a wave of her hand, indeed could have given it a decisive turn in our favour. The supposition was that we should come to an agreement with Russia and form the main front against the Anglo-Saxons. We had to seek an alliance for life or death with the Great Asiatic Power. So long as the Imperial Government hammered at Russia politically, and made the most public efforts to attain a firm relationship with England, we could not expect Japan to come to us. When we bent before Wilson's threatening Notes, Japan probably abandoned the idea of coming to an agreement with us.

The Japanese are rapacious and greedy of power. In this respect they are a primitive people; they want to have everything. But now that they have obtained the dominating position in Eastern Asia it would be foolish of them to quarrel with America about the South Sea Islands or the racial question. The main point of conflict ought to be China, whose market America does not intend to lose again, but the Japanese apparently hope to rule China as the Manchus formerly did. I do not believe that the Japanese reckon with China awakening in the near future. They will aim at getting China so firmly in their hands that she can no longer be a menace to them, but must become a tributary State.

If the Japanese were not opportunists in politics they would see that treaties with the Anglo-Saxons cannot avail them anything in the long run, and that their power is on an insecure basis so long as they are not doing everything to produce the best possible international situation for their reckoning with America. The special treaty which Japan concluded with the Czar in 1916 shows, however, that her diplomacy was seeking support wherever a determination to hold out against the Anglo-Saxons was to be found. Now that Russia and Germany have destroyed one another, the possibility of a Russo-Japanese-German alliance, which would have secured the liberty of the world, has disappeared for the time being, and Japan is compelled to carry along the enormous burdens which she has taken upon herself. The future of all non-Anglo-Saxon Great Powers is problematical.

III

Every warship constructed anywhere in the world except in England was ultimately an advantage for us because it helped to adjust the balance of power at

sea. Before the world-war, the omnipotence of England at sea, as well as on land, had not yet been declared sacrosanct. Just as Bulgaria or Roumania for
example were able to have, side by side with the great
land powers, armies of their own that were of no account in themselves, but which meant a great deal
under certain conditions owing to their alliance value,
smaller navies were being built side by side with that
of Great Britain which were important in the light of
the idea of alliance expressed by Bismarck. If an
English monopoly of the sea was recognized, then not
only the building of any fleet, not only any independent
policy, but, I may say, any feeling of freedom on the
part of other nations was out of the question. But
why did Japan, France, Russia, America, why did
Italy and the smaller States build warships?

If it is admitted that it would be useless to enter
into competition with the strongest sea-power, there
would be no point in any State having a navy. There
is no real reason why the interests of the various nations at sea should not be based on a principle of
mutual give and take, just as on land. As regards
the military side of the question, the strongest power
at sea has a greater advantage than the strongest power
on land, owing to the unlimited area that it controls.
But its omnipotence can be broken by the luck of
battle, which plays a more decisive part in a naval
engagement than in a land war, and secondly by
means of alliances. I maintain the view that naval
and alliance policy must supplement one another: the

one without the other loses its effectiveness. The map of alliances, however, was bound to have quite a different aspect according as it was drawn up from the standpoint of international and naval policy, or from the traditional quadrilateral of Berlin-Paris-Vienna-St. Petersburg which circumscribed the usual field of vision of the German diplomat. In this connection, many a small State might become more important than many an old Great Power. Germany acquired an alliance-value with regard to States that were separated from us by the ocean. And as the most compelling factor which had forced upon us the construction of our fleet for the protection of our influence at sea ran parallel with the interests of all other non-English powers who had built fleets, the Government, if it was not going to render worthless the whole building of the fleet, could and must partly extend its aims beyond this new point and partly restrict them.

It would take too long to discuss the omissions of our diplomacy in detail. In our position, one single ally worth mentioning would have been of decisive influence, whether it was Russia or Italy, whose naval armaments could have been constantly strengthened by us in the most opportune manner. Japan's benevolent neutrality would probably have hindered the outbreak of the war. A reliably neutral attitude on the part of Russia in the event of an Anglo-German war would have sufficed, in view of the status of our fleet in 1914, to have left our navy free morally and actually for an offensive against England. In order to estimate the strength of the trump card which our fleet put in the hands of an energetic diplomacy at this time, one must remember that in consequence of the concentration of the English forces which we had caused in the North Sea, the English control of the Mediterranean and Far-Eastern waters had practically ceased. Our actual policy of alliance demanded, to be sure, no other service from the German navy than the saving of the Dardanelles, which the British fleet could not force because too much of her strength was tied up in the North Sea. The sole use of Austria for our navy consisted in a refitting dock for our submarines in Pola and a submarine base in Cattaro. With allies who were powerless at sea and who prevented us from taking a part in real international politics, we entered upon a war in which the German navy was pitted against the fleets of the whole world.

Not only does Germany emerge from the war weakened, but also the bulk of those non-Anglo-Saxon Powers who allowed themselves to be trailed after the triumphal car of England. A German policy more venturesome and at the same time more cautious (we were incautious in spite of our nervousness) would have allowed the alliance-value of our fleet, the only trump card our geographical position allowed us in world-politics, to be played so as to ensure the peace of the world. As our diplomacy failed, the combination of alliance and naval policy, which would necessarily have resulted in a concentration of our means and ends, was not called into being.

Among other things, we had to do everything possible to win the friendship of our small neighbours. From the point of view of naval policy, a close relationship with Denmark would have been of the greatest use, in this connection much more important, for example, than our alliance with Austria, and I should have been prepared to make territorial sacrifices for a naval and economic agreement with this Germanic cousin of ours that would have made Danish feeling more friendly towards us again. In the course of various conversations with the Duke of Glücksburg, a connection of the Danish royal house, I touched on this idea of a revision of the Treaty of Prague. About ten years ago he was of the opinion that Denmark could have been won over by an arrangement with regard to the so-called Jutish enclaves of Northern Schleswig. I was not in a positon to deal officially with this private opinion. Such an understanding would of course have premised corresponding concessions on the part of Denmark. If Denmark thinks once more to turn our misfortune to account as at a former period when Germany was down, then let her remember the end of that epoch at Duppel, and avoid leaving another thorn in the heart of the German people.

I should have liked our representatives abroad to favour tactfully the interests of Scandinavian, Swiss and Dutch private persons in so far as these desired, and to look after them as if they were Germans. These small States, so important both for us and for the world, would have greeted the development of our power in a friendly way if they had found in us a natural support in any difficulty, and if we *had enabled them* to grasp the idea of "Europe" as persistently and skilfully represented by us. On the occasion of his Berlin visit Roosevelt said to me, "You would have to take Holland." Naturally that was a piece of bad advice, and its opposite was true for us. It was not permissible to conquer, but we ought to have won over, by bringing home to those small States with maritime interests of their own the certainty that their liberty, which was also our own interest, would be reliably protected against the omnipotence of Great Britain.

It was a misfortune for our nation that she was shown no great objective, and yet one lay so clearly before us. When I told Herr von Bethmann on one occasion before the war that we should have to set the nation definite objectives, he asked me in astonishment, "What sort of an objective?" In my opinion this objective ought to have been to bring together all free peoples away from the guardianship of the Anglo-Saxons. Big words only did us harm, but a definite propaganda in this direction would have helped us. Then the other nations of Europe would have been wise enough to look favourably upon our strength. The building of the fleet had obviously done the nation good; it had raised and strengthened the unity of the parties, national sense and pride, and the assurance of our position abroad. Also it had always been regarded favourably by all foreign nations, with the exception of the English. Our dignity as a people and as a State, however, demanded some supplementation of our fleet-building in foreign politics. The strong but peaceful support of the non-Anglo-Saxon nations in their freedom alone gave our increase of power any justification in international politics and any prospect of permanence. In its decisive years of development, such as we were passing through, a nation may not shrink from any obligation which is the direct consequence of its own development. All this will presumably come more and more to the front in the consciousness of humanity within the next few decades.

When war broke out I did not represent annexationist aims either in the East or the West. Even a Germanization of Belgium was not included in my wishes. But I did consider it necessary that the Belgian coast should not be allowed to fall under British domination, because this would result in the certain impoverishment of German labour and of German workmen.[1] I therefore desired the creation of an independent Flanders in which we should have the right of garrisoning Zeebrugge. It was not until during the war that Germans first grasped the industrial future of the Flemish Kempenland, and this produced a new reason for making the economic friendship between the Rhineland and Belgium free from British domination. I am convinced that in the course of time the inhabitants of the land round the Scheldt will

[1] Cf. Chapter XVII.

realize that this idea was also in their interest. The
small States of Europe will disappear in the trans-
Atlantic combine of the Anglo-Saxons, and the
strength of Europe, which reposes in the adjustment
of manifold independent civilizations within the nar-
rowest limits, will decay and therewith Europe's
wealth, its ascendancy, and the possibility of a position in the world for the States of our continent.
" The world is rapidly becoming English." Our war
was perhaps the last European fight for freedom
against Anglo-Saxon world-capitalism, or rather it
could and would have been if the Government had only
grasped and given effect to the idea of this war. Our
Social Democrats, wallowing in the delusion of fighting capitalism, have by their conduct during the war
and at its end certainly succeeded in destroying the
bulk of that German capital which they were attacking, but which gave the German workman his bread.
The result of this, however, is that the Germans are
now handed over to Anglo-Saxon capitalism, which
is far more brutal and unsocialistic in itself, and also
means foreign rule.

Confidence can only be aroused by a State which
possesses power and uses it both with firmness and
with wisdom. If we were to combat French propaganda in Alsace-Lorraine and Polish propaganda in
the East with full resoluteness, we ought to have met
a further advance of Danish culture in Northern
Schleswig, not with force, but with the methods of civilization (railways, schools, etc.). In this way we

should have shown that we could differentiate between vital and non-vital questions. How many times over we should have been repaid during the war if we had fulfilled the heartfelt desires of the Danish patriots in time of peace! Thus even during the war I myself was always in favour of showing the world that we represented the spirit of Europe more purely and more humanely than any of our opponents, in contrast to the hypocritical brute-force of the Anglo-Saxons and in complete contradiction of the calumnies in such expressions as " Boche " or " Hun." In this connection I wished that we had abstained from reply in kind to the barbarous custom introduced by England of interning defenceless and harmless civilians. I was also against initiating aerial attacks upon open towns and civilian populations begun by the enemy, so long as no appreciable military damage was done—and their effect was a mere pin-prick, compared with the concentrated use of the aerial weapon for definite and important military objectives (City of London and Docks).

IV

Our relations with *America* had undergone a needless change for the worse in 1898, owing to the appearance of our squadron off Manila. When I visited the Philippines officially in 1896 with the Far-Eastern squadron, the Islanders, who were then at war with the Spaniards, approached me with the idea of establishing a German protectorate there, and they tried to

persuade me to save a rebel leader who had been condemned to death by the Spaniards. Naturally I refused to intervene in this way; so far as I know, the
idea of extending German power to the Philippines
was never afterwards seriously considered in any
quarter in Germany. Whilst we appeared off Manila
during the Spanish-America war with a squadron
which was stronger than the American, we maintained
ticklish relations between the two navies, and on the
occasion of a collision with Admiral Dewey, Flag-
lieutenant (later Secretary of State) von Hintze upheld
German honour by his cool-headedness and prevented
the danger of a conflict. There remained, however,
in the United States, which had just stepped into
international politics with a definite purpose in view,
the suspicion that we had made an unsuccessful attempt to poach on preserves which they had discovered first. This vexation, which was skilfully fed
by the English press and diplomacy, swelled the suspicion that we were cherishing intentions on American
territory. The Americans were ignorant of European
affairs, and sensitive enough with their Monroe Doc-
trine to believe this kind of nonsense.

When in 1902 the English Government invited us
to take common action with Roosevelt's consent against
the brigand President of Venezuela, Castro, I advised,
in the conference at the Foreign Office, against compliance, basing my opinion on my impressions of
American character and English policy. Carl Schurz,
in whom German-Americans still had a leader at that

time, had warned me. I declared that if matters came to an armed conflict, the Monroe dogma might inflame America, in which case the English would probably leave us in the lurch.

Unfortunately this did actually happen. I had urgently recommended the Emperor before his journey to England to obtain an unconditional promise from the English that they would see us through. I do not know whether this was done; at any rate we accepted England's suggestion. Roosevelt, however, was not able to hold American indignation in check, even if he had wanted to do so, and the British press was base enough, with the tolerance of its Government, to face about, at once to rouse the Americans and attack us " Huns." [1]

There was no longer any hope of German interests being spared in those cases where both Anglo-Saxon Powers had to deal with them in common. Whether the upshot of it all would be that England would really become the " forty-ninth star in the Stars and Stripes,"

[1] It was at this time that Rudyard Kipling, who had been flattered by our Emperor, paid him back for the unfortunate " Hun speech " of the days of the China Expedition in his poem " The Rowers," in which he calls the Germans " Goths and shameless Huns." The same astonishing lack of conscience as in the Venezuela dispute was again shown by the English press, with the silent approval of the British Government, over the Hull incident two years later. For a short time the Jingo press raged against the Russians, who had bombarded English fishing-vessels in the North Sea under the impression that they were Japanese torpedo boats, a mistake which was not so unforgivable in view of the open support given to Japan by the British navy. Then on an invisible signal the rage of the press broke off suddenly and turned with redoubled force against Germany, who had no share in the affair at all! That was a plain lesson for anybody who had eyes to see.

as the American naval attaché said to our attaché in London, was a secondary matter for us. At the beginning of the century England had considered for the last time whether she should turn upon America or not, and had decided not to do so. My personal impressions took the same line as my political experiences, and our sentimental politeness towards the Union did not improve the situation. It was painful to me to have to attend the presentation of the statue of Frederick the Great to the sceptical Yankees. I never shared the illusion which is so fatally prevalent with us that the power of America might become some time and somehow a useful assistant to us against the British dictatorship of the seas. Moreover of all the greater navies, I have always put the lowest value on that of America as a possible asset.[1]

The longer our young sea-power was established, the more numerous and free were our chances in world-politics. Thus, provided peace was kept between England and Germany, the development of fruitful relations between America and ourselves was not at all out of the question. When Roosevelt, who knew me well and often engaged me in long conversations, advised me that Germany would have to regain control over the mouth of her main river and gather round her the small Low German States on the lower

---

[1] The American navy, treated as the passive element it was, was just as little dangerous as the French; it watched with a certain jealousy the German navy attaining a much higher fighting value, although the latter's building expenditure was smaller by some milliards.

Rhine and the Scheldt, he was being thoroughly honest and only speaking in his own fashion " roughly." He started from the assumption that England's world-power would gradually disappear and that we should become America's natural ally against Japan. The effect of the Anglo-Japanese alliance was to make Roosevelt attach great important to the growth of the German fleet. Before the American fleet was sent to the Pacific Ocean in 1908 (there was no Panama Canal then), Roosevelt asked me unofficially, through his ambassador in Berlin, whether I would take on the responsibility of this naval move if I were in his place. I replied, " I should risk it "; and I saw some advantage for us in this action. As a matter of fact one of the results of that American voyage was to make Australia lean strongly away from England towards America. We only drove back the colonies to the mother-country by the war. Later Roosevelt sent me his photograph with a flattering inscription signed : " From one who sent the American fleet round the world."

The natural sympathies of the Americans were with the English. But apart from this there existed inclinations towards businesslike relations between American policy and ours. The Americans took Germany very seriously in every respect before the war, and in spite of their collective idea of Europe they had a fine feeling for our rising power and a sober respect for the possibilities it contained. They were already reckoning with the chance of our economic and political

development being able to overhaul the English hand
over fist. At the same time the Americans regarded
themselves as the natural heirs of the English colonies. If we waited for things to develop in time of
peace, then those interests which were common to
America and ourselves grew by natural process from
year to year. When we slid into the war in 1914
one of the gravest consequences of this terrible fact
was that we brought to maturity the Anglo-Saxon
sense of common responsibility, instead of sending it
to sleep.

The Americans, who interpreted the firing of the
powder magazine on the *Maine* as a crime, in order
to be able to annex Cuba, would have regarded the
invasion of Belgium with a very cold eye if it had
agreed with their own interests. America is a world-
conquering Power, a fact which our democrats refuse
to realize. The outward superiority of our enemies
brought the Americans from the very first day to the
conviction that we should not win, and they defined
their attitude towards us on this principle. In spite
of this America was not yet ready for war against
us from 1914 to 1916, and was not able to fall upon
a fearless German war-policy. It was the length of
the war, the growing intertwining of interests with
the Entente, England's military needs, the illusory,
dilatory, and zigzag policy of Bethmann-Hollweg with
its transference of prestige in Wilson's favour, and
finally Zimmermann's Mexican letter which prepared
and facilitated America's entry into the war in 1917,

which could only have been effected by Wilson with far greater difficulty, perhaps not at all, in 1917, when I wanted the submarine campaign.[1] The determining feature was: we had to end the war swiftly and we could not afford to lose prestige.

The situation would have been quite different if the world-war had been avoided. The Anglo-Saxon family would never have suffered a military defeat of England. But a peaceful triumph over England by us would have been accepted as a natural thing, would have secured for " Germanism " a rising reputation even in the American hemisphere, and would have made us ultimately a real world-state and a desirable ally for the strongest power of the future. However Germany may now develop, these possibilities are past; and if ever our nation is again in a position to make useful alliances, this can only apply to Powers of another grade. Before the world-war we had rich possibilities of establishing a balance.

V

The construction of the fleet needed *peace* if it was to succeed. The nearer the fleet approached completion, the more it secured on its own part the peace which Germany needed more urgently for her continued prosperity, and which in view of her geographical position she found more difficult to maintain than any other big State. The decades before the world-war were characterized for Germany by the highest degree of prosperity and exposure to danger, together with strong, but not quite adequate, protection in her

own power. At several periods of his term of office
Bismarck was called a " juggler "; and the undoubtedly skilful personality of Prince Bülow received the
honourable appellation of " tight-rope dancer " on his
regrettable departure from office. In Germany's position only extraordinary attention to the changes in the
situation could secure her from harm. We could not
allow ourselves the luxury of making mistakes. Bismarck once said on hearing some complaints about
Caprivi's Chancellorship: " Just wait until you have
a real bureaucrat for a Chancellor, then you will see
what it is like." A stiff-necked illusionist like Bülow's
successor fell a victim to the complications of the
international situation owing to his inability to weigh
up a situation. The chief essential for a leader of
the German Empire was, and will always be, an understanding of foreign politics. This does not necessarily entail the black magic of diplomacy, but a
knowledge of the real fundamental condition of the
world, and a sense of the probable. Neither Chancellor nor democracy had any idea of the true difficulty
and danger of our position, which had to be tackled
with forceps.

But can a nation which shows no skill in its own
affairs, and which inclines to self-abandonment if it
has not the right leader, hope that Providence will
favour it again and again with a guardian like Frederick the Great or Bismarck? In our day we can see
the leaderless masses who have barely attained their
full power doing nothing more zealously than pulling

down and breaking up all that was left us of national
tradition, pride, and good-will. It is as though they
were afraid that a great patriot might again arise
destined in the future to bear the nation once more
across the broad stream of its self-humiliation.

Our lack of dignity in adversity, as well as our
insufficient restraint in good fortune, are due at bottom to the illusion that our encompassed position in
the world could be overcome by words and feelings,
instead of solely by power rigidly held and skilfully
applied.

It was a common fundamental failing of our policy
to use up piecemeal the great but insufficient reputation of power which Bismarck left us, by means of
repeated demonstrations, which showed our love of
peace but also our nervousness; it was too liable to
result in our giving way, and earned for us from the
enemy the fatal character of a *poltron valeureux*.
The bad habit of these sensational interventions such
as Shimonoseki, the Krüger telegram, Manila, the
China Expedition, Tangiers, right up to Agadir and
others, led to its culminating blunder in the ultimatum
to Serbia, July, 1914. Thanks to the respect inspired
by the old Prussian State and the thoroughness of
the German people we had managed to scrape along
for some time. But it would have been better to
grow in silence and to gather more power; for in
1914 we were near to the goal which made the mere
presence of our power suffice to maintain peace without any nervousness on our part. It ended in the

tragedy that the most peace-loving policy in the world
thought to better our unfavourable position by means
of an attitude which gave our malicious enemies the
pretext for putting upon us the suspicion of the will
to war, thereby disfiguring our image by one of the
most monstrous calumnies in the history aof the world.

We threw ourselves into the arms of others and
then offended them, and we scarcely neglected an opportunity of representing to them how wonderfully
well we had got on. We never saw ourselves from
other people's point of view. Admiral Seymour, who
was presented by the Emperor with the picture " The
Germans to the Front," said to a German naval officer: " You Germans have come on very much; if only
you would not always be ramming it down our
throats." We blew trumpets which were not in keeping with our position. Then all real or intended mistakes and injuries were magnified in an inflammatory
manner and dragged into the open, and in this way
our democratic press gave foreign countries apparent
proof that Prussian Germany was a house of correction.

The circumstances of my department caused me
doubly to condemn all these demonstrations in international politics. On the other hand, I saw with
anxiety how little the whole situation, political, strategic, and economic, its enormous prospects, and its
particular dangers was generally realized. The danger of a blockade, for example, or more especially
of a war with England, who could cut off our whole

position and future in the world as with a knife, was not viewed with the gravity it demanded, as I was often compelled to observe. In view of England's endeavour to encompass us with a coalition, it was a question of our keeping our nerve, continuing to arm on a grand scale, avoiding all provocation, and waiting without anxiety until our sea-power was established and forced the English to let us breathe in peace. We have done the opposite to all this, and thus at the very moment when relief was already in sight, the storm cloud, which had already begun to move away, burst over us. The possibility of a war with England ought to have been avoided in 1914 just as in 1904, and it could probably have been avoided too, as the naval gamble had already taken effect, if only our political leaders had clearly perceived the danger of this war at the right moment. If an actively developed sense of power and its governing laws had been able to prevent the growth of the illusion of a localization of the Austro-Serbian conflict in the German people and its political leaders in July, 1914, the world-war would have been avoided at that time.[1]

The difficulty of arriving at a bearable peace in the event of a war with England determined my vote in 1904, which I mentioned above. After the outbreak of the world-war, seventeen years of fleet-building had, it is true, improved the prospects of an acceptable peace with England, but only if our leaders showed

[1] Chapter XVI.

the utmost energy in war, diplomatic skill, and unselfish devotion. I therefore represented, with all the
strength I possessed, the only points which could
bring us this peace and keep destruction away from
us; the war at sea and the well-timed submarine campaign, the separate peace with Russia, and the unity
of the German nation in the face of the deadly danger
into which we had stumbled, and which had been
clearly seen only by very few.

I was beaten in this struggle; the German capacity
for self-delusion once more overcame Germans by
Germans. The end of my career and my faith in my
people was to see the war lost by weakness, blindness,
and party spirit.

I fought against our self-annihilation without possessing sufficient power to do so. Occupied as I was
with my own duties, I had never striven for political
power. In December, 1911, after the Morocco crisis,
when my quarrel with Bethmann began, the Chief
of the Cabinet informed me, as I was going in to
give my report to the Emperor, that the question
of appointing me to the Chancellorship was being considered. During the audience I pushed over to the
Chief of the Cabinet a note to the effect that I should
refuse such a proposal if it were made to me. At
that time it seemed to me unthinkable to become Bismarck's successor. It was only when I saw during
the war how the Government lost its head and its
courage and one irrecoverable chance after another,
and how the Empire was tottering towards the abyss,

that I probably should not have refused the Chancellorship, conscious though I was of my shortcomings, provided no more suitable person was to be found. For as our situation appeared abroad, my appointment would have meant a clear break with the existing system. Let us remember the joy in England when things were reversed, and the word went round " *Tirpitz exit.*" Our only salvation lay, not in any change of individual, but in this change of system.

The suggestion was several times made to me in those days, but not from the only quarters which had the power to act.

CHAPTER XV

I

THERE are many who declare that the German Empire would have been able to obtain a proper friendly relationship with England, and that it was only neglect on the part of German policy, and particularly the building of our fleet, that destroyed this prospect. If ever this idea were to establish itself in German minds, it could be taken as a proof of the saying that history is written by the victor; and in this present case the vanquished would be cheating in order to be able to pay allegiance to the Anglo-Saxon hegemony in its historical conscience.

But now the English are denying that they wanted the war against us. Anybody therefore in Germany who makes the building of the fleet responsible for the war cannot even bring forward the enemy as witness. This self-accusation is on the wrong track;

the historical truth lies much more in one of Bismarck's last statements in 1898, at a time when we had no fleet: " He was sorry that relations between Germany and England were not better than they are. Unfortunately he knew of no way to improve them, as the only means which he could think of consisted in our putting a check on German industry, and was not therefore applicable." We could not win England for a friend and supporter without sinking back to the level of a poor agricultural State. But there existed a means wherewith to improve our relations considerably—the creation of a German fleet which would make an attack upon German trade a more risky venture for England than it was at the time of Bismarck's utterance. In this sense the German fleet did its duty right up to July, 1914, in spite of the failure of German policy on different occasions, and it is not its fault that it was unable to fulfil its peace-preserving purpose better and longer. For me it is difficult to understand how Herr v. Bethmann-Hollweg continues to blame the " so-called naval policy," which he himself countersigned for eight years when he was Chancellor.[1] It is all the more difficult to understand because both he and Lichnowsky and other Foreign Office experts established a definite relief of the tension in Anglo-German relations during the years preceding the war, and because they all acknowledged that, as the German fleet approached completion, it did not prevent at least an improvement

[1] *Deutsche Allgemeine Zeitung*, November 27th, 1918.

in our relations with England. The outbreak of war,
however, was not due to any deterioration of Anglo-
Saxon relations; there is even a particularly tragic
association to be seen in the fact that Germany and
England had come closer together in 1914 than during the period when Germany was without a fleet in
1896, or when her fleet was weak in 1904 and Count
Bülow succeeded in crossing the danger-zone. The
German fleet preserved peace according to its aim
and purpose. To-day those parties concerned are as-
sailing this clear fact; and in addition there is that
German tendency to self-depreciation which is always
ready to believe unfavourable things, and is glad when
it can abuse as nonsensical to-day what seemed intelligent yesterday.

Up to the beginning of the 'nineties the old-estab-
lished prosperity of England had scarcely felt the parasitic existence of " Germanism " on the world's trade.
The growth of our industrial and commercial development was indeed begun by the alteration of our
customs policy in 1879, but it was not until after a
decade of internal construction that it became so pal-
pable abroad as to prepare the ground for a general
change of feeling in England. The latter first
counter-blow was the phrase " Made in Germany,"
and her first political outbreak followed the Krüger
telegram. In 1896-97 I came home from Asia and
America with the impression that England would do
her best to obstruct our future development. In the
middle of the 'nineties the principal clubs of the two

chief political parties, the experts of English society
in foreign politics, had united in the conviction that
Germany was the common enemy.   This was in accordance with the political principle practised by the
English for centuries.

As usual there was a certain interval between the
change of front on the part of the political wire-pullers
and its public expression.   Then followed the working
up of the English public on a grand scale; the tendency
of this campaign might be represented by the battle-
cry " Germaniam esse delendam," under which head-
ing *The Saturday Review* wrote the following notable
sentences in 1897 :

" Bismarck has long realized what the English people are also beginning at last to see, that there are
in Europe two great irreconcilable forces opposed to
one another, two great nations who would like to make
the whole world their domain, and exact commercial
tribute from it.   England . . . and Germany . . .
the German commercial traveller and the English
trader . . . are competing with one another in every
corner of the globe. . . . A million petty worries
are creating the greatest *casus belli* which the world
has ever seen.   If Germany was exterminated from the
world to-morrow there would not be an Englishman
in the world the day after who was not so much the
richer.   Nations have fought for years for a town,
for a right of succession: must they not go to war
for an animal trade of five milliards?"

If one gives to such prophetic utterances, which
were not isolated, but the leaders of a thousand-voiced

chorus of hatred, all the weight which they possess
to-day, one feels immediately that it could not have
been pleasant for the English to base the hatred which
they were hammering into their people so blatantly
in view of the decision that has been accomplished,
and so unpleasantly, simply on trade jealousy, which
was the really decisive factor. They needed pretexts.
As the first Navy Bill had not yet been introduced at
the time when the public was to be inoculated with
these ideas, the pretext of the navy was wholly lacking. Those who directed British public opinion therefore had to make use of hypothetical German designs
upon the Transvaal. When these were done with,
they made use of the German fleet, to which they
attributed the most grotesque offensive plans when
the bulk of the fleet only existed on paper—all for
the benefit of the English newspaper reader.

The Navy Bill provided the first opportunity for a
moderation of England's desire to destroy us, because
it would not have been so easily satisfied once the
fleet was completed. On the other hand, it goes without saying that the fact of our building a fleet was
felt by England to be an encroachment upon her monopoly of the seas, and that in this respect the building
of the fleet made our diplomatic position more difficult. The question then arose whether England would
not want to nip our fleet in the bud and therefore
force a preventive war because we were building a
fleet? As a matter of fact we were not very far off this
danger in 1904-5; at that time the seriousness of our

naval work was recognized on the one hand, and on the other our strength was still undeveloped.

It was only the unpreparedness of France and the English army which prevented the collision then. That was the danger zone which in Bülow's opinion and mine we had to pass through; in 1914, however, the bulk of it was overcome. Our navy had acquired too much respect for England to want to attack it without very weighty reasons. So the pugilistic tone of the 'nineties changed in time to a more cautious and sober view, as the German power at sea became more firmly established; and in this sense the German fleet acted after 1912 more and more as a factor for the maintenance of peace. No English statesman, if he was honest, has ever had any doubt as to the peaceful tendency of our policy at bottom, and the purely defensive intentions of our fleet.

The building of the fleet moreover did not prevent Chamberlain from seeking an alliance with us in 1901, in which matter he was at any rate comparatively isolated in the Cabinet. In reality, however, the fleet never stood in the way of an alliance if such a thing had ever been seriously considered by England; but even the Germany of the 'nineties, who had no fleet, tried in vain, as Caprivi told me in 1893, to secure an alliance with England.

England did not find it necessary and expedient to conclude formal alliances with other Powers, as we did with Roumania and Italy for example. She contented herself with establishing a general confidential relationship with those Powers, whom she could use for her main purpose, without binding her hands, which was more convenient in home politics and more effective in foreign politics. Before the building of the German fleet, that is before the beginning of the commercial jealousy, the foundation was laid for the policy of *entente* and encirclement against Germany.

The *rapprochement* between French diplomacy and England began in 1898-9 with the Fashoda agreement, which was so much misunderstood in Germany, and by January, 1901, there already existed within the British Cabinet a feeling in favour of an agreement with France and Russia at the cost of English sacrifices in Morocco, Persia, and China.[1] After that the Entente worked upon the public mind of all three nations with all the methods which German diplomacy despised, in order to bring them all into line on a common front against Germany, by suppressing their mutual differences. The reasons which appeared in the 'nineties, and urged the English either to overthrow or encircle Germany, continued to exist, and it could not be demanded of our fleet-building that it should alter the fundamental motives of English policy. It was enough for the fleet to provide the Government with an instrument which gave Germany more elbow-room, in spite of the policy of encirclement, through the fact that the mere existence of the fleet

[1] O. Hammann, *Zur Vorgeschichte des Weltkrieger* (1918), p. 124: H. von Eckardstein, *Diplomatische Enthüllungen zum Ursprung des Weltkrieges* (1918), p. 17.

continually widened the gulf between England's inclination to war and her resolve to make war.

Late in 1904 England gave an impressive proof of
her substitution of hostility to Germany in place of
the traditional enmity towards Russia, on the occasion
of the unscrupulous change of front in the Dogger
Bank affair. After Japan, in the capacity of a British
vassal, had beaten the Russians, England saw that the
hour had come when merely by pressing the button
she would be able to set France and Russia in motion
against Central Europe. This big offensive policy
against us was only hypothetically aggressive. A
peaceful encirclement would have been far pereferable
to Edward VII and his circle than the gamble of war.
The building of the German fleet was now improving
from year to year the conditions for an Anglo-German
understanding, for it was repressing England's own
inclination to war and was giving more sober-minded
English politicians the upper hand. Whilst the gigantic growth of German industry in the first decade of
the century was able to take place independently of
armed power, chiefly because France and Russia were
not " ready," the reverse was the case in 1914, for England had become the most hesitating party in the Entente with regard to the war. Without a German
fleet we should not have been able to continue for
long our trade competition with the three Entente
Powers. As a result of the fleet, however, the unal-
tered tension between England and Germany had
become less dangerous. According to the unanimous

judgment of the initiated, it was less dangerous during the time of the Austrian ultimatum to Serbia than during the long years before.

After 1903 at the latest, however, England's political principle was to suffer no longer the military weakening of France by Germany, or the military shifting of the European balance of power to the advantage of the strongest continent power, Germany. The unhappiest moment of German policy was when it forgot this fundamental fact in July, 1914, and confirmed the biting words of a certain French officer to a German medical officer: "*Vos armées sont terribles mais votre diplomatie—c'est un éclat de rire.*"

II

During the first years of the policy of encirclement the English did not yet take the building of the German fleet seriously. They were convinced that no first-class fleet could be built with the small sums that were expended. They considered that our engineering side was still too undeveloped, and our lack of organizing experience too great, and they were accustomed to see many Prussian and German shipbuilding programmes remain scraps of paper. Our naval programme was not regarded with different eyes until 1904. At that time all the ships which we possessed were paraded before Edward VII during Kiel Week against my wishes, and the Emperor gave as a toast " the reviving sea-power of the newly created German

Empire." King Edward's reply was cool, and during his inspection of our ships he exchanged many meaning looks and words with Selborne, the First Lord of the Admiralty, which impressed me unpleasantly. It seemed uncanny to the English that we should do so much with such small means, and show an organic development which surpassed their own in systematic thoroughness. The patient " laying one stone upon another " of the German method seemed to them dangerous in this instance too.

The ensuing concentration of British squadrons against us was stressed in February, 1905, by a speech from the First Lord of the Admiralty, Lee, who declared, without any tangible reason, that if necessary the British fleet would be able to deal the first blow before they had time on the other side of the North Sea to read the declaration of war in the newspapers. England's attitude in 1904-5 showed that England was strongly inclined at that time to destroy the whole of Germany's position in the world with one war-like blow. This inclination for war is comprehensible, because a war contained no risk at all for England. The English Admiralty, however, hoped to render the beginnings of our naval enterprise worthless, by proceeding in 1905 to the building of the dreadnought class, on the assumption that the German navy would not be able to get ships of similar dimensions through the locks of the Kiel Canal.

This chain of political and naval threats, accompanied as it was by a wild agitation of public opinion, created justifiable amazement in wide circles of Germany. On the one hand England's naval measures contained the admission that our fleet-building was being taken seriously. On the other hand the demand for our political humiliation, which had been going on for almost a decade, was now known, and the size of our fleet at. that time was too small to explain such measures as the concentration of British squadrons in the North Sea. At the bottom of it all there was the clear intention of making us afraid, and if possible of nipping in the bud our impulse towards international independence.

In consequence of this I was besieged on all sides by requests for a big increase of Germany's naval power, for the purpose of preparing us better to meet British threats of war, and to teach the English a lesson in politics. Even the Emperor was strongly impressed in favour of a propaganda campaign to this end on the part of the Navy League, and wanted me to demand in the Reichstag that the period of life of our big ships should be reduced. This period of life had in consequence of a parliamentary misunderstanding been put twenty-five years higher in the Navy Bill than was the case with foreign navies, and resulted in a considerable number of our ships being obsolete.

In spite of this I resisted the introduction of such a Bill, and also handed in my resignation in this connection at the beginning of 1906. The Bill which I brought in in 1906, and which was immediately passed

by the Reichstag, contained only the six big cruisers
which had been cancelled by the Reichstag in 1900,
but immediately announced by me as a supplementary
estimate for 1906. In addition I could not help asking the Reichstag for the increased financial means
necessitated by the transition to the dreadnought class,
which we were compelled to build, like all other navies
of the world, by the English. And finally, the means
had to be voted for the widening of the Kiel Canal
which was rendered necessary by this increase in the
size of the ships.

My restraint with regard to the pressure which
was brought to bear upon me to demand more ships
had a pacifying effect abroad and increased the confidence of the Reichstag. In the circumstances which
prevailed during 1904-5, any increased demands would
very probably have conjured up an immediate danger
of war; and on the other hand would not have brought
us any immediate gain, but would have proved too
much for the navy to assimilate at the time. The aim
which I had to keep in view, however, for technical
and organizing reasons as well as reasons of political
finance, was to build as steadily as possible. It proved
to be most advantageous if we could lay down three
big ships every year. This rate of building three ships
per annum, the so-called "three-ship rate," was not
provided for by the building programme of the Navy
Bill. We therefore aimed at grafting Supplementary
Bills on to the Navy Bill so as to stablize the three-
ship rate. After 1906 the easiest way to do this was

to shorten the lives of our ships after the model of
other navies, by accelerating the building of the new
ones to replace them. However, if this waś done the
stabilization of the three-ship rate was only approxi-
mately accomplished; for in consequence of the original Navy Bill, the new vessels followed one another
so closely for a number of years that sometimes four
and sometimes two ships had to be laid down. This
fluctuation in the rate of building was one of the blem-
ishes of a naval programme sanctioned by Parliament,
but one which had to be taken in with the rest of its
overwhelming advantages, for the Reichstag would
never have accepted the three-ship rate in 1898-
1900 whilst giving its imprimatur to the squadron
principle.

The moment at which we had to demand the reduction of the life of a ship was the financial year
1908. After there had been a regular race between
the Centrum and the Progressives for the adoption
of a Supplementary Navy Bill in the summer of 1907,
before we had actually decided upon the Bill at the
Admiralty, our request went without any difficulty.
For the first time the Progressives not only voted for
the ships as such, but also for the principle of legal
sanction.

This Supplementary Bill brought no increase in the
number of ships provided by the Navy Bill, but a considerable rejuvenation, and consequently an increase
in the fighting value, of the ships. The provision of
new ships also accelerated the building of dread-

noughts, which had shaken the general faith in the older classes.

According to the Supplementary Bill of 1908, the building programme provided for the laying down of four ships annually for four years, 1908-11, and then two ships annually, 1912-17, whilst from 1917 onwards the three-ship rate became permanent. In order to prevent too long an extension of the two-ship period, which had serious objections from the point of view of shipbuilding and finance, we definitely made up our minds at the Admiralty to break the two-ship rate in 1915 or 1916 by slipping in one or two new ships which we should ask for in due course. This possible (but by no means settled) future demand would then have been the sole, and indeed extremely inconsiderable, extension of the fleet over the original navy scheme of 1900; for as I have already remarked, we only restored in 1906 the Bill of 1900, and in 1908 we did not increase the number of ships at all.

These departmental considerations, which I could not altogether spare the reader, in view of their foreign political significance, resulted therefore in the following scheme:

1. Neither in 1906 nor 1908 did we exceed the original navy scheme of 1900 which was known to the whole world.

2. The life of a ship which we agreed upon in 1908 corresponded to the general principle of all navies.

3. The main thing from our point of view was the three-ship rate, and even if four ships were built

every year for four years, on account of the large
number of obsolete ships left over from the previous
period, this was balanced by a succeeding period in
which only two ships at most were built every year.

In spite of this existing state of affairs, the shorter
life of our ships, and probably more still the fact
that we were also able to build dreadnoughts, promised our navy such a considerable increase in fighting
value that the British experts, with Admiral Fisher
at their head, began to look askance at our Supplementary Bill. We had never hoped for British approval during the creation of our sea-power. The
navy scare, however, which Fisher now set going,
offended in our opinion against good manners in international relations, because the Admiralty and many
members of the Cabinet did not hesitate to stir up their
country with exaggerated and wittingly false statements regarding our building programme.[1] Chance
so willed it that the English only laid down four ships
in that very year. The British Government exploited
this fact to make palatable to the public the laying
down of four extra ships, *i.e.* eight dreadnoughts altogether in 1909. They made good use of the trick of

---

[1] In the spring of 1909 the foolish story was circulated that
we were secretly building beyond the sums provided for in the
Estimates. This untruth, which testified to a complete ignorance
of our Constitution, was repeated by Asquith, the First Lord
of the Admiralty, McKenna, and others in Parliament for several years, in spite of our repeated *démentis*. Winston Churchill
formally abandoned this dishonest procedure when he declared
in his first public speech as First Lord of the Admiralty (November 9th, 1911) that he was glad to be able to testify that the
statements of the German Minister regarding the naval programme are absolutely confirmed by events.

comparing the German fleet as it would be in 1920, with the British fleet as it was in 1908. The British taxpayer, who could not be so clearly aware of the actual overwhelming superiority of the British fleet as the British Admiralty, was filled with uneasiness by an official and press agitation as unscrupulous as they were clever, and he was thus rendered willing to make further financial sacrifices. Fear of invasion, and a nervous dread of German warships, Zeppelins, and spies, began to permeate English society and the masses of the people.

The German Ambassador in London, Count Wolff-Metternich, watched this increasing fear of Germany with growing anxiety. Until then he had taken up the right standpoint that the English must, and would accustom themselves to our Navy Bill. Time has shown that even our four-ship rate, which lasted for four years, did not constitute a *casus belli* for England. War, with its incalculable possibilities, seemed to them too serious an affair, and well-informed men in London were quite clear in their own minds that it would have been perfect madness politically, militarily, and economically for us to attack England. In the spring of 1909 Admiral Fisher even admitted quite frankly to our naval attaché that the navy scare was nothing more than one of the usual manœuvres to prepare Parliament and the nation for the acceptance of bigger Naval Estimates. The consequent perversion of British public opinion, and the growing influence of the bellicose Northcliffe press, had to be accepted by us into the bargain, as a regrettable but not a decisive evil. The anti-German agitation constituted as little a *casus belli* for us as our fleet-building for the British Cabinet, and in contrast to the *Germaniam esse delendam* of former years it represented a certain progress towards the securing of peace, for the British public to feel that Germany too was not unarmed. At the same time, however, it was hoped to make us fearful of our own courage by means of a loud outcry, and to prejudice us against our fleet, which was in itself the surest sign that we had taken the right path.

It is understandable if not quite excusable that Count Metternich should, under the strong pressure of English circles around him in 1908, begin to lose his sure judgment of the deeper-lying reasons of Anglo-German jealousy. It is understandable because a unanimous chorus of English opinion insisted that the German fleet-building alone was to blame for the straining of the good relations between the two countries. It is not quite excusable, because Count Metternich could and must have known the previous history of the Anglo-German tension during the period when we had no fleet, and on the other hand because he could and must have been convinced by the whole situation and the relative strength of both navies of the purely defensive line of our naval policy. But it is thoroughly German to be convinced by the enemy that the latter is really right; the German is unsurpassed in his capacity for seeing the other party's point of view, but finds it extremely difficult to fathom his opponent's real motives.

The reports of our London Ambassador caused Prince Bülow to enter into detailed discussions with me during the winter of 1908-9. Since January, 1909, I had declared my readiness, during the course of these conferences with the Chancellor, to allow the English Government to be informed by us that we would be permanently satisfied with a proportionate adjustment of the strength of the two fleets, which would allow a definite superiority to the British fleet for all time. As a starting-point for negotiations I first mentioned the proportion of 3 : 4, but later declared myself ready to accept the proportion of 2 : 3, and finally settled on the proportion of 10 : 16. This figure was ultimately proposed by the British Admiralty under Winston Churchill and was straightway accepted by me. Even though Churchill left himself certain back doors open which really guaranteed the English navy a greater superiority than 16 to 10, I passed them over in my conviction that the systematic completion of the Navy Bill would fulfil its defensive purpose, which was all we had ever aimed at.

The arrangement of a proportion between the two navies gave the British Admiralty actual proof that we did not intend on principle to build a fleet for offensive purposes. According to the views of all authorities on the science of naval warfare the numerical superiority, which under otherwise equal conditions gives the attacker at sea the probability of success, is

about 30 per cent. We conceded this advantage and
considerably more to the English. We could not
have given a more binding guarantee that offensive
intentions were far removed from our minds.

It was clear, however, that the English preferred
us to have not even a fleet which was 50 or even
100 per cent. weaker than theirs. On the one hand
naval history, accidentally perhaps, provides numerous examples of the ability of the weaker fleet to win,
if special conditions and the luck of battle are favourable to it. But by far the most important point about
the German fleet from a political standpoint was the
international alliance-value which it gave the German
Empire; and even though Germany's alliance-policy
had allowed itself to be pushed into the background
by British diplomacy these conditions might yet change
one day. Thus we could only obtain recognition from
England by abandoning the building of the fleet altogether. The untiring efforts of British diplomacy
were consequently aimed during these years at sicken-
ing us of the fleet, and at picking holes in the Navy
Bill, if possible, in order to wreck it.

The fundamental error which was at the root of
Bethmann-Hollweg's naval ideas was the belief that
certain concessions in the development of our fleet, little courtesies, so to speak, which we showed the English in naval affairs, might alter the fundamental and
political formation of our relations. A few ships
more or less were all the same to the English. The
reasons for their malevolence lay far deeper than the

discussion of the annual Naval Estimates which they kept going with masterly skill. Bethmann-Hollweg seemed to agree with me that the Navy Bill, the foundation of all our prospects in world-politics, must be preserved untouched. I for my part agreed with the Chancellor that everything must be done by us to effect an improvement in our relations with England. From the first days of his taking office, I supported the Chancellor in his endeavours to meet the English in various matters brought forward by them. In particular, I influenced the Emperor in this direction, and for my part I left nothing undone to keep in motion the negotiations regarding a naval agreement suggested in 1908.

In the course of these conversations, which were first carried on by private negotiators and often greatly delayed by the English, I received the impression, all the more strongly as time went on, that the English Government was not serious about a real naval understanding, but that it was only engaged in infusing more deeply into our Foreign Office belief in the legend that the German fleet was to blame for everything and that without it the Germans would be sure of a paradise on earth. It went to work in this matter with undeniable skill, as anyone will testify who has had experience of the mentality of our Foreign Office at that time and the Chancellor's inability to understand the political psychology of England. Our ambassador in London, von Kühlmann, was one of the principal supporters of the idea that German ambitions for world power might go hand in hand with those of England were it not for the obstacle of the German fleet.

It was proved later that the English government did not seriously wish to arrive at an understanding on a comparative rate of shipbuilding because our consent to English demands bore no results whatever.[1]

Above all, the real basis for any such understanding, limitation of naval shipbuilding by adherence to the numerical proportion that has already been mentioned, was only recognized by them in 1913, although Lloyd George had held out prospects of such a recognition years before. It was believed and openly stated by those in Germany most concerned that war with England was not to be feared on account of our fleet, but that danger of such a war would diminish yearly as the German fleet rose in the estimation of the English, and thereby made the prospects of war seem less safe even to the Jingo party. Rude utterances, such as those of the *Saturday Review* and Civil Lord of the Admiralty Lee were heard less frequently. After 1912 there grew up, especially in London, a tendency towards more businesslike treatment of relations between Germany and England. One instance of this was the Anglo-German colonial treaty which was ready to be signed in 1914.

[1] Among such demands may be mentioned the suggestion that German ship-building be inspected by the British naval attaché at Berlin, and British ship-building by the German naval attaché at London. I obtained the Emperor's consent to this plan with difficulty, but presented it to him in order that we might escape the odium of being the first to refuse.

III

The one real crisis between Germany and England during the years from 1904 until 1914 occurred in the summer of 1911, and was due to the manner in which the German Foreign Office tried to settle the Moroccan dispute then pending between France and us. The Foreign Secretary of State at that time, von Kiderlen-Wächter, lacked political insight, particularly as regards the English. Moreover, he did much harm by his slovenly methods of business. It was at his suggestion that on July 1st, 1911, the Chancellor dispatched the gunboat *Panther* to the Moroccan port of Agadir; and it was his fault that the British Government, which had demanded an explanation, was left in doubt and without an answer for several weeks. As a result Lloyd George delivered a speech on July 21st that had been prepared by the Cabinet which warned Germany that in case of a challenge she would find British power on the side of France.

As I was just starting my summer holiday trip I received unofficial information of the dispatch of the *Panther*. That the naval minister should not be consulted in a naval affair of such world-wide importance betrayed certainly a lack of organization in the government. I was clear in my mind from the first minute that this demonstration on the Atlantic was a political blunder, and I was strengthened in my belief when I learned that England had not been consulted. If Kiderlen thought it was necessary to make a military demonstration he should have made it on land and directed it exclusively against the French. Personally, I should have been against such a demonstration on principle. A flag is easily hoisted, but it is often a difficult matter to lower even a small one with honour. We did not desire to make war. The greatest mistake of our government, however, lay in keeping its intentions dark during the first weeks of July. Later Kiderlen gave assurances that the Chancellor had never for a moment thought of demanding territory in Morocco. But as these assurances followed Lloyd George's threatening speech it looked as if he had only drawn back before the raised sword of England. Our prestige all over the world received a blow, and even German public opinion was stirred by the impression that we had received a setback. "England stopped Germany," was the catchword of the press everywhere.

It was our first diplomatic reverse since Bismarck's administration, and it hit us all the harder because the structure of our position in the world was founded not so much on power as on prestige. At the time of Delcassé's dismissal (1905), prestige had proved effectual; but we now had proof that prestige by itself was a failing asset. If we kept silent in face of this rebuff we inflamed the "new spirit" of readiness for war on the part of France, and laid ourselves open to still greater humiliation at the next opportunity. Therefore it was unwise, as the government tried to do, to palliate the slap in the face we had received. We should have admitted it openly and taken prompt measures to reply in kind. For a state which is conscious that the welfare of its citizens rests not on glossing over humiliating experiences but on the prestige that is backed up by real power, there is only one means, after such an incident as the Agadir affair, of restoring its prestige:—to show that it is not afraid, and at the same time strengthen its defences in the face of an increased possibility of war. It was our duty to follow Bismarck's example in similar cases, and bring in a Defence Bill quietly and without irritating accompaniments.

With such an idea in mind I went to Berlin in the autumn and told the Chancellor that as we had suffered a diplomatic check it ought to be counter-balanced by a supplementary naval bill. The Chancellor not only denied that we had met with a check, but complained indignantly to the Chief of Naval Cabinet because such an expression should be used. Moreover, he feared, as a possible result of such a supplementary bill, war with England.

The supplementary bill which I had considered did not call for a decided increase in our fleet, but aimed at improving its preparedness for war. The weak point in our naval defence lay in the annual autumn arrival of recruits, which, coupled with our short term of service, paralysed the striking power of the fleet for a certain period of the year. A means of increasing our preparedness for war without at the same time making a considerable addition to the number of ships was to put a reserve squadron on active service, so that in future we could have three instead of two squadrons permanently in service. Through the ability thus acquired of leaving a crew on the same ship almost interruptedly during its term of service we simplified greatly the complicated business of living quarters on shipboard, and set the officers and petty officers free for more important tasks and for sea voyaging on a large scale. A greater consideration of the *personnel* who had been wearing themselves out in strenuous service under unfavourable conditions was necessary in order to preserve the necessary energy in those who were ambitious and wanted to rise. This reform made it necessary to build only three additional large ships within the next twenty years, and attained a vital improvement in the navy with a very slight outlay. No one cognizant of British policy could possibly believe she would be stirred up to war by an increase of three ships in twenty years, unless she had already made up her mind to go to war. Our ambassador, Count Metternich, agreed with me that danger of war was very slight. But from 1909 until towards the end of the World War, lack of real discernment has been the characteristic of our foreign policy. For this reason the struggle between Imperial bureaucracy and the reform of the fleet arose because we feared we might provoke England to war. We could not have givn the English a more welcome line to follow.

The Agadir and Congo negotiations were plausibly

interpreted by the Foreign Office as diplomatic successes, although the resignation of Colonial Minister von Lindquist and other unpleasant incidents disputed such a complacent point of view. I consented to withhold the Supplementary Bill for a time in order not to render the negotiations that were proceeding more difficult for the government. The Emperor, too, who without any knowledge in advance had begun to uphold in public the re-enforcement of the fleet, decided on the advice of the Chancellor, in the beginning of October, upon postponement. To make a political impression the Defence Bill should have been presented at the beginning of the autumn session, and might then have prevented the Morocco debate (in November) which further impaired our prestige. Such a debate ought to have been avoided altogether. But the course this debate took made hesitation impossible, in my opinion, both as regarded home and foreign policy. Now was the time to declare what we intended to do and would do, all the more because England, after the settlement of the Morocco question, could not make the Supplementary Bill a *casus belli*.[1]

[1] From a purely departmental point of view I could stand a year's postponement of the Bill. I must here mention a third advantage which this Bill possessed, besides improved readiness for war service and freeing of the training personnel,—namely, the interruption of the two ship rate. If the two ship rate, as settled in 1908, were continued uninterruptedly for six years, there would suddenly be needed in 1918 an increased sum of sixty million marks in consequence of the three-ship rate which would then recommence. As a result, if the Chancellor of the Exchequer in 1918 compelled us to defray the entire extra expenditure by taxation, we might on account of the financial

On November 14th, the Emperor commanded the Chancellor to include the Supplementary Bill in the Budget of 1912. Bethmann declared his willingness to do so, to me, but apparently left himself a loophole. He next urged the Minister of War to bring an Army Bill into the background, and then he pleaded the coming Reichstag elections as an excuse for publishing the Budget minus the Navy Bill. From the point of view of domestic politics this amounted to a surrender of the Bill, and from the foreign political point of view, after all that had gone before, it lowered our prestige still further. In the beginning of January, Kühlmann sent a message from London in which that most unhappy diplomat erroneously stated that the success of the pending understanding with England in regard to colonial possessions depended on the abandonment of the Supplementary Bill. Later, he was equally mistaken in 1916 when he prophesied a declaration of war by Holland, and thereby influenced the decision of the Imperial Government in

condition of the Empire have been placed in a nice predicament. For this reason, bridging over to the three-ship rate by alternating with the two-ship rate was of the greatest value in the period between 1912-1917. But I did not need the Supplementary Bill for the budget of 1912. Another need of the navy which I advocated in 1911 was that large cruisers be given preference in our building programme, and this measure would have added to our war strength because the English were behindhand in building ships of this very type. Bethmann's opposition, however, forced me to withdraw this measure so that I might at least put through the more important part of my plans. By forcing me to abandon this measure,—a regrettable act from a military point of view,—before Haldane came to Germany, and then neglecting to turn this action of his to account in the course of the negotiations with Haldane, the Chancellor absolutely threw away a very effective weapon.

the U-boat question. In this same month of January
the Chancellor, without consulting me, proposed to
the Emperor that the Supplementary Bill be laid before the Reichstag not in statutory form but as a
yearly grant.

When the Emperor refused, the Chancellor fell
back on the demand that the formation of the third
squadron should be made gradually and that the building rate until 1917 should only include a third ship
every other year.

I was already placed at such a disadvantage by
the many disappointments I had met, which were accompanied by acts of financial and political finesse
on the part of the Secretary of Finance, Heermuth,
that I acquiesced in the modifications demanded by the
Chancellor, but I demanded in return that no further
changes be proposed. The Chancellor evaded a direct
promise. On January 13th, 1912, I requested the
Emperor to come to a decision which should put an
end to this backing and filling and wrangling, so
harmful both at home and abroad, which, with the
best will in the world, could not be concealed. The
Emperor thereupon commanded the Chancellor to declare his opinion of the Bill fully and freely; and
the Chancellor again tried to gain time by not coming to a final decision. On January 25th, the Navy
Bill was ready, and on February 7th was announced
in a speech by the Emperor the day after the English
Minister of War, Haldane, who had been invited by
the Imperial Government, arrived in Berlin. This was

a new phenomenon in the opposition of inner political circles to the necessary improvement of our naval equipment, this arrival of a foreign competitor. What were the preliminary deliberations precedent to inviting this British statesman to Berlin are unknown to me.

IV

As I was kept quite in the dark by the Chancellor as to his aims and expectations, it was only during the course of these negotiations with Haldane, and especially from their London sequel that I was able to understand clearly the attitude of the English cabinet at the time. Kiderlen's careless neglect was followed by Lloyd George's heavy counter-blow, and this, in my opinion, was followed by an undignified attitude on our part. Our assiduous courtesy produced in England the feeling that they could do what they liked with us. If we asked the English to Berlin we must be prepared to sacrifice something to spare ourselves the further embarrassment of a fruitless invitation. Bethmann's reluctance to uphold the Supplementary Bill in the Reichstag gave the English the cue to our weak spot, and showed them how they might even confuse the whole scheme of fleet construction as well as widen the breach within the Imperial Government. So the English accepted the invitation. Sir Edward Grey's confidant, the Minister of War, Haldane, who on account of his skill in reconnaissance, exhibited on the Russian General Staff in 1906, was also considered very acceptable to Germany, was sent to Berlin with the purpose of disgusting us as much as possible with the Supplementary Bill, and indeed with the whole scheme of fleet construction. As they recognized the Chancellor as an ally, and as Haldane moreover did not come as a petitioner but as a guest, there was no need for the British Cabinet to furnish him with offers to us that were seriously meant. Nevertheless Haldane brought with him a pretended present, of which more later. In spite of the open opposition of the Chancellor to the Supplementary Bill, which had already greatly impaired its value in foreign eyes, this Bill still afforded an adequate means, by skilful negotiation, of reaching an understanding on the basis of real give and take, even although there was not much inclination on the part of the English to negotiate with us as equals.

On the 4th of February the Emperor had informed the Foreign Office privately that Germany was ready to meet England halfway on the question of the Navy Supplementary Bill, provided she could at the same time receive sufficient guarantees of a friendly policy on the part of England, so that both powers might agree to take no part in any combination or military entanglement directed against each other. Such an agreement would at the same time make possible an understanding as to expenditures for armaments.

For the negotiations with Haldane himself the Emperor laid down the following principles:

1. The Navy Supplementary Bill is to be retained for the present.

2. England is to declare what programme she will follow (a) with regard to the Supplementary Bill, (b) with regard to the existing naval programme.

3. Discussion of a German-British alliance or a treaty for mutual neutrality, in connection with which the German Supplementary Bill might be retarded.

4. A demand that England give up the proportionate strength of 2 : 1, the "two keel to one standard," in favour of a proportionate standard agreeable to Germany.

The Chancellor was directed to ascertain whether Haldane had been authorized by his government to enter into preliminary negotiations or whether he came in a more or less private capacity to feel his way. As this question was answered the Chancellor was to speak in the name of the Emperor or merely as a private individual expressing his own views. In addition, the Emperor warned him not to play our trump card too soon, and to lay stress on the right of every state to decide upon its own defensive power. Finally, until we had obtained a promise of English concessions, progress of the Navy Bill must not in any way be retarded.

Just because we were disposed to take a compliant attitude, we should, in my opinion, if we wished to accomplish anything, assume an attitude of reserve, all the more because Haldane, an able and extremely clever lawyer, belonged to the class of British statesmen who considered it an easy matter to hoodwink our politicians. From some papers abstracted from the entourage of the British statesman we are in possession of accounts of the hour and a half conference which Bethmann held with Haldane on the afternoon of February 8th.[1]

If these are correct, the Chancellor assured the British Minister of his continuous endeavours to come to an understanding with England, and displayed an unofficial inclination, yielding to Haldane's suggestion, to distribute the building of ships called for by the Supplementary Bill over a number of years. In return he proposed an agreement for neutrality by both nations under certain conditions. Haldane evaded this proposal, and emphasized the " unconditional loyalty of Great Britain towards the entente with France and Russia," and, according to his report, called the Chancellor's attention to England's military duties in behalf of France, Belgium, etc., in the case of certain eventualities. Further, he warned the Chancellor against a German Supplementary Bill which England would be compelled to reply to with a " two keels to one " standard. He did not, as has been stated, consent to any agreement for neutrality, and the utmost he would offer was a noncommittal promise to undertake no "unprovoked attacks." Thus Haldane adhered to the traditional policy of England towards us.

[1] *The Vindication of Great Britain* and the *Manchester Guardian*. While correcting the proofs of this book a third version has been sent to me from an issue of the *Daily Chronicle* translated into German.

At this preliminary conference the Chancellor's mistake lay in disclosing the contents of the Supplementary Bill, including the changes which he himself wished to make, to Lord Haldane. Had he only chosen the original Bill as a basis for negotiations, he would have left a far greater means of compensation in our hands. But to emphasize his own pacific desires, Bethmann considered it advisable in conversation with the Englishman to side against the departmental representatives of German defensive power, those "naval fellows." This course produced an excellent impression on Haldane and made it easier for him to widen the breach in the German government revealed by the Chancellor, and also to conjure up a fictitious "war party" against which the Chancellor was to contend.

On February 9th Haldane was received by the Emperor, who had wished to be present at the conference originally planned for Haldane and myself. The audience was preceded by a luncheon at which the Chancellor was also present. While we did not talk politics at lunch, a decided air of tension prevailed. When I entered, the Chancellor asked me not to mention a fleet building programme in the proportion of two to three. Why he did so I do not know; perhaps he did not consider the plan sufficiently favourable for England. I was not informed by the Chancellor as to any part of the negotiations, particularly the proposal for mutual neutrality. Before the audience that followed, Bethmann retired.

During this audience my part was chiefly that of a witness, as the Emperor himself led the conversation. At first Haldane declared that he spoke in tne name of the British Cabinet and with the consent of the King, while toward the end of the conference he contradicted himself and said that he was present merely in a private capacity.[1]

Haldane began by holding out to us the prospect of a great African Empire. Although the Emperor, as late as January, had regarded such colonial offers with deep and justifiable distrust, it had proved possible in a few weeks to excite his ambition by the prospect of very valuable acquisitions to the Empire. But he did not stop to consider the difficulties that lay in the way of such a tempting prospect. The generous offer of colonial possessions, which, by the way, the English neither possessed nor had the right to dispose of, was artfully calculated to take advantage of the Emperor's disposition. This offer, so crude and obvious, made a painful impression on me. Once before, in 1908, England had tried to tempt us by offering the Portuguese colonies, while at the same time they stiffened the determination of the Portuguese not to sell. In the present case the acquisition not only of Portuguese, but also of French and Belgian territory was discussed. By such a scheme England planned not only to keep us in leading strings but to furnish proof to the French

[1] The *Manchester Guardian* of Sept. 1st, 1917, said that Haldane had previously received full instructions from the Cabinet. He was not to negotiate as to a treaty, but he might talk and entangle us as he thought best and report the course of events to the Cabinet.

and Belgians of our ambitions, and thereby strengthen their dependence upon her.[1]

I certainly admired Haldane when, during the drawing up of these provisional and very dubious schemes, he modestly remarked that he " only claimed the Cape to Cairo line as England's share." This meant Africa for England! When the ultimate superiority in power was added to the English skill in negotiation, woe betide Germany! Haldane makes me think of the words of the American who said to a German admiral that when he compared the leading statesmen of England and Germany whom he knew, and put them opposite one another at a conference table, he would be surprised if we still retained Potsdam at the end of the negotiations.

For my part I began by declaring that I would welcome an understanding. When in the course of the conversation Haldane designated the two-power standard as the British tradition, I proposed an ar-

---

[1] With reference to Portugal compare the declaration of the Prime Minister on March 20, 1912. That the scheme of the Entente was a question of rousing Belgian distrust of us instead of satisfying German colonial ambitions was proved by the French Ambassador at Berlin in April, 1914. The German Government, in their desire to come to an understanding with the Western Powers, and particularly with England, had hesitated between sacrificing the fleet or the colonial plans. During the astonishing conversation held at the time mentioned above with Jagow, he disclosed to the French representative his private opinion that Germany, France and England should economically develop the Belgian Congo. Cambon, the French Ambassador, immediately rejected such an idea emphatically, and made good use of Jagow's naiveté by egging on Belgium against Germany. Perhaps he remembered Bismarck's masterly turning to account of the far greater blunder of Benedetti in regard to that same Belgium.

rangement in the sense of a proportion between the
two fleets of 2 : 3; that is, I offered what Lloyd George
and later Winston Churchill had proposed. Haldane
rejected this politely; England had to be equal with
her fleet to any possible combination. When I returned
that our army must in that case also be equal to any
combination, although it was hardly so strong in
numbers as either of the two neighbouring Powers,
Haldane replied that that was quite a different matter.
He did not propose a naval concession on our part as a
necessity which he demanded, but he opined that the
spirit of the whole agreement would be bound to suffer
by the Supplementary Estimates. He next came out
with a proposal of a certain delay in the building of the
three ships, whether we could not distribute them over
three years? I tried to make clear to him the difficulties which a further change in the Bill would occasion us, as we had already reduced our programme
considerably out of regard for conciliatory feeling in
England. During the negotiations it seemed to me
right on principle, only to yield so far as was unavoidable, because it was always possible for us to give
more ground. I also represented that Haldane must
remember how His Majesty was bound by the Speech
from the Throne. Haldane admitted this, and inferred
that our system of service necessitated a third squadron
in commission. Demands with respect to the commissioning of ships and the *personnel* of the fleet were
matters of indifference to England. He only wanted a
token of our readiness to meet England, more for the

sake of form—for he was not concerned with expenditure.[1] Ought I then to have been satisfied with offering the prospect of a general naval *rapprochement* in the event of a political agreement, or was it more correct to define the limit of our *rapprochement* in this interview? I took the latter course when Haldane himself proposed that we should retard the rate of our increase "in order to lubricate the negotiations," or that we should at least cancel the first of the three ships. He outlined in writing of his own accord the same proposal which I had previously fixed upon in my own mind as a possible concession. I therefore sacrificed the ship.

I would have sacrificed the whole Bill for a really solid agreement of neutrality, as I had let the Emperor know beforehand. All through these years I was fully conscious of the grave responsibility, and I always had before my eyes the possibility of making concessions as far as naval armament was concerned (for I had never considered this as an end in itself) in return for real international equality and for the freedom of the seas. This peaceful purpose of our fleet-building was considerably nearer to its fulfilment two years later, as Churchill's consent to the 10:16 formula showed. But at the beginning of 1912 when our fleet was weaker than it was two years afterwards, I could not know exactly how great was the possibility of a political agreement. The Chancellor had never said

---

[1] The Supplementary Estimates meant an increase of only nine millions per annum.

to me plainly : " this and that is the concrete objective which we want to attain." When working with him one was always groping more or less in the dark, and so I gave away the third ship against my real principles and without any return, so as not to obstruct negotiations which could possibly promise success.

Owing to the fact that the Chancellor had already given away the *original* Supplementary Estimates, I had no more compensations to offer in return for little gifts, which were paid out to the tune of future colonies. I could only sacrifice military values on principle in return for actual, and in a certain sense final, guarantees, either naval (the proportion of 2 : 3), or political (an agreement regarding neutrality). To have dropped Supplementary Estimates without any positive compensation would have meant giving way in too one-sided a fashion. This was just what we had to avoid most of all if we did not want to return to the period of English threats such as in 1896 or 1904-5, or to put an eternal screw upon ourselves. We had to deal with the English on the basis of like to like, if we wanted to secure permanently our mutual relations in spite of the mistakes made in July, 1911.

I was therefore uncertain whether I had not already gone too far in reality, in sacrificing as a proof of our compliance a part of the Supplementary Estimates which had already been reduced. My doubts were soon dissolved by my seeing clearly the real aims of the English. For after Haldane had pocketed this

concession without giving anything in return, and had
declared himself satisfied with it, he went farther and
cautiously touched upon the question as to whether the
Navy Bill itself had to be carried into effect.   Here the
Emperor intervened and so Haldane withdrew his
feeler.   In spite of this I still felt certain that the real
desires of the English were not directed against the
bagatelle of the three supplementary ships, but against
the Bill itself.   Haldane admitted on various occasions
during the conversation that the increase of the fleet
by the three supplementary ships did not materially
matter.   After we had apparently achieved unanimity,
and sacrifices had only been made on Germany's side,
Haldane declared, as I said, that the whole thing was
a private affair.   Although the later negotiations in
London came to nothing, I kept to the sacrifice of the
one ship so as to leave no doubt about our good-will.

A really businesslike deal with Haldane was rendered difficult by the presence of the Emperor.   When
the conversation turned upon the point that was
decisive for us, the political agreement, Haldane
evaded it: a neutrality clause, he said, would not
be possible on account of England's relations with
France.

As we left the Castle, Haldane expressed himself
satisfied with the conversation.   I had deduced from it,
(1) that the Supplementary Bill was actually im-
material to England, but that her real object was to
cripple the development of our fleet, and (2) that *no*
agreement was offered by the English which would

have meant an honest naval understanding on the basis of the proportion suggested by Lloyd George in 1908. Rather was the "two-keels-to-one" standard, which took all the value out of our fleet, to be rigidly recognized by us on principle, and this would be equivalent in the long run to a reduction in our Navy Bill. If we accepted the "two-keels-to-one" standard, then England could content herself with building four or even three ships for a succession of years, and curtail our own programme by two or one and a half ships per annum according to agreement. This would be an end of the Navy Bill; apart from this, the principle of our naval speculation cited above would be killed, and our fleet would lose its justification for existence and Germany her international alliance-value. They thought that they could expect us to give way in this fashion because we were apparently urging so strongly for an "understanding" at any price. I deduced further, (3) that Bethmann's formula of neutrality did not come into question, but (4) that our naval subjection was to be rewarded solely by reversions in the African possessions of the English *protégés,* French, Belgians, and Portuguese; these reversions were calculated to suit the Emperor's imagination and the desire of various diplomats to achieve a success.

Haldane did not therefore proceed on strictly business lines: he tried first of all mock negotiations, ready to sugar our subjection and to grant us the appearance of a political agreement and the acquisition of colonies, if we practically entered into a vassalage in return for this.

England's real face was revealed a little more clearly by Winston Churchill, the First Lord of the Admiralty, who on February 9th, at the same moment that Haldane was descending the steps of the Castle at Berlin with the bronze bust given him by the Emperor under his arm, made the luncheon speech in Glasgow in which he described the German fleet as a luxury.

So long as the idea of a luxury fleet prevailed, and so long as the proportion of 2 : 3, once proposed by Lloyd George, was rejected by the English Cabinet, it was, considering the mentality of our Government, useless, and produced only diplomatic disadvantages, for us to invite British Ministers to Berlin, who offered us nothing, but skilfully sowed discord among us.

If Haldane had shown any inclination towards a reasonable and proportionate arrangement of the fleets, I was prepared to say to him: when the proportion of 2 : 3 is once established and a solid friendship has taken root between our countries, then the time will have come to discuss a proportionate reduction of the Navy Bill itself. The procedure of the English statesman, however, which aimed at deceiving our illusionists and not at a square deal, naturally made me keep back this idea, which could only be properly accepted when England recognized our position in the world and offered us tangible compensations. If it was at all possible to bring England to serious negotiations instead of to this mockery, this could only be done by steadfastness in the main issue, the Navy Bill.

What deductions did the Chancellor make from the failure of his attempt at an understanding which had failed to realize the soul of England from the very outset, and had been based upon unreal premises? He looked round for a whipping-boy and of course found me at once, because I did not give up the German fleet blindly without any compensation.

As to the final conversation which Haldane had with the Chancellor on February 10th, the report published in *The Manchester Guardian,* says: "Haldane was interested mainly in the navy question, and his whole argument throughout, that a political understanding remained unreal so long as Germany did not make some concessions in her fleet, did not help the Chancellor's depression, who was decided, however, if he could do anything at all, not to let the idea of an understanding with England be wrecked by Tirpitz."

I leave the reader to examine this plea in connection with my version of Haldane's conversation with me as I have reported it; it follows from this latter that my naval concession was absolutely uncompensated, and that Haldane himself did not treat the Supplementary Estimates as vital. Even with the Chancellor, Haldane seems therefore to have aimed ultimately at the collapse of our Navy Bill.

The negotiations were then continued in London. Their course showed more and more clearly that Eng-

land was only engaged in making us give one-sided
concessions in the construction of our fleet without
receiving anything in return. The Foreign Office could
not expect to complete this one-sided subjection, and
now urged me to drop all the three supplementary
ships. This demand was equal to the abandonment of
the whole of the Supplementary Estimates, for we
could not then ask for the *personnel,* since the whole
justification of these Estimates became illogical once
the ships were dropped. The Foreign Office did not
take into account that apart from the weakness incurred militarily by the stoppage of this reform, and
especially after the Emperor had come to an agreement with Lord Haldane, the result was an unwarrant-
able loss of prestige, and that we had started down a
slope on which there was no stopping. The further
history of the sufferings of the Supplementary Bill,
which cannot be related here in detail, showed that
our diplomacy allowed itself to be brought more and
more to the standpoint that England really had the
right to determine the limits of our armament. The
Emperor's firmness finally suppressed any suggestion
that the Supplementary Bill, which had been solemnly
announced in a speech from the Throne, should be
dropped without any concessions on the part of the
English. The Chancellor must have felt, in view of
the course which this affair had taken, that our representative in London was not equal to his task, for our
ambassador there was relieved by the best diplomatist
we possessed, Freiherr von Marschall.

V

Although very anxious about the improvement of Anglo-German relations, Prince Bülow preserved Germany's dignity completely in 1908-9. On the other hand the negotiations adopted by us in 1912 called forth a domineering attitude towards us, which they abandoned, however, quite correctly when they noticed that it was not our intention to accept subjection. The improvement which was so perceptible in Anglo-German relations after this turn of events in 1912 induced even Bethmann and Kühlmann to declare frankly during the pre-war period that my standpoint had been correct. Statements to this effect by both statesmen were reported to me. On April 23rd, 1914, the Chancellor had a conversation with the Ambassador von Wangenheim, in the early morning before he left Corfu, the contents of which were given by the latter to a companion in a form which was handed on farther in an official report drawn up on the same day. According to this the Chancellor said: " There is no question that Tirpitz's policy in 1911-12 was the right one, and that we owe our present promising relationship to England to this naval policy alone. I myself was unable to estimate it as such at the time, but I now acknowledge Tirpitz's standpoint." Even in July, 1914, Bethmann showed by his attitude that he saw in me an instrument of peace. Then when the misfortune of July, 1914, arose from reasons which were very remote from the German fleet, Bethmann-Hollweg, to

be sure, slipped back into his " whipping-boy " theory
of 1912 and received ample applause; this proceeded
from the English on the one hand, who as they did
not want the war, according to their own assertion, had
to distort the matter and stamp me as a war agitator,
and on the other hand from German democracy, which
is glad after the result of the war solemnly to abjure
the understanding they showed from 1900 to 1914 of
Germany's need of foundations of power. I shall not
deny myself the insertion of the following sample of
contemporary German history-writing. The *Frankfürter Zeitung* writes, 1918, No. 330: " Was not Lord
Haldane in Berlin, and did he not propose a treaty
which would only have left us a *moderate distance*
behind the English fleet? Bethmann did not accept
this proposal, and we know well why. Not because
he did not want to do so himself, nor because he had
not recognized that this solution was wholly sufficient
for Germany's justified interests, but because he was
miserably afraid of Tirpitz and his journalistic com-
panions, of the impudent, criminal propaganda which
the Admiralty was carrying on at the expense of the
German taxpayer." The low-mindedness that, apart
from the untruth, speaks out of such press utterances,
which unhappily are not isolated, relieves England of
the trouble of producing the proof of her generosity
and of German roguery. In reality it so happened that
Haldane's proposal amounted to the abandonment of
the German Navy Bill, and I heard from the *Frankfürter Zeitung* for the first time the incorrect opinion

that the Chancellor also recognized this abandonment of the Navy Bill to be sufficient for Germany's justified interests. I must therefore have been the departmental goat which had frustrated Haldane's honest attempt at reconciliation.[1]

Is Germany really doing well for her own sake to allow all those people to be defamed who once laboured for her safety and protection?

From its own standpoint the *Frankfürter Zeitung* is justified in asking why the Chancellor did not decide to let me go, if my activities were so fatal (I made it very easy for him in 1911-12 and several times offered the Emperor my resignation) or refuse his responsible counter-signature.

For my part I put one question to those Germans who assume that the English did not go to war to maintain the continental balance of power or for reasons of the old trade jealousy, but for the sake of Germany's naval policy. Do they think that the Supple-

---

[1] The tendency of the book inspired by Haldane, *The Vindication,* to construct a peace party (Bethmann) and a war party (Bülow, the Crown Prince, and myself) and the desire to draw the Emperor over to Bethmann's side probably explains a misstatement in the book, that the Emperor had cancelled the third ship "against the wishes of his Admiral." In reality, the conversation went so that I asked Haldane, "What do you mean by lubrication?" He mentioned the reduction of the Supplementary Estimates and wrote it down himself. I replied, "We can accept that." Hereupon the Emperor agreed. Haldane's historical error was explained by an evil conscience: in order to get rid of England's blame for the war he had to invent a war-party in Berlin. It is not worth while discussing the perverted version in *The Manchester Guardian.* I remained silent with regard to Haldane's publications in 1916-17, because I had to leave the reply to the Emperor at that time.

mentary Bill of 1912 or the completion of the Navy
Bill would have matured a resolve to make war?

The first possibility practically settled itself. If
England preferred peace on principle before 1912 she
would hardly have changed round to war owing to
the two ships of the Supplementary Bill. Or would
England perhaps have not used the situation that had
arisen in July, 1914, as a *casus belli,* and not have de-
fended Belgium and France if I had abandoned all
three supplementary ships instead of one and had purchased a diplomatic defeat into the bargain? If, however, England was resolved to go to war on my account, then it would be simpler to bring a reproach
against me for conceding anything at all, and thus
making me to a certain extent an accomplice of those
of our Ministers who did harm to our armaments on
land and sea by an inexcusable policy of economy during the years preceding the war, and consequently
helped to lose the war. The sole question therefore—
and the answer to it is, to be sure, more a matter of
opinion—is whether we ought to have decided upon
and put into execution any Naval Bill at all. It is
useless quarrelling with those people who preferred
that German overseas trade should wither in peace,
rather than make an attempt to protect is by a "bal-
ance-of-power" policy at sea, and the unfortunate outbreak and course of the war will justify them against
those others who regarded the course of events as an
inevitable fate instead of a series of unavoidable mistakes. I should not have built a fleet for my country

with all my heart, if I had not believed in its ability to become a real free world-power. Perhaps I was deceived in this. The self-humiliation of our democracy at least raises the suspicion that I deceived myself as to the inner forces of the nation. Its world-political course has been broken by its disunity, not by outside conditions; this is my firm conviction, from which all the noise of the historiographers will not dissuade me.

This attempt on the part of German democracy to clear itself of our previous endeavours to secure peaceably a position in the world would only produce cool contempt from the English, once they had attained their object. The future generations of Germany, however, will experience whether the Anglo-Saxons will allow a Germany that is impotent at sea to thrive as an industrial State.

There are some political bookworms who say we ought to have refrained from building a fleet for a few decades like Bismarck did, and thus have abstained from provoking England until we had acquired a dominating position upon the Continent. Let these people who thus cling to Caprivi's standpoint remember what Bismarck himself said about the unavoidable German tension and its causes. According to her political principles of three hundred years' duration, England would never have permitted a close economic competitor, least of all us, to have acquired a dominating position on the Continent, quite apart from the question that the latter was an object worthy of our endeavour. England would, however, have opposed

even by force of arms any expansion of our power
on the Continent all the more ruthlessly and dispassionately the less she herself feared us.   On this account the opposition to France and Russia was eased
in England in the 'nineties, and turned in our direction.   In 1914, on the other hand, protected as Germany was by the construction of our fleet, which had
almost passed through the " danger zone," we had
practically won by peaceful methods the rank of the
fourth world-power, without England having found
an opportunity as yet to intervene.   Extraordinary
clumsiness on our part contributed to give her this
opportunity at such a late hour.   A prominent German
statesman characterized this achievement as a first-class
piece of diplomacy—in a negative sense, however.
There was no other way to the position of world-power
than by building a fleet.   The highest prosperity is not
given to a nation for nothing.   Sea-power was a natural and necessary function for our national economy,
the world-wide influence of which was disputing the
palm with England and America, and had already
overtopped the other nations.   Such a position is
dangerous, and it becomes untenable unless a navy
which inspires respect increases the risk run by a competitor in any attempt to strike down his rival.   It
will indeed be scarcely possible to make German doctrinaires understand that such developments as those to
overseas trade and sea-power cannot be commanded,
but must proceed organically from the inmost development of the nation, and that a nation of seventy mil-

lions will literally starve on a confined territory without a dominating export trade.

VI

The years following Haldane's visit brought an improvement in Anglo-German relations which was unanimously welcomed in Germany, but, as events were to show, wrongly estimated in part. Our naval policy had proved its love of peace in 1912 by its one-sided sacrifice of the third ship, and (this was the main point) by the reduction of the four-ship rate of building to the two-ship rate in 1912. From a military point of view this was not without its dangers, as it increased England's advantage over us and actually worsened our prospects in a naval engagement from the autumn of 1915 onwards. But this actual proof of our love of peace, which could not be explained away by any sophistry, contained a political value which bore fruit, and would have borne still more if the events of July, 1914, which I shall come to later, had not cut short its development.[1]   It is with a certain melancholy that I look back to the short time in which Freiherr von Marschall acted as our Ambassador in London. Marschall had dealt with naval questions from time to time in the Reichstag as Foreign Secretary before the appearance of the Navy Bills, and a former official of the Foreign Office gives him the following testimonial for his activities in these matters:

[1] For the rest, the best proof that we are not to blame for the race in naval armaments lay continually in a comparison of the Naval Estimates of the various naval Powers.

" that no Minister had done more than Marschall to awaken some understanding of the political and economic disadvantages of our not having a fleet, before the period of systematic popular instruction which began with the appointment of Admiral Tirpitz to the Admiralty." [1] His long exile in Constantinople had brought the statesmanlike qualities of this outstanding mind to full maturity, when the Emperor nominated him in May, 1912, to succeed Count Wolff-Metternich in the most important foreign political post of the Empire.

Contrary to his predecessor Freiherr von Marschall immediately began to study seriously the concrete numerical and constructional proportions of both navies, without a knowledge of which it was imopssible to deal properly with England. In this endeavour he came to see me shortly before his departure for London, and in the course of a long conversation we achieved perfect unanimity with regard to the naval policy to be pursued. Marschall had been recognized as an equal opponent by the English statesmen at the second Hague Conference in 1907, as well as during his successful activities in Constantinople. There he had had occasion to observe the power of England at one of its international focuses, and he had succeeded in getting the better of the English at the Sublime Porte. His appearance in London now interrupted for a time the German method of running after the English and being impressed by their ways. Marschall

[1] O. Hammann, *Der Neue Kurs* (1918), p. 175 *et seq.*

knew that the Briton becomes more polite, the more resolutely his competitor maintains his own stand-point. He declared that Germany could not carry out her economic policy without possessing a power at sea which could protect us against the necessity of yielding to England at every turn. When he handed in his credentials at Buckingham Palace in July, 1912, the King honoured him with an address in German, where-upon Marschall for his part gave the English Ministers present an opportunity, by using the German language all through the audience, of exhibiting a surprising grasp of our language hitherto unsuspected by any German diplomat. On this solemn occasion, Marschall complained that he saw his otherwise so good and promising reception compromised by the English press, in consequence of another navy-scare speech by Churchill: if things went on in this strain, he added, he felt that he would be exerting himself in vain.

This scene was described to me by an eye-witness, Captain Widenmann, our naval attaché, who said that the effect of this dignified and firm manner, which was based upon an exact knowledge of the circumstances, was significant. Never before during the years of the Anglo-German tension had a German statesman found such consideration and esteem in England, and Admiral Sir John Jellicoe expressed the general feeling in a conversation with Dritten when he said of Marschall: " he looks like a tower of confidence." His early death (September, 1912) was a loss of incalculable effect to Germany, who was so poor in real statesmen.

In discussing the growing English inclination towards an understanding I would restrict myself to
those systems which lie within the province of the
navy. The First Lord of the Admiralty, who had still
hoped in 1912 to persuade our " luxury fleet " to the
" two-keels-to-one " standard through the agency of
Haldane, accepted in 1913 the 2 : 3 standard which had
been proposed by Lloyd George in 1908 and by myself in 1912, in the approximated form of 10 : 16. By
this means the Anglo-German naval agreement was
practically achieved, and as we had no more Supplementary Bills in contemplation, Anglo-German naval
discussions were finished in the main, and this bone
of contention was done away with as far as one could
see.[1] I did not want to endanger this development by
any means. The reliability of German policy was our
best weapon. I was therefore in opposition again,
when in 1914 the German capacity for self-deception
was once more over-estimating the improvement in
Anglo-German relations. At that time the Emperor
wanted to lay more stress on our foreign service, which
in itself was quite in my line, and he desired to introduce an additional estimate for the preparation of four

[1] In a very involved form, Churchill made one more attempt
to break the neck of the Navy Bill by proposing a year's
holiday from naval shipbuilding. The unfavourable reception
of this idea in England, however, relieved us of the necessity
of going into it in any detail. I will only mention by
the way that Bethmann, Kühlmann, the Foreign Office, and
the party leaders of the Progressives and the Centrum refused
most resolutely at that time to entertain at all seriously this
proposal of a year's respite, for from 1912 onwards, and indeed
for ever as it seemed, there prevailed the most complete unanimity regarding our naval policy.

more small cruisers, which were permanently to represent our rising political interests in the Mediterranean. I raised the strongest objections to the sudden introduction of an additional estimate on these terms, for it might produce political complications, as the sending of the German Military Mission to Constantinople, which had been done without my previous knowledge and to my regret. I asked through the Chief of the Cabinet to be relieved of my office, whereupon the proposal was dropped. In the autumn of 1914 I wanted to propose a supplementary estimate for the purpose of sending a battleship division to San Francisco for the World's Exhibition, and thereby to ask, by means of the budget, for the means which we lacked for keeping more ships in commission abroad. Even in the distant future there was no occasion, as far as one could see, for the introduction of a new Supplementary Bill. I never intended a further increase of our battleships, but on the contrary I had in view the possibility of reducing their number in the event of a continuation of the huge increase in the size of the ships.

After Haldane's visit, when our extravagant desire for an understanding led the English to believe for a time that they could treat us like Portugal, the Government in London refused an agreement of neutrality, but was ready to promise not to take part in " unprovoked (!) attacks " on us. For this meaningless kindness they put two conditions to the Emperor, firstly that the Supplementary Bill should be dropped alto-

gether, and secondly that Bethmann should remain
Chancellor. The Emperor formally rejected this demand as an interference in our domestic affairs. When
the interests of two nations who stand quite naturally
together under the right policy, such as for example
the Germans and the Russians, converge, the mutual
confidence between the statesmen can never be too
great. When, however, unbridgeable differences are
held in check and cannot be turned into common interests, as is the case between Germany and England, a
liking for one man cannot exceed a certain temperature
without becoming dangerous. Yet England's desire
was fulfilled and Bethmann remained. When the Emperor told me about this request, he added that I had
been described as " a dangerous man " at the same
time. I replied that no greater praise had ever been
given me in my life.

At the time I was not yet sufficiently acquainted
with the mentality of many Germans, which differs
from the political instincts of other nations, and which
considers the fact of a statesman being testified as
" harmless " by a foreign political opponent is sufficient
to recommend him to his own country.

CHAPTER XVI

THE OUTBREAK OF THE WAR

I

During Kiel Week in 1914 our London Ambassador, Prince Lichnowsky, told me that England had agreed to the present German rate of shipbuilding; a war about our fleet or our trade was now out of the question; our relations were satisfactory, and the *rapprochement* was growing. Here he added the question whether a new Navy Bill was to be expected. My reply was: " We have no need of any more."

In this same Kiel Week a British battleship squadron was our guest for the first time in nineteen years, as a symbol of our improved relations. I had some English officers and the English Ambassador to lunch on board when the news arrived of the murder of the Austrian Heir-Apparent. Two days later the English ships sailed away. On July 2nd I went to Tarasp to take the cure, as I had planned. That piece of news had moved us all in an uncanny fashion. It was expected that some satisfaction would be required for the dark deed, and as a consequence of certain tension also throughout Europe I did not fear the possibility

of a world-war. Who was to take on the responsibility
for such a thing? Moreover, our military intelligence
showed that an attack from Russia was not to be
reckoned with till 1916 at the earliest, if at all. It
was not suspected that the murder in Serajevo had
been contrived with the knowledge of the Czar or of
England.

Daily reading of the English newspapers, together
with official reports, had kept me in touch with the
diminution of the agitation against us, and the easing
of the tension between England and Germany. The
fundamental feeling that we ought to be repressed
had not altered, and it could not be forgotten for one
moment that it was still England's political principle
to hem in Germany's influence. But the moment for
striking us down was felt by wide circles in England to
be past. In 1897 the destruction of the German
Empire, which had no fleet then, was discussed in cold
blood. In 1905 the Civil Lord of the Admiralty openly
threatened the still tiny German fleet with an annihilating attack. In 1908-9 a navy scare at least accompanied the Bosnian crisis, although there were no
threats; the sword no longer sat loosely in the scab-
bard, the tone was no more arrogant and brutal, but
it was still very much excited. During the Agadir and
Haldane period, 1911 and 1912, a certain self-control
and growing caution were mingled in the hostile tone.
When the last attempt to force upon us the English
hegemony, as expressed in the 2 : 1 proportion of the
fleets, was defeated by us in 1912, the British Ministers

soon afterwards expressed themselves satisfied with our building ships in the proportion 10 : 16, and showed us more respect in every way. In 1912-14 they encouraged our support of the Austro-Hungarian standpoint, but we shall not discuss how far the secondary result of this, the emphasizing of Russo-German differences, was felt to be desirable. In July, 1914, England showed a desire at first, as I found out later, not to let loose a world-war on Serbia's account. This desire was actuated by the need, which is so strong in a commercial people, of preserving the general peace so long as their own interests were not endangered. It would be wrong to explain this attitude as friendship for Germany. England would have availed herself of every unobserved moment to reduce the German people to the condition of poverty from which the State of the Hohenzollerns and of Bismarck had alone raised it.

Meanwhile, the strengthening of Russian power had brought the danger of a world-war, on the whole gradually nearer since Russia had joined the Entente, and our Russian policy, which was wrong in so many ways, had not succeeded in easing the tension between us. The preparations for war of both Russia and France had been advanced to the utmost limits. The fact that England favoured these preparations, and the desire for conquest which was behind them, renders England's historical guilt irrefutably clear, particularly because she herself was much more cautious with us in consequence of the increased risk of war, and to a certain extent balanced by her cooler temperament the increased explosive force of the Entente, within the unstable European situation brought about by her.

For the half-century of peaceful growth had now made us difficult to attack. Both Cabinet and public opinion in England found it more and more to their own interests to let us take part in the business of the world as their best customers. While England became more accustomed to this idea, those people in Germany who regarded England's predominance as a sort of divine right, and German power as something unusual and inadmissible, withdrew into the background. Even those who had hitherto taken the line that England should not be " provoked " by a navy of our own began to take heart in a Fatherland which was respected and protected by its own strength, in consequence of the more polite treatment of the reinforced German Empire. We had almost passed the unavoidable " danger zone " of our fleet-building, and our object, the peaceful equalizing of our rights with those of England, was within sight of fulfilment.[1]

England did not fear an attack from us. She had a guarantee against this in our unfavourable strategical situation in the " wet triangle," which did not in-

---

[1] The predominant opinion of political circles was summed up by a progressive Reichstag Deputy, Heckscher; I quote from a pamphlet: " Why did England abandon the policy of encirclement against us? We owe this to the creation of the German fleet." The illusion, to be sure, now swung over in German fashion to the opposite extreme. Instead of rejoicing in the position that had been won and the security of peace, people were intoxicated with the idea that the policy of encirclement had been " abandoned " at one stroke. These exaggerations in one direction and another were fatal to us.

crease, but limited, the effectiveness of our fleet, and together with our lack of any strong naval allies could not produce a desire for war in any responsible German. There was another guarantee in the proportion of five German to eight English squadrons, with which we had declared our ultimate aim satisfied, and further in the Emperor's notorious love of peace, and over and above everything else in the simple and fundamental fact of our position in the world, that we gained in and by peace more than was ever imaginable in the most glorious war.

England and Germany both experienced in themselves the truth of the old saying " *Si vis pacem, para bellum,*" which the German did not grasp until the coming of the great Prussian kings after unhappy centuries of self-annihilation. Trade and travel increased in both countries by leaps and bounds. The military burdens were borne with a jest, and had productive results in the fullest sense of the word. A real balance of power was appearing on the political horizon.

British statesmen naturally did not stress the fact, in their conversations with Germans, that it was mainly the presence of our nearly completed fleet in the North Sea that had produced their respectful tone, and had lessened the probability of a British attack. Of course they only spoke about their peaceful inclinations, and less of the facts which strengthened these inclinations. To-day the English are glad that the war has come, in the same sense as the American Ambassador Gerard said to me after the outbreak of war, that he could not understand our allowing the war to happen, for we should have outstripped the English by peaceful means within a few years. But the English could hardly imagine in July, 1914, that our Government would keep the German fleet from striking. They did not think of war at all light-heartedly therefore. That stroke of genius, the policy of encirclement, which was to drive the noble quarry, Germany, to its death, was on the point of being broken by the growth of our power.

So far as I had honourably contributed to the preservation of peace, I looked back upon my life's work with satisfaction, and felt that the conclusion of the Navy Bill was not far off, when I could lay the completed task in the hands of my successor. He could then stand at the wheel in the petty war of officials and parliament; the German navy had done its work, in the sense of Stosch and of myself, if it maintained by its strength peace and liberty upon the seas.

Never before in the course of her long history was Germany more powerful and more respected by the greatest ones of the earth than in these days; never had she thriven more richly. In the judgment of experienced men of affairs, such as Prince Bülow for example, in his *Deutsche Politik,* we were to all intents and purposes "over the hill," and we had asserted our right to a place in the world. German civilization and economy were making up in full measure, in Eastern Asia, Africa, South America, and the Near East, for what our history had neglected to do. Just a few more years of calm and skilful leadership and we could not have been uprooted as a world-state in the sense of Roosevelt's words spoken in 1904: "The prosperity of a nation has not normally the significance of a threat, but of a hope for the other nations." A chance, which in a certain sense is symbolical of the tragedy of the world-war, decreed that the Anglo-German colonial agreement was sent over to our London Ambassador in its final form for his signature on the very day of the declaration of war.

The ill-will of the Entente Powers ought at no moment to have been under-estimated. But in spite of this, the situation was not lost for German diplomacy when the Serbian challenge was sent to Austria in the summer of 1914. It only had to be handled frankly and at the right moment. An immediate request from our Emperor to the Czar, asking the latter to assist in obtaining satisfaction, might have been successful, and would at least have favourably influenced our political situation.

So far as Germany was concerned there was never a menace of any moment in the will to war, but it rested solely in the fatal mediocrity of the politicians in office.

II

On July 5th, 1914, the Austrian Ambassador handed in to the German Emperor at Potsdam a letter from the Emperor Francis Joseph, which had been brought by Count Hoyos, the Chief of Cabinet of the Austro-Hungarian Foreign Minister, Count Berchtold, to-gether with a memorandum which had been drawn up

before the assassination. This stated, as was reported
to me when I was in Tarasp, that the threads of the
conspiracy stretched to Belgrade; the Austrian Government would approach Serbia with a demand for the
fullest satisfaction, and if this was not given would
march her troops into Serbia.

The Emperor William, with his chivalrous feelings,
promised loyalty and support against the Serbian mur-
derers in reply to the Austrian Emperor's personal
request. According to the statements which he made
to my deputy in the park of the Potsdam Neues-Palais
on the morning of July 6th, the Emperor did not consider an intervention by Russian to protect Serbia as
probable, because the Czar would not support the assas-
sins of royalty, and moreover Russia was at the time
militarily and financially unfit for war. The Emperor
proceeded to argue in somewhat sanguine fashion that
France would put the brake on Russia, because of
France's unfavourable financial position and her shortage of heavy artillery. The Emperor did not mention
England; there was no thought of complications with
this State. Thus the Emperor himself regarded any
far-reaching dangers as improbable. He hoped that
Serbia would give way, but he considered it necessary
to be prepared for any other issue of the Austro-
Serbian settlement. For this reason he summoned in
due course on July 5th the Imperial Chancellor von
Bethmann-Hollweg, the Minister of War von Falken-
hayn, the Foreign Under-Secretary Zimmermann, and
the Chief of the Military Cabinet von Lyncker. It was

decided that measures which were calculated to arouse political attention or incur special expenses were to be avoided.

After this decision the Emperor went on his previously planned Scandinavian voyage on the advice of his Chancellor.

It was the constitutional duty and the supreme obligation of the Chancellor to examine the promise to Austria from the political standpoint of Germany's interests, and to keep its execution in hand. The Chancellor approved of the Emperor's decision, assuming as he did that Austria's crumbling position as a Great Power would go to pieces if it did not receive any satisfaction from the acquisitive Serbian State. The memory of the Bosnian crisis may also have had some influence.

I am not informed about the political activities of the Emperor during his Scandinavian voyage. I have reason to believe, however, that he did not notice any grave danger to the world's peace. When the Emperor did not consider that peace was threatened, he liked to give free play to his reminiscences of famous ancestors. In moments which he realized to be critical, on the other hand, he proceeded with extraordinary caution. If the Emperor had remained in Berlin, and if the normal Government machinery had been at work, then the Emperor in spite of his sporadic dealings with foreign policy would probably have found ways and means of evading the danger of war about the middle of the month. As, however, the Chief of the General Staff, the Minister of War, the Chief of the Admiralty Staff, and I were kept away from Berlin during the succeeding days, the whole business was monopolized by the Chancellor, who, having no experience himself of the great European world, was unable to estimate correctly the value of his collaborators in the Foreign Office.

The Chancellor at any rate did not write to me for advice.

The events of July, and particularly Germany's part in them, are now so completely exposed by a series of partly official publications, that it does not seem to me to be in Germany's interests any longer for me to conceal my opinion.

After the experiences of the world-war the question might be raised whether the German nation ought not to have come to an agreement in time with the neighbours and heirs of the Austro-Hungarian monarchy as to their partition. But if the opposite policy was pursued, which was in keeping with a sense of loyalty and with our historical development, and if the integrity and status of the Hapsburg monarchy as an ally was maintained, then the Chancellor was right when he considered that sufficient satisfaction must be given by Serbia to Austria. For it was only by this means that Austria could once more be made a useful member of the Triple Alliance, and her internal decay perhaps stopped. The mistake made in Berlin and Vienna only began with the treatment of the whole affair. In spite of Count Tisza's warnings, Bethmann and Berchtold were unable to imagine that sufficient satisfaction could be obtained in other ways than by threatening an advance by Austrian troops. So Berlin laid itself out from the first to achieve the double aim of giving tottering Austria the necessary support for swift and sudden action, but on the other hand of "localizing" the conflict. In the event of the Serbian reply proving insufficient, which was considered probable, Austria was to insist on satisfaction by marching her troops into Serbia; and Vienna intended to give Bulgaria an opportunity of joining in any military operations, but this idea was received sceptically in Berlin. Every nerve was to be strained, however, to prevent this local and limited Balkan war from spreading to Europe. In spite of the most energetic endeavours on the part of the Chancellor, however, to maintain peace among the Great Powers, the world-war broke out. Consequently the question arises, how in spite of Austria's indubitable right to satisfaction, and to a clearing out of the Serbian nest of conspirators, it has been possible for the enemy, regardless of all the efforts of the German Government to keep the peace, to convince almost the whole world of Germany's guilt in the world-war?

I intend in the following pages to contribute a little to the solution of this riddle, and that is only possible by discussing the political psychology of Bethmann-Hollweg.

As early as July 11th the Berlin Foreign Office was convinced that the Entente had advised Belgrade to give way, though I learnt this some years afterwards. In this the Chancellor had the means wherewith to untie the knot. He drew, however, from the assumption that the Entente did not want a war, the short-sighted conclusion that Austria could probably force an entry into Serbia, regardless of the Entente, without endangering the peace of the world. For, as Zimmermann has said, on July 8th it was assumed in Berlin "that if Austria advanced into Serbia, England and even France would combine with us to influence Russia so as to localize the conflict." The strength of the connection between the three Great Powers was under-estimated, and therefore the danger of a universal war also. The perfectly comprehensible disinclination on the part of human beings to confess to mistakes that they have made makes it difficult for the Chancellor and his following to confess frankly to their optimism, which was so ruinous for Germany at that time. I possess, however, in the reports of my department sufficient reflections of the atmosphere of the Wilhelm-strasse in those days. On July 13th the Chancellor had been informed on the essential points of the intended ultimatum, upon which I received a communication in Tarasp from my deputy. The portion of the letter sent to me ran as follows:

"Our Ambassador in Vienna, Herr von Tchirschky, has learned privately, and also from Count Berchtold, that the Note to be sent by Austria to Serbia will put the following demands:

"1. A proclamation from King Peter to his people,

calling upon them to dissociate themselves from the Greater-Serbian agitation.

" 2. The participation of a high Austrian official in the inquiry into the assassination.

" 3. The dismissal and punishment of all officers and officials who are shown to have had a share in it."

I knew nothing about the Entente having advised Belgrade to keep the peace as was optimistically assumed in the Wilhelmstrasse at the time. It strikes me as peculiar to-day, that the Entente has not been able to bring forward conclusive documents proving its intervention in Belgrade in the interests of peace. The Serbian murder could not indeed very well be countenanced by any civilized State. When I received that communication in Tarasp, my very first impression was that this ultimatum was unacceptable to the Serbians and might easily lead to a world-war. I never believed in the possibility of "localizing" the Austro-Serbian passage of arms with regard to Russia, just as little as I had any faith in England's neutrality in a continental war. I wrote to my deputy in this sense and recommended an agreement with the Czar.

This suggestion had no effect.

I saw that the danger of the situation lay particularly in the fact that England formed the final link in the Entente chain.

The traditional hostility of Pan-Slavism towards the German Empire and the Austro-Russian jealousy in the Balkans continued to exist in spite of the Potsdam meeting in 1910, and the Russian *intelligentsia* had allowed themselves to get heated about our Balkan policy between 1908 and 1914. The circles represented by the *Novoye Vremya* wanted the war, although not before 1916. Yet Sassonov and the Czar still had the reins sufficiently in hand so that German policy could in my own firm conviction steer off the Russian impulse towards expansion from us and Austria-Hungary, by giving it an opening on other fronts that were not vital to us. It was only the clumsiness of our policy which brought the Russian war-party to the top and ultimately made it possible for Suchomlinov to deceive the Czar.

Russia certainly had no right to make a war out of the chastisement of Belgrade, but the danger that large Russian circles would demand a war ought not to have been under-estimated. I was convinced even before the ultimatum that the St. Petersburg warparty would be held in check if we treated with the Czar in confidence; if we acted too directly, then we might almost certainly reckon that England would let loose the war in conformity with a century-old political tradition of the maintenance of " continental balance of power " as she understood it. I laid stress on this danger of arousing the slumbering English will-to-war in a conversation with Prince Henry, who visited me in Tarasp in the middle of July. My views were shared by Minister of State von Loebell, and the Saxon Ambassador von Salzo, who were both staying there.

The question of interrupting my cure was then settled by the Chancellor asking me not to return to Berlin, so as to avoid sensation. As late as July 24th the Chancellory telephoned to the Admiralty that my return would render the situation more acute. I could not consider that a return on my own account would be either correct or useful, particularly as the Chancellor, who had been upset by the issue of the Supplementary Bill dispute in 1912, kept me out of foreign affairs with a certain jealousy, and had begun to weave stories about me to the effect that I interfered with his policy. For the rest I was unable to obtain a clear picture of what was going on from the daily reports of my department, which was naturally only badly informed by the Foreign Office, and in consequence I received the impression that no Power would take upon itself the responsibility of a bigger conflict. We had been accustomed to these tensions for years. Bülow had always mastered them. The intensification of the situation after the delivery of the ultimatum, and particularly the news of the return of our fleet into home waters, finally caused me to return home on July 27th without consulting the Chancellor.

The ultimatum was handed to the Serbian Government on July 23rd; July 16th had originally been agreed upon for this, but Vienna postponed the event in order to wait for the departure from St. Petersburg of President Poincaré, who was working for war. This postponement was regretted in Berlin because it led to the fading of the fresh impression of the assassination and consequently of the motive for intervention. This difference of opinion between Berlin and Vienna was dominated by the endeavour of both Governments to maintain the peace of the world, and they only differed in their views as to the method of how to tackle the Serbian wasps' nest so as to not endanger peace. Berlin's standpoint was probably the more correct. If an advance was to be made into Serbia at all, which was indeed far more dangerous than the originators of the idea considered probable, swift and impressive action should at least have been taken so that negotiations could have been introduced all the more readily after a pledge had been secured.

German policy gave up the most difficult psychological problem, when the Serbian reply was known.

On July 25th, Serbia accepted the demands of the Austrian ultimatum in the main, and declared her readiness to negotiate the rest. How far England, Russia, France, and Italy had helped Austria to a certain diplomatic success by pressure on Belgrade, I do not know. At any rate it cannot be denied that the Serbian reply showed an unexpected compliance, and I do not think that the Austrian Government showed a right sense of proportion when it declared this reply to be unacceptable as a basis for further negotiations. But Dethmann-Hollweg and Count Berchtold did not grasp the tangibility of the diplomatic success which had already been achieved. As Austria's honour had been saved, and Bethmann-Hollweg also had endeavoured to prevent a European war, the danger of war could probably have been regarded as averted if Austria had been satisfied with her success. She could have given the Serbs a short space of time for the immediate fulfilment of the desired concessions, as a condition for negotiations regarding the other demands. Even if international supervision had then been imposed for the other demands, the high value to Austria of the accomplished humiliation of Serbia with England's consent would not have been diminished.

Things went otherwise. The helm was put over the wrong way and the ship continued to turn in the direction that had been taken. Bethmann and Berchtold did not clearly see the imponderabilia which would result if they made the Serbian reply a ground for marching troops into the country. Although the reply offered a possibility for future negotiations, this was passed over, and it was not seen how dangerously the St. Petersburg war party was strengthened thereby. Trust in the peaceful intentions of the Entente, and England particularly, gave rise to a hope in the statesmen of the Central Powers of localizing the Serbian conflict, and led to a stiffening of Vienna's tone towards Serbia. In order to put a complete stop to the undermining of Austria by the Serbs, they plunged into a far greater danger, and jumped out of the frying-pan into the fire.

The acuteness of the situation now caused the Chancellor and Sir Edward Grey to put forward proposals of mediation. I cannot touch upon the mistake which

the Imperial Chancellor made, in my opinion, in his
treatment of the English proposals of mediation which
began on July 25th, without previously acknowledging
Bethmann's good intentions.

The Chancellor diplomatically announced in absolutely conclusive fashion his endeavour to prevent the
world-war. I may mention here the resumption of
the Austro-Russian negotiations which had stopped in
consequence of a Russian misunderstanding; further,
Bethmann's direct and moderating influence upon Vienna, beginning after the rejection of the Serbian
reply; and finally the spontaneous offer of the proposal of mediation, and to limit the Austrian occupation of Serbia to holding that country in pawn until
Serbia had given satisfaction. These proofs of Bethmann's desire for peace are followed by others which
will be discussed later. How was it possible, then,
that peace should be wrecked in spite of so many good
intentions? Because the fundamentally false hope of
a real will-to-peace on the part of the Entente and
England particularly, which had created the belief
in a localization of the chastisement of Serbia, still
continued to take effect, and lowered still further the
slight diplomatic skill of our leaders.

When Sir Edward Grey suggested on July 26th
that England and Germany, with France and Italy,
should undertake mutual mediation, the Chancellor
did not realize the opportunity which offered itself,
just as in the case of the Serbian answer. Caution
was, to be sure, advisable with English proposals of

conference. It had been Germany's experience to find herself at a disadvantage in conferences of the Great Powers, as a result of the superior diplomatic weight of the strongest sea-power and the corresponding partisan attitude of the assembly. At this point, however, the European " areopagus " (as Bethmann called it), proposed by Grey, ought not to have been refused, because it offered the sole possibility of still averting the world-war. Bethmann could have accepted Grey's proposal of an ambassadorial conference immediately, on the condition that Austria-Hungary might secure for herself a pledge in Serbia, as Grey conceded later (July 30th) at Bethmann-Hollweg's suggestion. The Chancellor, however, took up a standpoint which gave the enemy a pretext for asserting that the Chancellor considered it beneath Austria's dignity to accept the "good services " of four Great Powers; that in addition, Germany did not want to interfere in the Serbian affair; and further that the Austro-Serbian conflict had occurred and was unavoidable. His argument was that one could only try to localize it. Accordingly he telegraphed to Lichnowsky on July 27th: " It is impossible for us to allow our ally to be brought before a European court in this dispute with Serbia." A report of the Austrian Ambassador says that on the same day Jagow informed him of the disinclination of the German Government to take up Grey's proposal of a conference.

There could have been doubts about the degree of loyalty in Grey's proposal. Such doubts, however,

ought not to have decided the question of acceptance.
The Central Powers should have reserved guarantees
for themselves: as I have already mentioned, Grey
raised no difficulties on July 30th when Bethmann
demanded such a guarantee of a pledge for Austria.
If Grey did withdraw his proposal of a conference
before Bethmann-Hollweg's refusal of it was known
to him, it is not certain whether he was influenced
by a desire to render the negotiations more difficult.
Even he could have promised himself more from direct
Austro-Russian negotiations at that time. He would
then have found himself in agreement with the Chancellor, who, although he rejected the idea of a conference, was trying to mediate directly between Vienna
and St. Petersburg.

The secondary mistake committed by Berlin in refusing a conference was just as great as the primary
one of relying too much on the disinclination of the
Entente to go to war. Bethmann showed himself
over-sensitive for the dignity of the Austro-Hungarian
State, which was not identical with the German Empire, but which the policy of the Chancellor at that
time had bound to us for life or death. Bethmann
contended further that we should not interfere in a
procedure which had been approved by him and the
Foreign Office since July 5th. Jagow was so little
interested in the Austro-Serbian conflict that he con-
fessed to the German Ambassador on July 27th that
he had not yet found time to read the Serbian reply
to Austria. How are such diplomatic mistakes at a

fatal hour to be explained? They can only be explained by the general characteristics of the political system which we had had in control of the Empire since 1909. The question at issue was indeed the avoidance of a world-war, but as a Royal Prussian Assize Court would certainly have decided that the just Austrian and the unjust Serbian causes were a purely Austro-Serbian affair, Grey's proposal to a different effect had to be interpreted as not being to the point. Legal narrow-mindedness is not, however, sufficient to explain the complete absence of instinct with which the Chancellor proceeded in this matter. The real explanation is that deeper quality which sealed the fate of most *démarches* during his Chancellorship, the lack of the sense of reality in so many Germans.

III

Bethmann-Hollweg had been building for years at a "house of cards," as he himself afterwards called it—in other words, an Anglo-German understanding that was not based upon facts, but upon diplomatic flattery.

Outsiders may think that if only one arrives somehow at a conference table and exchanges friendly words across it, clearing up misunderstandings and opening up prospects into the distant future, a great deal will have been gained. English policy has only used such things to inveigle others; England herself, however, allowed the issue of the negotiations to be

determined by the unspoken realities which remained
under the table. After Bethmann had been prevented
in 1912 from exchanging for English kindnesses and
promises the only reality which had any weight in
our favour—that is, the German fleet—the prospects
of a permanent and real understanding had perceptibly
increased. But those realities which weighed in England's favour ought not to have been overlooked. The
world obeyed in general the command of the strongest sea-power. We were its most powerful counter-
part, but we had to be careful for that very reason
not to go further than our interests unavoidably demanded. Those illusions about England which almost reduced our naval armament below the safety
level in 1912, and would have determined the inevitable but probably slow ruin of Germany, were now
suddenly endangering peace. The motives which had
prompted England to "loyalty" towards Austria and
us during the Balkan wars of 1912-14 were idealized,
and it was consequently believed that even a Balkan
war in which Austria herself would take part could
be localized within the storm-centre of Europe.

As far back as July 9th the sober view had been
represented in the Foreign Office that if, contrary to
all expectation, the maintenance of the world's peace
was not accomplished, England would probably immediately join in on the side of our enemies, without
waiting to see the course taken by the war. The
peaceful attitude of the English Foreign Office in the
ensuing weeks deceived the Bethmann circle more and

more, however. There was even an inclination towards a peaceable view of England in the General Staff. When Grey's warning words were known after the delivery of the ultimatum: "The situation would be very dangerous, and a war between the four Great Powers might easily ensue," the learned ones of the Wilhelmstrasse squeezed out of this sentence the assurance that Grey wanted to stress the fact that no danger of war existed with the fifth Great Power, England. Jagow, Stumm, and others strengthened the Chancellor in such ill-founded ideas. They also succeeded in winning over the Emperor to them. When the fleet, which was in Norway, received orders to return home on July 25th, the Emperor wanted to send all the big battleships into the Baltic. The Foreign Office desired the same, so as not to provoke England. The Emperor, however, bluntly told the Commander-in-Chief of the Fleet at the time that no doubts as to England's peaceable attitude were allowed; the whole fleet therefore would be held in readiness against the Russians. Technical reasons alone caused him to consent to a part of the fleet going to the North Sea.

I must raise against the British Cabinet the grave charge that, although it was well aware of Bethmann's love of peace and his whole nature, it brought upon itself a large share of the responsibility for the outbreak of war by its vagueness as to England's attitude during the crisis, even though it is granted that the English Cabinet really wanted peace at first and

had not any *arrière pensées* from the outset of allowing Bethmann to run his head into a noose. Grey
would have been able to preserve peace if he had made
clear in time to Bethmann England's attitude in the
event of the Austro-Serbian conflict extending to the
rest of Europe. That he omitted to do this is more
surprising than the fact that Lloyd George did not
hesitate to threaten us openly at the instigation of
the Cabinet in July, 1911, although the situation at
that time was by no means so acute. This time a
corresponding private warning was even avoided.
Grey's silence about England's attitude strengthened
in their opinion those Berlin politicians who favoured
invasion of Serbia. Grey and the English Cabinet knew exactly that Bethmann would do everything
to avoid a war with England. They also knew that
there were very few politicians in Germany who had
any adequate idea of England's ability to annihilate
another nation without mercy. Only a few of us could
look into England's soul, with its cold indifference
towards subject peoples, like the Irish or the Indians
for example; it is the year 1919 that first brought
this home to the average German. Previously many
people in Germany had the idea that the more defenceless Germany was, the more free play England would
give her. If only our politicians had realized the true
spirit of English policy, they would have armed to
the utmost on the one hand, and would have diplomatically exercised the greatest caution on the other,
so as to give England no opportunity for annihilating

our people. The British Ministers knew in what state of terrible delusion many Germans lived as to the dangerous nature of Germany's position. They also knew that Germany could not make a vital question for herself out of the plus or the deficit of Serbia's satisfaction. In spite of this they omitted to give any timely warning. Whether history will succeed in bringing to light the real extent and the reasons for this British ambiguity, I must leave to the future.

In the days of July the German Government brought upon itself grave blame with regard to the German people, but not England or the Entente, by its ignorance of the world. England, who had whipped up the French desire for revenge for the already half-forgotten Alsace-Lorraine, and had made important concessions to the Russians in order to orientate them against Germany, was only reaping the fruits of her own endeavours when matters came to war. Strong tendencies to attack us were still in full swing in England, just as in Germany there existed a justifiable anxiety aroused by England that the policy of encirclement would some time and somehow change to one of force. The question whether England considered that the given moment had come in July, 1914, retires in view of this. Some time in July a moment did occur in England, of which Grey had said to Sassonov in September, 1912, " that if the circumstances in question were to come to pass, England would do all she could to inflict a most sensible blow on the power of Germany." Doubt can only exist as to the exact

point of time in July at which this change was effected
in the British Cabinet. England was geographically
and militarily in the fortunate position of being able
to keep in the background, and with her usual mastery
to keep her puritanical humanitarian face at the very
moment when she had decided to go to war. In
doing so the British Cabinet corrupted not only the
English nation, but also the German, which has always fallen a victim to foreign hypocrisy ever since
the time of the Goths. Suchomlinov would never have
set the machinery of the war in motion had he not
been certain that the British power was ready to
join in.

After the events of the last year there was scarcely
any possible doubt that England would never countenance a military weakening of France by us, and in
the event of an invasion of Serbia the possibility of
a war with Russia and consequently with France had
to be taken into account when the matter was looked
at from the most unfavourable point of view. As
Bethmann, however, was not willing to recognize that
England's peaceableness was a result of our growing
sea-power, but preferred to interpret it sentimentally,
he also lacked all feeling for the real *limits* of this
peaceableness. The inclination for an understanding
which was rising in England in spite of everything
reposed, as I have said, principally upon a sober estimate of the decreasing profitableness of a war. England had begun to acknowledge our power so long
as in English opinion we acknowledged hers. We

might regard this as going too far, but we had to adapt ourselves to the general situation. Bethmann on the other hand, who had failed to appreciate German interests in 1912, now failed to realize the extent of England's claims, and in July, 1914, he once more hoped for a settlement made in good heart instead of with an eye on the main chance. His same insufficiently developed sense of reality, which dealt feebly with the requirements of the State, also saw the British line of thought unclearly, and thus supplied by his lack of dexterity the opportunity for the Entente to draw its net tight.

England wanted to allow Austria some diplomatic success over Serbia, but she could not permit a diplomatic defeat of Russia, without shattering the artificial structure of the latter's power which she had erected against Germany. Bethmann's and Berchtold's policy of invading Serbia was on the contrary based on the expectation that the love of peace shown by England in recent years would go so far as to cause the Czar, if the worst came to the worst, either to refuse his traditional patronage to the Serbs or to venture on a continental war without England's help. German politicians failed to perceive that this would threaten to cut the sinews of England's Entente policy.

Just because her relations with France, and with Russia too, were not based upon a formal treaty of alliance, but upon looser agreements, England had accompanied on principle every kindness towards us, during the ten years of the encirclement period, by

unmistakable signs in the other direction. During
that visit of the English fleet to Kiel at the end of
June, 1914, the British Ambassador in St. Petersburg,
Buchanan, announced the conclusion of an Anglo-Russian naval convention. The charming wife of the
commander of the English squadron in Kiel, Lady
Warrender, an Anglo-Saxon of the type of those political women which we scarcely know in Germany, was
rather embarrassed when I referred to this fact with
gentle irony. I said that it was all the same to us
whether in the event of war British and Russian
squadrons operated together or apart, but it might
easily lead to a misunderstanding if such trains of
thought were voiced at that moment. She described
Buchanan as a simple-minded blunderer. Whether
rightly or not, the fact of the convention as such
ought to have sharpened our wits.

Whilst we gave England the choice, by means of
an unskilful and clumsy imitation of the Bosnian crisis
in 1908-9, of either putting the Grand-Ducal party
out of humour or of opening the war under particularly advantageous conditions, there came to the surface the feeling of those London clubs whose minds
were steadfastly fixed on the war and left it to a favourable moment to decide when we should be struck
down by force. When in the course of July, England
realized the *cul-de-sac* into which Bethmann had got
himself, she turned away from the businesslike peace
policy of an understanding, which she kept up until
Grey's proposal of a conference (if we are to believe

her assurances) and turned to the no less business-like policy of war in order, in her character of " perfidious Albion," to make Russians and Germans kill one another. The opportunity which we offered them could never again return so favourably. They now had the possibility of putting us morally in the wrong, and of interpreting the follies of our policy as agitation for war. They could throw the overwhelming power of the world against us, and by making us appear as the attacker—which Bethmann never thought of—deprive even our own alliances of their legal value.

Finally the moment itself was tempting strategically to the English, which Bethmann did not know, and he did not consult me about it. Although the British Cabinet only came into the war hesitatingly, the will-to-war in it gained the upper hand in the situation, and ultimately put the match to the fuse by means of secret encouragement of the French, and consequently of the Russians.

Bethmann did not want a world-war, and did not expect that one would break out. He therefore believed that Austria might venture on a local war. Neither he nor Jagow had the power of reversing the actual situation; they did not see that the Entente Powers showed on the one hand a certain degree of readiness to settle this local crisis mutually, but on the other hand they were not at all frightened of a world-war. Bethmann and Jagow persisted in their conviction that the Austro-Serbian conflict was unavoidable, but could be localized, for irretrievable

days, until the forces which were working for war
within the Entente, and were grossly under-estimated
by them, had won the day. It now happened that
French chauvinism and Pan-Slav anger had risen in
the same degree as the English desire for war had
decreased. Certainly the deciding power was England,
but she only kept the bellicose forces in check so long
as peace seemed more advantageous to her than war.
Fear of Europe's "intervention," and the hope that
the Entente "faced by an unalterable fact" would
adjust itself to it, had induced Bethmann-Hollweg
to give a free hand to Austria's policy of invasion.
So that he believed that he could steer past a general
conflict by a short local war. Then when, contrary
to expectation, Serbia's reply was not altogether "negative," and when Grey "intervened," Bethmann lacked
the instinct to grasp the whole new situation.

They had in the Wilhelmstrasse a peculiar conception of the possibilities of securing the earnestly desired peace by means of a nervous preparation for
war, which was mere weak pretence in the main.
These politicians who never wanted to draw the sword,
and who were unfortunately unable, as results have
shown, to judge the military requirements of a preparation for war, believed that they were able to
threaten with uncertain military measures which they
themselves did not take seriously.

The political sense of proportion of these men fills
one with amazement. On July 20th the Secretary of
State, von Jagow, declared to a representative of the

Admiralty Staff that, if it came to a war between the Triple Alliance and the Dual Alliance, England would probably not join in. He, Jagow, had an idea, however, by which one might still increase the inclinations of the English to remain neutral, and this was to threaten the English with the immediate occupation of Holland if they declared war against us. The whole thing would naturally only be a bluff. The next day, after discussing the matter in the Admiralty, the Admiral told Jagow that his "bluff" would be the surest means of compelling England to come in against us. The reflected splendour of Bismarck's authority, that still lay over the Wilhelmstrasse in the eyes of the officers of my Ministry, was fast fading away, and the incident was reported to me with the comment: "One could only ask oneself again: how is it possible that the conduct of German foreign policy is entrusted to such a personality?" Jagow had been put at the head of the Foreign Office by Bethmann on account of his cautious nature which rendered any decision difficult for him. He would have been the last person to occupy Holland, an action which would have been contrary to all German interests. He now thought that he could make an impression on England by a "strong" gesture, with just the same *naïveté* with which he had displayed to the French Ambassador a few months previously an appetite for Belgian colonies that Germany did not really possess in view of her almost unopened African territories.

When Bethmann later became aware that England would seriously go to war, he broke down completely. But why did he rely so long with regard to England on his own political reckoning which had so often been wrong? Why did he pay no attention during those long three weeks to all the warnings that reached him from England and about England? Why did he not endeavour to procure some assurance as to England's attitude in the event of a continental war? This riddle too is explained by the peculiarity of his fundamental scheme.

IV

On July 8th the Under-Secretary of State, Zimmermann, issued directions that all conspicuous measures, such as interruption of leave, etc., were to be avoided, just as the Emperor's voyage had not been abandoned. For the main essential of the success of the localization of the war would be to avoid the impression that we were inciting Austria.

During the negotiations of 1911-12 it had struck me that Bethmann-Hollweg avoided straight and open discussions, and preferred to settle even such questions, the nature of which demanded general deliberation, suddenly with an accomplished fact after long and hesitating delay. In addition there was Bethmann's capacity, which had been early noticed by one of my colleagues, and also by his admirers, "of asserting something which would not be taken at all seriously, and of not merely putting the matter objec-

tively, but subjectively also." [1]   The aim of the procedure which he had chosen here was good—the avoidance of the world-war.   But the means used to this
end were unskilful; for they helped considerably to
promote the world-war.   Bethmann did not see that
ambiguity did not bring us any respect in such a
matter, and was extraordinarily dangerous.   The
world would not believe that Austria had sent Notes
to Serbia without our having previous knowledge of
them.   For this bureaucratic method of catching people napping, brought to bear, as it were, on a European
affair, and on statesmen of the rank of the English
instead of an open discussion which would have
awakened confidence, changed the already heavily
laden atmosphere to a higher state of tension.

From reports of July 11th, I find that it was con-
jectured in the Foreign Office at the time, that the
Austrians would have preferred us to have refused
them our help as an ally against Serbia.   Our ally
knew so little what she wanted, it was said, that
she now asked us what she was actually to demand
of the Serbs.

This impression was scarcely correct.   It showed
how little Berlin ought to reckon on Austria remaining firm in the course which she had taken to save
her honour.   In spite of this the Chancellor failed to
realize how unenviable his position and how enormous his responsibility before history would be, if

---

[1] H. Kötschke, *Unser Reichskanzler sein Leben und Wirken*
(Berlin, 1916), p. 17 *et seq.*

he appeared as the man who had left Germany's
future in the hands of the Vienna Government without any further control.

This attitude was bound to deprive our policy of
the reputation for straightforwardness which Frederick the Great and Bismarck had won for it. Trust-
worthiness is also an asset of power which must be
carefully treasured, and it is a remarkable phenomenon that politicians with only a slight understanding
of real power generally have no fine sense for the
imponderabilia of prestige.   When Grey's proposal
of a conference arrived, Bethmann thought he had
better stick to his attitude, and so he refused the
proposal; in other words, he stood by his declaration
of "non-intervention" in the Austrian affair, which
meant that the decisive moment for a possible action
in favour of peace was lost.   Thus Austria was able
to intensify the situation by her declaration of war
on Serbia (July 28th) whilst German policy stood
spellbound within its self-imposed limits.

The English with their cool way of discussing
questions of power could or would not understand
Bethmann apparently standing aside, although his
doing so actually purposed the localization of the conflict and the maintenance of peace between the Great
Powers.   It was, however, remote from their own
way of thinking to assume that a German statesman
might think it wrong openly to support Austria and
talk about Germany's interests of power and prestige.
They noticed that German diplomats were partly too

distrustful and partly too confiding. At the same time they saw the most favourable opportunity for war approaching. In the inconsistency of our policy of invading Serbia we offered the Entente the pretext for imputing to us the *preventive war*. The grave charge of war agitation, which has done us such immeasurable harm, was raised.

The encirclement policy of the Entente had at any rate several times occasioned some nervousness in Germany. For it evinced indubitable symptoms of a conspiracy. Since the end of 1912 we knew that the Serbs were intended for the part of the Piedmont of the Balkans, of beginning the disintegration of the Hapsburg Monarchy when the time should be ripe. We were not far from stamping out these sparks then before they could burst into flame, and indeed this was seriously considered by Austria in 1913, but turned down by Italy and us. Further, we had heard of Russian utterances to the effect that something was going to begin in 1916. Consequently one occasionally met with the view expressed by irresponsible and half-informed people, but solely by such people that " *If* the war cannot be avoided, *then* the sooner the better." The Russian armaments, which " were to be ready in 1916," were not to be taken too lightly on account of the St. Petersburg war-party, which actually availed itself of the European confusion in the last week of July, 1914, to set going the whole conflagration. In spite of this a German preventive war against Russia could never have been justified. Moreover, our caution with regard to England, not to mention France, ought not to have slumbered. If the British lion had cringed more and more since 1912, we had still to reckon with the possibility of this only being the crouch before the spring. Slight doubts of this kind, however, did not exclude co-operation on a large scale with England on a real foundation. Only we ought not to have given it any cause to spring. England's ententes were only loosely woven until the treaty of September, 1914, and a peaceful solution of the policy of encirclement seemed possible, however, in view of the English fear of the risk, provided Germany was at the same time courageous and cautious, and armed herself undismayed, but avoided leaving any excuse for the enemy's will-to-war.

The story that Germany worked systematically for the war is a wild fable which is best refuted by our unpreparedness for war, as I shall show later. For the rest, General von Moltke, who was taking the cure at Carlsbad during the critical weeks, assured me later that he had nothing to do with the negotiations, and had never recommended that the ultimatum to Serbia should be used as a test to see if the Entente wanted war, or did not yet consider itself strong enough.

If the Chancellor had consulted me, as was his duty —he must reconnoitre the military possibilities in every direction before taking such a course—then I should have had to tell him that from the standpoint of the navy the danger of war, which was undesirable in itself, would not offer any favourable strategical opportunities. The building of dreadnoughts, by the introduction of which England automatically doubled the fighting force of our navy, had only been going on for four years. The Kiel Canal was not ready. The fleet would not reach its maximum until 1920. Several weaknesses which were inherent in our navy, particularly in its leadership, in consequence of its youthfulness would only disappear in the course of time. Even if the number of ships did not increase, the navy became better and better every year, like young wine. The mechanical comparison of the number of ships lost its significance as the psychological moment of internal organization grew in importance. The French had openly expressed their doubts as to whether we should really be so " foolish " as to reduce the number of our ships in building from 1912 onwards according to the Navy Bill. We had dared to do so, and thereby given England sound proof that we were not taking part in a race of armaments. In spite of this fact, and although our alliance did not guarantee us any important or certain support at sea, I reckoned that from about 1916 onwards an English attack would no longer be probable from a naval point of view. Every year of peace was therefore an inestimable gain for us. I left no doubt as to these views of mine in my conversations at Tarasp.

If the Chancellor had only consulted his colleagues in his treatment of this question, as no other statesman would have failed to do, he would have divided

the responsibility. I for my part should have advised
against the ultimatum.

In his fear of clearness, the Chancellor was so little
prepared for the war that collective consultations between the political and military leaders never took
place, either on the politico-strategical problems of the
conduct of the war or even on the prospects of a world-
war at all. I was never even informed of the invasion
of Belgium, which immediately raised naval questions
when it took place. It might here be interjected,
whether I for my part was not in a position to urge
for the preparations of a mobilization of the whole
Government in time of peace? Nobody who knows
the conditions that existed in our governing bodies
at that time will ask this question.

Bethmann's greatest mistake from the point of view
of the history of the world does not lie in his mis-
calculations of July, 1914, but in his failure to make
preparations beforehand during the years when the
enemy coalition was collecting all its forces, and
strengthening by means of warlike preparations the
resolve in its continental members to avail themselves
of any opportunity for an armed battle against Germany. With little trouble and at an expense that
would have been scarcely perceptible in the long run,
the German nation could have been guarded against
the blow of this war, even though constant fear of
it had occasioned the necessary measure of precaution. The danger was there; the consequences had to
be deduced from it. For France and Russia had

reached the limit of their powers in their armaments, and France had even exceeded them in a certain sense. Germany and Austria-Hungary on the other hand had not nearly found the limit of their powers. How is this terrible omission to be explained, which would have raised the gravest charges against the responsible statesmen in any established nation?

The Chancellor, supported by the Secretary of the Treasury Wormuth, was afraid of the expression "armament race." He thought to serve peace by restraint in warlike preparations for war. By this means the Entente was to be convinced of our peaceful intentions. The whole world knew in truth that we wanted to keep the peace, but it raised such a shout of indignation at our insufficient Defence Bills, that it could hardly have been louder if we had really made thorough-going preparations for war. The insufficiency of our armaments, however, loosened the sword of our neighbours. If we had drawn the natural inference from the growing strength of Russia since 1909, and had actually kept pace with our opponents' armaments, then peace and friendly relations with Russia based upon respect would have been secured. It was an enormous mistake in method for us not to secure the highest degree of military defensive strength in view of our disadvantages in diplomacy and geography. What would have become of Prussian Germany if Frederick the Great and his father had been afraid of a race in armaments with Austria? A nation which was taking part in such a race for the economic mastery of the world, as we were before this war, must not be afraid of the suspicions of rivals and pacifists unless it is going to lose everything.

This truth, upon the realization and pursuit of which the development of the German State has reposed according to the different stages of its career since the time of the Great Elector, has remained unknown to German Radical democracy.[1] But our political leadership was in league with its own illusions and not with the political wisdom and traditions of our difficult historical progress and suffering.

A not inconsiderable portion of these omissions could, however, have been made good in July, 1914. On July 5th the Emperor said that in spite of the improbability of a world-war, one had to be prepared for the possibility of a collision. It was obvious from the interconnection of the European system of alliances that we had to be prepared for the worst in such a crisis. But what happened?

In July, 1914, we exported considerable quantities of grain to France. There was a shortage of saltpetre which became almost a vital danger to the army.

---

[1] If I am often obliged to attack the blindness of wide democratic circles in foreign affairs, I know quite well that there are numerous honourable and patriotic Social Democrats and Radicals who have shown complete understanding of the needs of the German State. By the word "Democrats" I mean, in this book, the powerful tendencies represented by Scheidemann, Gotheim, Haase, and the *Frankfürter Zeitung,* which had in effect undermined the strength of the State. My attitude in this matter has nothing to do with home politics.

Copper, nickel, and other materials necessary for war were very short, and every opportunity of supplementing our supplies of them unostentatiously was disregarded almost intentionally. In order to prove the actual harmlessness of Berlin, even if it meant the ruin of the country, the simplest measures of precaution both economic and industrial were not taken for times of stress.

Apart from the desire to raise no false suspicions in the minds of the Entente, the instinct of keeping scrupulously to the Budget ought to be taken as a guide. We ought to have been able to buy in on a large scale and to be indemnified by the Reichstag if peace should prevail. The event of war was apparently no longer taken seriously. The Government left every department to itself, and quite in the dark as to the views and intentions of the others. Whilst the various military organizations only needed to press the button for mobilization, there was no general scheme for the event of a world-catastrophe. The end of July, 1914, found us in a state of chaos, and indeed with a talent that was not quite equal to the English gift of improvisation, in which our moral conscience could not console us by the fact that the German Empire had been least occupied of all the Great Powers with the possibilities of war. In spite of these suicidal proofs of our love of peace, the world allowed itself to be persuaded of our guilt owing to the mysteries of our policy in July, 1914, which looked like war-agitation. We were the sheep in wolf's clothing.

V

In discussing the guilt question a twofold mistake is easily made in Germany. In the first place political circumstances are construed in too logical a manner. Many persons seek to prove from a multitude of various symptoms that the world-war could not have been arrested in view of the enemy's malevolence. I consider this view to be wrong. There can indeed be no doubt about the malevolent intention of England, France, and many Russians to smash our Empire. But we ought to have taken all the more care not to have given them an opportunity of carrying it out. As I said in 1904, every opportunity by which we offered the enemy a pretext for war was to be scrupulously avoided because we were not then equal to England in war, and consequently, could not save our extensive foreign trade. The severing of this artery also became an essential reason for our losing the war in 1918. Things would have been just the same in 1904; above all we could not protect our trade and our existence by a victory over France alone. So long as things stood like this, it was madness to give the enemy pretexts for war. So long as the policy of encirclement persisted, there was actually only one way for us: to build a good fleet, to seek support, and to avoid friction.

If we could have succeeded in allaying the crisis in 1914, and if only we had been given two more years for the growth of our fleet, then, as I must repeat,

England's love of peace would probably have risen to the decisive point. Personally I am unable to get away from the dreadful fact that a more cautious policy, which had not made war so easy for the enemy in 1914, would probably have secured for ever our economic position which was already almost equivalent to that of the English, and would have brought our foreign trade and our whole national life a still more brilliant future instead of dreadful ruin.

In July, 1914, we could probably have blocked the way to the enemy's desire for war by a more skilful handling of the Serbian affair. Whether the world-war would have broken out in spite of this, say in 1916, who could prove? I personally am definitely persuaded that every year of peace gained at that time founded peace still more firmly, provided we always had at heart the serious position of our nation and gave corresponding attention to our armament. It is, to be sure, only men with a firm hand and a cool head, who are known to be able to carry through a war, that can also maintain peace in such acute situations. The man who works too strongly and too openly for an understanding moves away from peace, and he who does not uphold the dignity of the nation as high as possible is unavoidably brought by the hard selfishness of all neighbouring nations to a persistent decay of his nation's welfare and prosperity.

The second mistake in judgment I consider to be in the fact that the Austro-Serbian conflict and the world-war were not kept sufficiently sharply divided from one another. Not only the German nation, which is on the whole one of the most peace-loving in the world, but Bethmann-Hollweg's Government also, is perfectly innocent of the world-war so far as its own will is concerned. On the other hand this German Government had a share in the development of the Austro-Serbian affair, for it assumed (what has proved to be wrong) that the *castigation of Serbia* by Austria-Hungary *would prevent* the threatening dis-integration of the Hapsburg Monarchy and the *world-war* which, in their opinion, must necessarily have proceeded from such an eventuality.

How is the whole question of guilt then to be answered?

The *causa remota* of the world-war lies, according to the judgment of all honest observes of European events—the Belgian Ambassador for example—in the English policy of encirclement which originated in the 'nineties in trade jealousy, then hid behind pretexts (Transvaal, Navy), poisoned the press of the world, linked up all the anti-German forces in the world, and created a tense atmosphere in which the slightest mistake could cause a most terrible explosion.

The mistake of our Government lay in the belief that an Austro-Serbian passage-of-arms could be lo-calized. Confiding in the peaceableness and justice of England in particular, it considered a thorough cor-rection of Serbia to be necessary for the restoration of Austria-Hungary to health, without a world-war arising therefrom. Everything in the actions of our

Government which might be interpreted as war-agitation by the enemy refers principally to Serbia and to the desire to preserve Austria from adopting a weak attitude towards this rapacious little State. Terror overcame the Chanceller when the Russian war-party seized on his mistake, and he became aware that his steadfast belief in England's peacable intentions had deceived him. Under the hypnosis of this faith he had not even prepared our country for a world-war. In the above-mentioned conversation between the Chancellor and Wangenheim, according to the latter's version of April 23rd, 1914, Bethmann also spoke about " policy without war " and the dangers of a preventive war, and he stated that our national capital was increasing so rapidly that in ten or fifteen years we should have outstripped all other nations. Then we should have had an assured place in world-politics, which were ultimately the politics of economics. It would be our task to get through this period without any great conflicts.

Thus thought the Chancellor, who three months later dealt with the Serbian affair alone with the Foreign Office, in the absence of the chief military representative. A man who thinks like this is not contriving a world-war. The Chancellor naturally knew that a sharp Austrian ultimatum was to demand satisfaction from Serbia, even though he did not know the text of it. But it is a lie on the part of our enemies to say that Bethmann intended by this means to break the peace of the world. It was on the contrary his hope, although short-sighted enough, not only to maintain, but permanently to secure the peace of the world by his procedure.

Nobody knows the wrong conclusion of our Government with regard to England and their lack of skill in foreign politics better than I do. I can therefore confirm perhaps* better than others on this account the fact that the Government was not driven to take its false steps by a desire for war, but by a fear of war. Their short-sightedness, not their ill-will, assisted the English policy of encirclement to its success just before the door was shut. Bethmann and Jagow had thought to be able to strengthen Austria by means of a diplomatic demonstration. When they saw that it had failed and that war threatened, they were themselves horrified at what they had done. How can one speak on the question of guilt without placing this most important fact in the foreground? The mistakes of our leaders weigh lightly from a moral point of view in comparison with the enemy's attitude. Whoever is acquainted with the reports of the Belgian Ambassador and the innumerable documents on Russia's preparations for war, and has followed the general development of the last two decades, must ask himself in amazement how the opinion could possibly arise that Germany was the guilty party in the world-war.

By its attitude in 1919 the Entente has itself given judgment for every survivor—perhaps one may no longer count upon the present generation, over-fed as it has been with lies. With devilish ferocity a whole nation, which would in itself be innocent of any mistakes on the part of its Government, has been subjected by the English, the French, and their following, to the most grievous tortures in body and soul that ever a nation in the Christian West has had to suffer. A master nation is to be reduced to a pariah, robbed of the dignity of humanity, and only left a hungry scanty prison-existence, just enough to allow it to give service and tribute to its slave-masters for an unlimited time. And why?

In September, 1912, Sassonov was in London. I take the following excerpt, to which I have referred above, from his report to the Czar, published by the *Pravda,* and give it in this connection:

" Grey declared without hesitating that if the circumstances in question were to come to pass, England would do her utmost to inflict the most sensible blow upon German power.

" The King, who touched upon this same question in one of his conversations, expressed himself much more emphatically than his Minister. With evident excitement His Majesty mentioned Germany's striving to become Great Britain's equal with regard to sea-power, and he explained that in the event of a conflict this would have fatal consequences not only for the German navy, but also for German trade at sea, for the English would sink every German ship which came into their hands.

" These latter words apparently reflect not only the personal feelings of His Majesty, but also the prevalent feeling in England with regard to Germany."

When the British statesmen encouraged the Russians in this case, as so often in the years before the
war under the usual pretext of the navy scare, that
they could build upon a steadfast desire in England
to annihilate Germany, they knew with 100 per cent.
certainty that the Emperor and Bethmann-Hollweg
were striving for nothing but peace; they also knew
just as certainly that a war-party, which was attaining the strongest influence, existed both in St. Petersburg and Paris, and they patronized them with all
means in their power. At that time there was spreading in Entente countries an atmosphere that made
wide circles of public opinion feel that war was inevitable; this atmosphere also sprang from the Entente countries over to Germany, and produced here
the anxiety which I find for example in a letter from
our naval attaché in Tokio of June 10th, 1914, expressed in these words:

" I am struck by the certainty with which everybody here considers the war against Germany assured
in the near future . . . that scarcely tangible but
yet so clearly perceptible something that lies in the
air here like the kind of pity over a sentence of death
not yet pronounced."

If the archives of the Entente were opened before
the most incriminating documents have disappeared
from them, the friends of humanity in England and
America would be staggered by the most murderous
of all lies with which they could indict their own

Governments, who imputed to Germany desires of world-conquest, of which nobody in Germany had dreamed in 1914, in order to render the annihilation, disintegration, plundering, and outlawry of the German nation palatable to their own peoples. In 1914 the German nation had outstripped the English in many matters of economics which England regarded as her domain. In trade with many countries Germany was already ahead of England, as well as in the production of steel and other things. In this economic race for the first place, we were inexperienced politically and easily vulnerable; since 1909 we were obviously badly led. The giant Germany could and was to receive the deadly blow, the knock-out, which was to make him a dwarf again. As soon as Bismarck had given us a State, we had by German diligence caught up and out-stripped all other nations in economic prosperity. Thereby we became a nuisance to others; what right had we to disturb the fat livings of the older World-Powers? England and France have pursued the aim of *Germaniam esse delendam* with Roman severity, and thanks to our mistakes they have achieved it. They stand there to-day as successful culprits, who have thrown off the mask now that they have made good their schemes. If the German people had realized in time the whole risk of Bismarck's creation, they would not have made themselves defenceless and thereby have accomplished the enemy's desires. We were too careless epigones. But now we experience the sight of the wolves who are devouring the sheep playing the part of judges over this " criminal " victim.

I can produce yet another valid proof that our Government did not want the war. It was convinced from the very beginning that we should not win. Now one can indeed credit the Government with great lack of skill, but never with the criminal action of desiring a war when it itself was most deeply convinced of its hopelessness. Scarcely anybody in Germany could rightly understand before the outbreak of war, and after it, how great the danger actually was. We were partly wrapped up in *bona fide* illusions, and partly rather supercilious. A materialistic view of life or inherited party feelings clouded the vision of many. Thus we omitted to do what would save us. This incompetence is our guilt.

VI

On July 27th, when I arrived in Berlin, there still existed, so far as I now see the situation, a bare possibility of bringing the ship of peace past the rocks and getting her clear of them. At the time I had a false picture of the situation just like the Emperor, who had returned home of his own accord against the Chancellor's wishes, and my ministerial colleagues who were streaming to Berlin. The key to the understanding of it now got lost in the Wilhelmstrasse. I heard of Russia's preparations and I now believed that I must interpret the chance of mobilization of the English fleet, which had been going on for months, as a threatening measure. Over Bethmann's action to save peace at this stage, there were written the words, as so often before: "Too late by half."

Early on July 28th the Chief of the Naval Cabinet, von Müller, visited me and gave vent to his horror at his most recent experiences with Bethmann. He considered a change of Chancellor and the substitution of Hintze for Jagow to be unavoidable. Müller did not review the actual situation.

As soon as the Emperor arrived in Berlin he developed a feverish activity to maintain peace. The Chancellor had not known how to keep the Emperor really in touch with events. The Emperor found it difficult to find a clear starting-point for effective diplomatic action. He said he didn't know what the Austrians wanted; the Serbs had conceded everything but a few bagatelles; since July 5th the Austrians had said nothing about their intentions.

This statement was made in the evening of July 29th in the Neues Palais at Potsdam, whither the Emperor had invited the military chiefs in order to inform them of his negotiations with the Chancellor, who had collapsed completely. We had no idea at that time of the doubts which Bethmann must have had about his policy during the first weeks in July. We only saw with consternation what was taking place before our eyes, including the Emperor's, who expressed himself without reserve regarding Bethmann's incompetence, as he had done many times before; he gave the opinion, however, that he could not separate

himself from this man now, as he enjoyed the confidence of Europe. The Emperor informed the company that the Chancellor had proposed that in order
to keep England neutral we should sacrifice the German fleet for an agreement with England, which he,
the Emperor, had refused to do. Consequently after
his return from Potsdam on the evening of the 29th,
the Chancellor had to put some restraint upon himself
with regard to the fleet, when he summoned the British
Ambassador to him and made high offers for England's neutrality in the event of a Franco-German war.
The offers he put forward on this occasion, as well as
the cutting reply given him by Sir Edward Grey, are
known from the English Blue Book (Nos. 85, 101).
The public, however, did not know that the Chancellor
was prepared once more, as in 1912, to sacrifice the
German fleet in the strange conviction that England
would then consent to a German victory over France.
The attempts at capitulation began therefore even
before the war, and when there was still time to prevent it. The Chancellor had two unhappy ideas: the
Austrians must march into Serbia, and the German
fleet stands in the way of England's love. In the event
of his Belgrade policy giving the enemy an opportunity for war, he was now covered at any rate: the
German fleet was to blame for everything. The Chancellor's naval policy of July 29th, as well as that of
1911-12, unfortunately cast its shadow across the war;
for our conduct of the war at sea, as it was desired
and carried out by the Chancellor, meant at bottom

nothing less than the slow sacrifice of Germany's navy and future, which he had been forbidden to give up at one stroke.

That day Prince Henry arrived in Potsdam from England with the message from George V that England would remain neutral in the event of war. I doubted this, whereupon the Emperor replied: "I have the word of a king, and that is sufficient for me."

The confusion which agitated all Europe and prevented anybody from reviewing the whole situation seemed to clear favourably on July 30th. England agreed to a proposal of mediation from the German Emperor which had been accepted in Vienna also. A complete material agreement had been arrived at between us and London. I learnt this on July 30th at midday by a letter from the Emperor, which enabled me to breathe again.

In the early hours of July 31st, however, I learnt from the Admiralty Staff that in the Foreign Office the war was regarded as inevitable, and that Jagow had asked whether we were ready to attack the English fleet.

The contradiction was cleared up for me when I received the news of the Russian mobilization between noon and one o'clock.

At half-past twelve the Chancellor had sent for me, and when I saw him he had the Imperial order for the "threatening state of war." I drew Bethmann's attention to the agreement that had been effected be-

tween us and London, and I read to him the Emperor's letter of which he did not know anything.
The Chancellor thought that the Emperor was con-
fusing several things.   The Russian mobilization, he
said, would be such an unheard-of proceeding against
us that we could not put up with it; if Russia continued, we must also begin to mobilize, and an ultimatum had had to be dispatched to the Czar so as
not to bring our mobilization too much in arrears.
That was my view too.   The blood-guilt of those
responsible for the Russian mobilization is not lessened
by any bungling on the part of our Government.   In
spite of the agreement which had been established at
the eleventh hour between us and England, the Russian mobilization had made war inevitable unless a
miracle happened.   Longer hesitation on our part
would have delivered our territory to the enemy, and
would have been inexcusable.   In reality the Russians
had been mobilizing since the 25th, and this advance
did us considerable harm when the machines of war
began to move.   I gave the Chancellor to understand,
however, that it seemed to me right to stress more
in the ultimatum the fact that positive agreement existed, and a favourable mediation was in progress.
The Chancellor replied with some warmth that this
had been said all along and Russia had just answered
it by mobilizing.

I often wondered later whether the Emperor ought
not to have sent somebody to St. Petersburg in time.
The most suitable man for this purpose, Hintze, was,

to be sure, in Mexico. I knew definitely, however, that the Czar appreciated the point of view that Germany and Russia could gain nothing by tearing one another to pieces, but at the best a third person would do so. It was naturally too late to send anybody on July 31st. It may also happen that I shall be told that I over-estimated the power of the Czar, and under-estimated Pan-Slavism. I can only state here that, following my instinct more than my reason, I advised the Chancellor to insert a peaceable paragraph into the ultimatum. I scarcely hoped thereby to hold back the wheel of fate which the Russian mobilization had set in motion, but in any case to shift the responsibility for all that was coming more exclusively upon the enemy.

On August 1st I learnt in the Federal Council that we had sent a declaration of war against Russia after the ultimatum. I considered that very unfavourable for Germany. In my opinion we ought to have turned to account diplomatically the advantage that we were militarily on the defensive with regard to Russia, by leaving the declaration of war to the Russians. We ought not to have inspired the moujik with a conviction that the Emperor intended to attack the White Czar. The depreciation of our alliance treaty with Roumania was also of importance. This treaty, just like that with Italy, had been made by Prince Bismarck for defence; both States were only pledged to help us if Russia or France attacked us. By our declaration of war on Russia we formally gave the Rou-

manians the right to leave us alone in the war, just
as we did to the Italians later by our declaration of
war on France.   Did not Bethmann really consider
the enormous disadvantages which were created for
us by our not leaving the act of declaration of war
to the enemy?

I had the impression that our action even in this
direction was completely unconsidered, and took place
without any system, and my feelings revolted at our
having to assume the odium of the attacking party in
the face of the world, on account of the jurists of the
Foreign Office, although we could not at all intend to
march into Russia, and although we were in reality
the attacked party.   I therefore asked the Chancellor,
as the meeting broke up, why the declaration of war
had to coincide with our mobilization?

The Chancellor replied that this was necessary because the army would immediately send troops over
the frontier.   The reply astonished me, because at
the most it could only be a question of patrols.   But
through all these days Bethmann was so agitated and
overstrained that it was impossible to speak with
him.   I can still hear him as he repeatedly stressed
the absolute necessity of the declaration of war, with
his arms uplifted, and consequently cut short all
further discussion.

When I asked Moltke afterwards the actual relation
between the crossing of the frontier and our declaration of war, he denied any intention of sending troops
over the frontier forthwith.   He also told me that he

attached no value to the declaration of war from his own point of view.

Thus the riddle, why we declared war first, remains unsolved for me. It is to be assumed that we did it out of formal legal conscientiousness. The Russians began the war without any declaration, but we believed that we could not defend ourselves without such a statement. Outside Germany there is no appreciation of such ideas.

Summoned to the Castle in the afternoon for the signing of the mobilization order by the Emperor, I arrived late in consequence of a break-down in the traffic, after the order had already been signed. I heard, however, that a Russian acceptance of our declaration of war had not yet arrived, and I therefore made a last attempt with my suggestion that there was still time, until the Russians had acknowledged our declaration of war, to send a gentler message after it. I was unable to rid myself of the impulse to at least shift from ourselves the odium of the declaration of war, although the last spark of any possibility of peace was really extinguished. I therefore asked whether hostilities were to be opened on our side without the Russian Government's acceptance, for in view of our advance in the west, our movements in the east could only consist of bluffs and demonstrations. As our patrols, according to Moltke, would not cross the Russian frontier for some days, we did not yet need to stand there as the attacker.

My question was overwhelmed by the arrival of a
dispatch from Lichnowsky which impelled us to make
a last effort for peace. I actively supported Bethmann
in this, and later in reply to his question whether we
could promise the English not to attack the French
coast, I answered in the affirmative, and recommended
him to include the offer in his speech to the Reichstag.
This peace-move was condemned to failure owing to
a misunderstanding on Lichnowsky's part, although
he at least proved once again that Germany did not
want the war. During the night of August 1st-2nd,
the dispute about our declaration of war, this time
with regard to France, was repeated in the Chancellor's house. The Chancellor opined that we must
declare war upon France immediately, because we
wanted to march through Belgium. I interjected that
I had not understood why the declaration of war on
Russia had been made public at the same time as the
mobilization; I said that I could see no advantage in
launching the declaration of war against France before we marched into France. I referred to reports
from the Ambassador in London, according to which
the advance through Belgium would immediately result in war with England, and I touched upon the question as to whether it was possible for the army to retard the march through Belgium. Moltke declared
that there was no other way. I got the impression
that it was impossible to interfere in the machinery of
transport. I declared that we must then reckon on
immediate war with England. Every day would be

a gain for the mobilization of the navy. Therefore the intimation to Belgium must be delayed as much as possible. I was promised that it should wait until the second day of mobilization, but this was not done. I did not know then that on July 29th Bethmann-Hollweg had revealed to the British Ambassador, and consequently to all the Entente Powers and Belgium, the possibility of military operations taking place in Belgium. This had been done with the idea of preserving a confidential relationship with England in spite of the war on the Continent.

The impression of the stupidity of our political leadership became more and more disquieting. The march through Belgium did not seem to have been an established fact hitherto to the Government. Since the Russian mobilization the Chancellor gave one the impression of a drowning man.

Whilst the lawyers of the Foreign Office immersed themselves in the academic question as to whether we were now at war with Russia or not, it came out that they had forgotten to ask Austria whether she would fight with us against Russia. This had now to be done. Italy likewise had not been informed of our declaration of war against Russia.[1] When we went

---

[1] At that time I could not foresee that Austria would consider her own declaration of war on Russia for some length of time, and thereby give us some bad hours. As late as the morning of August 5th, the Admiralty urged the Foreign Office, in writing, to obtain Austria's declaration of war on account of our ships in the Mediterranean. Moltke told me to my horror that if the Austrians drew back we should have to conclude a peace at any price. But the management of the Serbian affair had been thoroughly inadequate. The diplomatic situation was

out, the military expressed their indignation to me
about the condition of the political leadership. None
the less I was troubled by a feeling that the General
Staff was not correctly estimating the meaning of a
war against England and was heedlessly going on with
the war against France because this apparently meant
only a short war. The decisions of the hour were
never guided by previously considered politico-strategical plans of mobilization for the whole war.

When the Emperor realized the failures of his efforts for peace, he was stirred to the very depths. An
old confidential friend of his who saw much of him
during the first days of August declared that he had
never seen such a tragic and disturbed face as that
of the Emperor at that time.

The agitated discussions between Bethmann and
Moltke were continued in the Emperor's presence in
the Castle on August 2nd, myself being present.
Moltke attached no value to a formal declaration of
war on France. He pointed to a series of hostile acts
on the part of the French, which had been reported to
him; the war, he said, was actually here and its development could not be withheld. I represented again

made more difficult by Austria declaring war on Serbia without
invading the country, and negotiating about a pledge which she
did not possess. If they intended to invade the country, they
would have had to occupy Belgrade the moment the ultimatum
expired, before the Serbs had time to blow up the Semlin Bridge,
and to negotiate after the pledge had been seized. Thus we had
not Austria in our hands, either with regard to the ultimatum
or with regard to the world-war. I will not speak here about
our omissions with regard to Italy. Afterwards I did everything
I could, so far as my position allowed, to secure the sending of
Prince Bülow to Rome.

and again that I could not understand why a declaration of war had to be sent to France at all, for it would always have an aggressive flavour; the army could march up to the French frontier without such things.

The Chancellor declared that he could not hand over our terms to Belgium without a declaration of war on France. I have never been able to understand this reason.

The Belgian question ought to have made our diplomacy tread with particular caution from the very beginning. The General Staff had for decades considered the possibility of an invasion through Belgium all the more seriously since the French policy of revenge began to support itself on the Russian armies. There could not exist a doubt in the whole world that the French were at least intellectually the aggressors in a Franco-German war. In warding off a French war of revenge, which threatened us on the Vistula just as much as on the Meuse and the Moselle, our march through neutral Belgium could only be justified in the eyes of the world if the political offensive of France against us was made as clear as day.

Those who were specially engaged on this question in the General Staff, who naturally were especially conscious of the terrible gravity of Germany's position, had been led to the conviction by many symptoms during the few years before the war, that the French and the English would march through Belgium to attack the Rhineland. As a matter of fact, the French in

1914 attacked in Lorraine, just as Schlieffen had always prophesied. But we had proofs at our disposal
that the Western Powers had Belgium in view as the
theatre of war. Moreover, there were voluminous
signs of a leaning on the part of influential Belgian
circles towards the Entente, both politically and militarily, even before the Belgian archives were opened.
As the Chancellor then must have been informed on
the Belgian question, it was his duty to make the
corresponding diplomatic preparations for the march
through Belgium, which the General Staff considered
to be necessary to meet a Franco-Russian attack.
Nothing was done in this direction. Politically Germany's strategical offensive through Belgium was a
matter for the gravest misgiving; this could only be
allayed if our policy clearly convinced the world, with
redoubled caution and skill, that we were *politically*
on the defensive. If, however, we gave ourselves the
false appearance of being the aggressors politically,
then the invasion of Belgium, which was actually a
pure emergency measure, appeared in the fateful light
of a brutal act of violence. The enemy received
overwhelming material for slandering us, if after the
ultimatum to Serbia, after the refusal of Grey's proposal of a conference, after a formal declaration of
war on Russia and France, we proceeded to march
through Belgium. How doubtful and ambiguous was
Belgian neutrality and its armed defence by England!
It was only our complete lack of political skill that
wove the legendary martyr's crown for this country.

We were to the fore in everything, as though we wanted to facilitate the enemy's schemes. The General Staff was not the authority to take the sole responsibility of judging the political reaction of strategic necessities. The "wrong" done to Belgium, which Bethmann revealed, gave the enemy, however, the desired confirmation of their calumnies against us and further confused our own nation's feeling of justice in the most baneful manner.

I only arrived at these reflections on the Belgian question during the war, as I was not informed on anything to do with this matter in time of peace or at the outbreak of the war. The diplomatic mistakes, however, which we made when opening our operations in the west were straightway clear to me during that conference.

After the Chancellor had left the meeting, Moltke complained to the Emperor of the "deplorable" state of the political leadership, which had made no preparations for the situation and was now still thinking of nothing but legal Notes, although the avalanche was on the move.

I declared to the Emperor that in my opinion the Foreign Office had not functioned for many years; it had, however, not been my affair to advise the Emperor in this matter; but the gravity of the hour impelled me to over-step for once the limits of my authority. I concluded: "The Chancellor is my superior, and I am not here to judge him; but let Your Majesty recall Hintze and put him in Jagow's place."

Hintze was actually recalled from Mexico and made his way to General Headquarters. From there, however, he was appointed to Peking at the instigation of the Foreign Office, and for a second time he had to betake himself round the world in disguise. He had had a number of experiences which, comparatively speaking, probably fitted him best of all for the purpose of making a separate peace with the Czar, which could have been obtained and would have decided the war in 1916.

VII

On August 6th I was visited by Jagow to impress upon me that the Admiralty should not give political information to the Emperor—which as a matter of fact had never happened.[1] I remonstrated with him on account of the complete *déroute* of the political leaders, who ought to have given the event of war a certain amount of preliminary consideration. Now we had to turn all the strength at our disposal against

---

[1] I have often been reproached with pursuing a policy of my own, and particularly with influencing politics by means of the information department. This is quite untrue; on the contrary, I have always imposed upon myself the greatest restraint in this matter, even during the war, as must be quite plain from the hitherto unknown information contained in these Memoirs. This still holds good if a zealous officer here and there in the information department should actually have overstepped the limits of his authority without my knowledge and against my wishes. Just as untrue is the assertion, with which Bethmann even used to work on the Emperor, that I had any connection with or influence on that excellent writer, Count E. zu Revent-low, during the war, although this gentleman, together with Rohrbach and Jackh, placed their journalistic talents at the disposal of my deputy when the war began.

the mightiest of our enemies. In reply to my question, what would happen if we beat France and Russia but not England, Jagow shrugged his shoulders. The conflict of opinion came to the surface when I said: "Couldn't you promise Russia the passage of the Dardanelles and anything they like, to prevent the war?" Jagow replied: "If you had only brought us a little naval agreement with England, the war would not have been necessary."

After all that the Foreign Office must have known relating to the outbreak of war, it needed some boldness to describe the German navy as the cause of the war. But henceforward the Chancellor and the Foreign Office applied considerable care and tenderness to the spreading of this legend. This joined hands with the far more fateful campaign against the German fleet, to withhold it from striking in the war.

If Germany's armies had marched into Belgium and France, indeed if we had wrestled successfully with Russia and France, a Germany without a fleet would still have had England for an enemy. In keeping with her traditional policy, England would never have suffered our superiority on the Continent, even if she had had no formal *ententes* with the other Powers. If the German fleet played any part at all in the general situation of July, 1914, it acted as a brake on England's temptation to go to war and caused Grey's efforts to maintain peace. England's attitude during the years when we had no fleet, or when our fleet was

weak, proves that she would not have passed over
even then any opportunities that were offered of striking us down with foreign help, and of preventing our
hegemony—indeed, that she would probably have
seized them more readily than when she set the instrument of the *ententes* in motion against us in 1914.
I am saying things that are self-evident, but the eager
tendency of the Germans to self-annihilation enabled
the Chancellor and his helpmates in the autumn of
1914 to sow suspicion against Germany's sole means
of salvation at that time—the fleet. The result of this
was to obliterate in the minds of many people all
traces of those weeks of July, the real origin of the
war. Soon I heard from a reliable source that an
understanding had been effected between the Chancellory and the editors of certain newspapers, by which
I was to be regarded as being to blame for the war.
Undiscerning Germans were soon imitating the enemy
and saying that autocracy and a military caste had
caused this war; and those persons who were in
reality, though not consciously, the prime movers in
the destruction of the Monarchy and who shook the
foundations of German strength and independence,
pressed forward after the Revolution for the osten-
sible purpose of telling the " truth " before a State
tribunal.

The ambiguity of Bethmann's policy in July, 1914,
has not only worsened our diplomatic position in the
war and at the conclusion of peace, but it has also
strengthened the German tendency towards self-hu-

miliation in a degree which threatens to overshadow the whole distant future of our nation. For the enemy, who wanted to put the blame for the war upon the German people found ready agents in the very bosom of the German people to persuade us that we had started the war. I have hinted at the mistakes of German policy during these weeks, and they are not to be glossed over. But we are not to blame for the war. Those in authority in London, Paris, and St. Petersburg are solely to blame for the war, as well as for the barbarous way in which it was conducted. Besides, how could there be the slightest doubt about it? How can the German nation forget that the Belgian Ambassadors, keener-eyed than the German diplomats, unmistakably revealed, several years before the war, the Entente's will-to-war and the conspiracy that it had woven around Germany? The Entente's guilt is also established in its deeds. The Entente, which tore Alsace-Lorraine from the German motherland; which made the German people the hirelings of Anglo-Saxon capitalism, and wanted to dissolve the Austro-Hungarian Monarchy and annihilate the Turkish Empire; which fought with sword, hunger, internment, theft of trade, and moral poison, until the death of our nation was sealed; which translated immediately into fact the enmity that it had shown for decades, as soon as the negotiations of July, 1914, offered a particularly favourable opportunity,—this Entente will not be able, by hypocritically turning to advantage our unhappy policy, to avoid for ever the judgment of the history of the world upon the crime that it has committed on the spirit of humanity.

VIII

I have expressed myself so definitely in this statement because official quarters are still endeavouring to obliterate the mistakes that have been made. The moral guiltlessness of our Government at that time can, however, only be made clear by a frank statement of their diplomatic inadequacy; and only by this means can it be proved historically that the Emperor had no share in the mistakes made by the Government. If other authorities committed errors, this was not due to a desire for war, which they lacked altogether, but to an absence of clear, straight thinking.

Our nation now streamed to the colours, and in the jubilant spirit of sacrifice of August, 1914, and in a fullness of strength of the Prusso-German State that will never be witnessed again by German eyes, sought to ward off the attack which a short-sighted diplomacy had enabled our watching neighbours to make. National spirit was then on the rise, a fact which was proved by the German nation in 1911, when it refused to allow itself to be pacified by a weak Government in the matter of the insult that was offered it. It proved it again with moving power when the Emperor sent forth the call to arms. Our nation did not know at that time what mistakes our political leaders had made, and under what unfavourable conditions it was going into an unprepared war. It knew that it was free from blame, and was so in reality. But none of the innumerable peace offers of our Government moved England to mercy, after she had realized the weakness of our Government and had deduced from this the certainty of our defeat in spite of Germany's great strength and health at that time.

And yet the world-coalition would not have succeeded in conquering us, in spite of its unparalleled superiority, if our inner unity had been upheld with those means which corresponded to the traditions of our fathers and the danger of the hour. No matter what heroism was shown by our troops, the hereditary faults of the people and the destructive elements were fostered by the Government at home, until England's desire was fulfilled and the most prosperous and best nation on earth had been reduced to the lowest level.

So the old pirate State, England, has again succeeded in letting Europe tear herself to pieces, and by throwing in her own power and applying the most brutal methods, she has secured a victory which accords with her material interests. The liberty and independence of the people of the European continent has now vanished and the bloom of their civilization is perhaps destroyed for ever.

But England's day of judgment will have its birth in this very success.